Palgrave Hate Studies

Series Editors
Neil Chakraborti, School of Criminology, University of Leicester, Leicester, UK
Barbara Perry, Faculty of Social Science and Humanities, University of Ontario, Oshawa, Canada

This series builds on recent developments in the broad and interdisciplinary field of hate studies. Palgrave Hate Studies aims to bring together in one series the very best scholars who are conducting hate studies research around the world. Reflecting the range and depth of research and scholarship in this burgeoning area, the series welcomes contributions from established hate studies researchers who have helped to shape the field, as well as new scholars who are building on this tradition and breaking new ground within and outside the existing canon of hate studies research.

Jon Garland · Irene Zempi · Jo Smith
Editors

Hate Crime Perpetrators: New Perspectives from Theory, Research and Practice, Volume I

Understanding Offender Profiles and Motivations

palgrave
macmillan

Editors
Jon Garland
Department of Sociology
University of Surrey
Guildford, UK

Irene Zempi
Department of Criminology & Criminal Justice
Nottingham Trent University
Nottingham, UK

Jo Smith
Brighton Law School, School of Business and Law
University of Brighton
Brighton, UK

ISSN 2947-6364 ISSN 2947-6372 (electronic)
Palgrave Hate Studies
ISBN 978-3-031-92665-5 ISBN 978-3-031-92666-2 (eBook)
https://doi.org/10.1007/978-3-031-92666-2

This Palgrave Macmillan imprint is published by the registered company Springer Nature Switzerland AG
The registered company address is: Gewerbestrasse 11, 6330 Cham, Switzerland

Acknowledgements

We would like to thank all of the authors who contributed to this edited collection.

In addition, we would like to thank the staff at Palgrave for their support in the production of this text.

Jon would like to thank Karen for her support throughout the time this book was being put together. He'd also like to thank all those involved in the British Society of Criminology Hate Crime Network for being such good people and such fun to work with, including and especially, his co-editors.

Jo would like to thank Simon for his support during the work on this book. Both Jo and Irene echo Jon's thanks to the members of the BSC Hate Crime Network and the co-editors. It's a privilege to stand side by side with you in the fight against hate.

This book is dedicated to the memory of Sylvia Lancaster and to the continuing work of the Sophie Lancaster Foundation. Sylvia was a force of nature who worked tirelessly to combat prejudice in all its forms and to get hate crimes against alternative subcultures onto the broader hate crime agenda. She was also a kind and generous person who, while she didn't suffer fools gladly, could also see the good in people, despite everything she'd been through. Her achievements as a campaigner have left a lasting legacy that continues to inspire new generations who learn of Sophie's story. It is hoped that this book does that legacy justice.

Contents

Contributors

Imran Awan Department of Criminology and Sociology, Birmingham City University, Birmingham, UK

William Bergstroem Department of Sociology, University of Surrey, Guildford, UK

Ian Brunton-Smith Department of Sociology, University of Surrey, Guildford, UK

John Clayton Department of Geography and Environmental Sciences, Northumbria University, Newcastle, UK

Ben Colliver Department of Criminology and Sociology, Birmingham City University, Birmingham, UK

Catherine Donovan Department of Sociology, Durham University, Durham, UK

Lexi Faulkner College of Criminology and Criminal Justice, Florida State University, Tallahassee, FL, USA

Jon Garland Department of Sociology, University of Surrey, Guildford, UK

Jane Healy Department of Social Science and Social Work, Bournemouth University, Bournemouth, UK

Valerie Houghton Edinburgh Napier University, Edinburgh, UK

Darrick Jolliffe Department of Security and Crime Science, University College London, London, UK

Brendan Lantz College of Criminology and Criminal Justice, Florida State University, Tallahassee, FL, USA

Stephen J. Macdonald Criminology and Disability Studies at Durham University, Durham, UK

Cristhian A. Martínez Department of Social Psychology, University of Groningen, Groningen, Netherlands

James Pickles School of Humanities and Social Science, University of Brighton, Brighton, UK

Jo Smith Brighton Law School, School of Business and Law, University of Brighton, Brighton, UK

Irene Zempi Department of Criminology & Criminal Justice, Nottingham Trent University, Nottingham, UK

List of Figures

Populism and Hate Feelings

Genocide: An Alternative Lens to Explore Hate Crime Offending

List of Tables

Female Hate Crime Offenders: The Theoretical and Policy Implications of an Under-Researched Phenomenon

Introduction

Jon Garland, Irene Zempi, and Jo Smith

Over the last twenty-five years or so the scholarly body of work in the field of hate studies has grown significantly. From the time it first established a foothold in North America with the work of Barbara Perry in the early 2000s (see, for example, Perry, 2001) hate studies has developed from almost a footnote in criminology and sociology into a noted area of enquiry in its own right. Innovative research has been undertaken

J. Garland (✉)
Department of Sociology, University of Surrey, Guildford, UK
e-mail: j.garland@surrey.ac.uk

I. Zempi
Department of Criminology & Criminal Justice, Nottingham Trent University, Nottingham, UK
e-mail: irene.zempi@ntu.ac.uk

J. Smith
Brighton Law School, School of Business and Law, University of Brighton, Brighton, UK
e-mail: j.smith12@brighton.ac.uk

J. Garland et al. (eds.), *Hate Crime Perpetrators: New Perspectives from Theory, Research and Practice, Volume I*, Palgrave Hate Studies,
https://doi.org/10.1007/978-3-031-92666-2_1

into the frequency, nature and impact of hate crime victimisation (see, *inter alia*, Burch, 2021; Paterson et al., 2024; Wilkin, 2020; Williams & Tregidga, 2013; Zempi, 2016), as well as the effectiveness of police and criminal justice responses to this victimisation (Walters, 2014) and the utility of the suites of legislation that has evolved around the world to help protect victims and punish the perpetrators of hate-motivated offences (Mason, 2014). Other areas of investigation have included the extreme right and related political movements (for instance, Perry & Scrivens, 2019) and the experiences of those groups who are victims of targeted hostility but are not officially recognised as hate crime victim groups, such as sex workers (Campbell & Sanders, 2021) or members of alternative subcultures (Garland & Hodkinson, 2014). Along with this growing body of research, hate studies has established its own conferences and symposia, active networks within learned societies, book series, special editions of journals and, via the International Network for Hate Studies, a genuinely global network of academics and practitioners working in the field.

Unfortunately, this expansion in research and related activities has occurred against a very troubling backdrop of global events that has demonstrated why working in hate studies is so important. In June 2016, in the midst of the emotive and sometimes histrionic debates surrounding Brexit and the United Kingdom's relationship with its European neighbours, sitting Labour member of parliament Jo Cox was murdered by far-right extremist Thomas Mair. This occurred during a decade-long period that saw significant year-on-year growth in police-recorded hate crime (Home Office, 2024). Significant events since then have included; the election (twice) of Donald Trump to the office of President of the United States, a man whose politics are hard to categorise but are undoubtedly towards the far right of the political spectrum; the storming of the Capitol building on 6 January 2021 by disparate groups of Trump supporters and far-right militias in an attempt to overturn the 2020 US presidential election result, and the growth of conspiracy theories during the Covid pandemic of 2020/21 that were tinged with antisemitism and other forms of racism, and which were often fuelled by the activities of extremist groups sensing an opportunity to gain influence among a concerned public (Lawrence & Davis, 2020).

In parallel with these developments has been a groundswell in the popularity of far-right political parties across Europe, which has recently seen Alternative fur Deutschland come second in the popular vote in the German 2025 general elections (Kirby, 2025) and National Rally third in the National Assembly elections in France in 2024 (Cokelaere & Goury-Laffont, 2024). Meanwhile, the populist/radical right has also made significant gains in countries like the United Kingdom, where Reform UK, fronted by arch Brexiteer Nigel Farage, polled over 14 per cent of the vote in the 2024 UK general elections and appears to be a serious threat to the Conservative and Labour parties. The Conservative government of 2019–24 was, at times, openly hostile to the idea of hate crime which it, along with a number of sympathetic journalists and commentators, saw as part of a liberal/left 'woke agenda' that was a threat to free speech and civil liberties (Vaizey, 2021). The investigation of non-crime hate incidents was subsequently deprioritised by the police following interventions by the then Home Secretary Suella Braverman (Home Office, 2023). Within this hostile political climate, we have also seen an increase in popularity of the former leader of the far-right English Defence League (EDL), Tommy Robinson, among some sections of the white working class; this popular support does not seem to have waned despite Robinson being sentenced to multiple periods of imprisonment. Recasting himself as a 'citizen journalist' rather than a political activist, Robinson has become the focal point and 'poster boy' of the 'post-organisational' far right, achieving numbers in the tens of thousands on marches in support of him and his causes in the early-to-mid 2020s that the EDL did not get anywhere near to achieving, even at the height of its popularity in the early 2010s (Sherwood & Quinn, 2024). In some ways, given this backdrop, the riots of the summer of 2024 that were flavoured with virulent anti-Muslim and anti-immigrant sentiment and influenced by various far-right groups (Deo & Malik, 2024), should have come as no surprise.

Given these alarming developments, the growth of the academic field of hate studies is to be welcomed, particularly given some of the significant 'real-world' influence and impact this work has produced. However, it has, and for good and understandable reasons, often focused on examining the experience of victims. The study of perpetrators—who they are, what their histories are and what motivates their actions—and the ways in which wider society creates a climate within which intolerance can flourish, has received much less attention. This is why we believe that this book, which showcases the work of leading scholars researching hate crime perpetration, is so timely. The book explores developing theoretical perspectives, current research into hate crime perpetration, and scholarly analysis of legal frameworks, policy responses and criminal justice practice that aim to combat hate crime at individual and societal levels. The book highlights links between different forms and arenas of hate crime offending, providing new perspectives on the nature of contemporary hate and intolerance, how it can be understood, and how it might be effectively tackled. We therefore hope that this book will add fresh dimensions to hate studies whilst making a worthwhile contribution to wider debates around hate perpetration and to relevant policy and practice around dealing with hate offenders.

Outline of Chapters

This collection opens with Darrick Jolliffe, Ian Brunton-Smith and Jon Garland undertaking 'An Examination of the Differences and Similarities Between the Profiles of Hate Crime Offenders and Those of Non-Hate Offenders.' This study, the first to examine recidivism in hate crime offenders, is also the first to evaluate the extent to which the reoffending of hate crime offenders may be distinguishable from non-hate crime offenders. Drawing on data recording the reoffending behaviour of all adult males released from short-term incarceration in England and Wales in one year, the chapter argues that hate crime offenders may be distinguishable from non-hate crime offenders in the signature of their reoffending. However, it was not possible to disentangle the form of this 'difference,' and so the authors conclude by recommending that future research on hate crime offenders should focus on understanding this 'difference' so that the profound harm of this form of offending can be mitigated.

Chapter, 'Who are the Perpetrators of Online Hate? A Case Study of Islamophobia,' sees Imran Awan examine Islamophobic hate crime through the lens of hate speech. The author, in noting that social media remains an unregulated platform, identifies that those committing hate crimes in cyberspace have often been overlooked by policymakers, academics and wider stakeholders. To begin to rectify this, the author draws from content analysis to propose a unique typology of the perpetrators of online Islamophobia following trigger events, using this to contextualise the hate crime offenders' motivations and key characteristics. Awan concludes that a new international and national online cyber hate strategy should be adopted which highlights the manner in which online Islamophobic abuse occurs and identifies ways in which the authorities can deal with such incidents more effectively.

Disablist hate crime offending is explored in chapter, 'Towards a New Typology of Disablist Hate Crime Offenders: A Contextual Analysis.' This chapter sees Valerie Houghton and Jane Healy use several datasets to develop a picture of disablist hate crime offenders, and differences between disablist acts are identified: in the context of the incidents, the relationships between perpetrators and victims, and offenders' potential motivations. The findings from this chapter demonstrate that in most of the police and safeguarding cases that were analysed, perpetrators were known to their victims rather than being strangers, and that disablist hate crimes are dynamic and that perpetrator actions can indeed be diverse. The typology offered by Houghton and Healy is useful for understanding how and why disabled people are victimised in contemporary society, but importantly positions the perpetrators' acts (rather than victim vulnerability) as central. Whilst the authors acknowledge that the typology needs further exploration and empirical research to test for its validity and applicability across a larger dataset, ideally working with disablist perpetrators directly, the importance of the foundations laid in this chapter cannot be understated.

Chapter 'Familiar Faces: Hate Relationships and the Everyday-ness of Hate Offending,' by John Clayton, Stephen J. Macdonald and Catherine Donovan explores the important issue everyday experiences of 'hate relationships'; that is, hate which is considered 'low level,' and concentrated in and around the home and neighbourhood. Drawing on research in North East England, this chapter reflects on perpetrator profiles, roles and actions towards victims. The authors challenge the stereotype of hate as perpetrated in public spaces by strangers who hold extreme views and interact with victims infrequently, by focusing on perpetrators as 'familiar,' by making three arguments. Firstly, it is argued that perpetrators in hate relationships are not isolated individuals, but rather they operate within the context of peer pressure and friendship groups and in the transmission of ideas and practices of 'othering.' Secondly, the perpetrators of hate relationships are not necessarily 'offenders' in the sense of having been prosecuted for criminal acts. Finally, perpetrators in hate relationships are 'ordinary,' but they are not ordinary strangers, in the sense they are known to victims. It is concluded that we should pay attention to the everyday temporality, spatiality and sociality of hate relationships, and that we must do more to combat exclusionary behaviours in ways which acknowledge challenges that transcend the victim/perpetrator binary.

The multifaceted nature of transphobic hate discourse, as situated within its broader historical and political contexts is the focus of James Pickles and Ben Colliver's work in the next chapter, 'Perpetrators of Transphobia and Transphobic Hate Crime.' The authors document how transphobic rhetoric, particularly within the framework of 'gender critical feminism' has transitioned from academic claims into mainstream media and public policy, so influencing societal attitudes and behaviours. The chapter outlines poor legislative responses to transphobic hate crime and identifies significant disparities in the punishment of transphobic hate crime perpetrators, highlighting a legal system that often fails to adequately protect and value trans lives. The authors argue that these legal inconsistencies not only perpetuate a hostile environment in the legal system but also show the urgent need for more equitable and effective policy interventions. It is concluded that further work should examine the profiles of perpetrators in transphobic hate crimes, and explore how the spectrum of anti-trans hate-based violence and the rise in transphobic rhetoric can lead to transphobic hate crime.

In chapter 'Populism and Hate Feelings,' Cristhian A. Martínez observes that a new wave of right- and left-wing populism has been on the rise since the 1990s, fuelling polarisation and conflict around the world. Seeking to explain how the populist worldview might progressively lead to the emergence of hate feelings, the author proposes a three-phase theoretical model. This model establishes the links between the three main features of populism (people-centrism, anti-elitism and Manicheism) and discreet negative emotions, which blend together to constitute the recipe for hate. By providing the reader with an overview of the distinctive features of hate, and an outline of the three-phase model of the emergence of hate in the context of populism, Martinez is then able to consider the implications of populism instilling hate. This is compared to the role of discrete negative emotions in generating intergroup conflict.

In the following chapter 'Genocide: An Alternative Lens to Explore Hate Crime Offending,' Will Bergstroem draws from a selection of key theories and models on hate crime offending to undertake intersectional assessment of hate crime and genocide. Calling for an interdisciplinary exploration of hate crime and genocide, which can be useful for genocide prediction and prevention, the author presents three key arguments. Firstly, Bergstroem notes that there is a clear relationship between the concepts of hate crime and genocide, which warrants an interdisciplinary approach to the topics. Linked to this, it is then argued that hate crime can play a key role in the development and stages of genocide. Finally, Bergstroem advocates for the use of models of hate crime offending to demonstrate the role of and overlap between hate crime and genocide commission. This chapter therefore successfully highlights the benefits and importance of intersectional approaches for developing new perspectives and knowledge around hate crime and genocide.

Next, the chapter by Brendan Lantz and Alexis Faulkner, 'Female Hate Crime Offenders: The Theoretical and Policy Implications of an Under-Researched Phenomenon', details the contemporary research being undertaken into female hate crime offending in the United States. The chapter assesses the extent of female hate crime perpetration and how this may differ from that solely perpetrated by males. It also discusses the significance of examining these issues via an intersectional framework as a mechanism for 'doing difference' across multiple social domains. The chapter argues that understanding hate crime offending within this framework has fundamental implications for understanding hate crimes as a mechanism of social stratification and the production of societal inequality.

In the chapter, 'Perpetrators of Hate Crime in and Around the Space of the Mosque' (the first in Volume II), Mikahil Azad employs interviews and ethnographic work to examine how different kinds of Islamophobia can manifest in the spaces in and around two mosques based in Birmingham, England. He outlines the nature of the physical and verbal actions of perpetrators of hate incidents that he observed, noting their overtly hostile nature towards local Muslims, making them feel unwelcome in the environs of their own mosques. He argues that these sentiments are typical of those found nationally, which are historically deep-rooted yet which cause so much damage to contemporary Muslim communities.

In the following chapter, 'The Strategic Use of Gender-Based Hatred on TikTok: Hate Stratagems, Information Manipulation and Incel TikTok Creators' (in Volume II), Anda Solea examines the issue of online hate and specifically how incel TikTok creators weaponise their misogyny via targeting women online. The chapter analyses 332 videos shared by five incel-specific TikTok accounts and reveals that these harmful videos degrade women by using hateful discourse to portray women as a threat to all men. The chapter argues that appeals to emotion and pseudoscience are used to validate, promote and normalise the incel 'blackpill' ideology that states that physical attractiveness defines society hierarchically, and that women, being inherently 'lookist,' place incel men at the bottom of this hierarchy, fuelling their sense of resentment, bitterness and misogynistic hatred. Women and girls are therefore left at heightened risk of being targeted, suggests the author, due to gender not being recognised as a protected characteristic under hate speech legislation.

Following this, the next chapter 'Mapping the Complexity of Hate Studies: Taking Stock, Moving Forward' (in Volume II) by Matteo Vergani, Alexandra Lee, Haily Tran, Imogen Richards, Greg Barton and Cam Smith, recognises the difficulties in defining what constitutes a 'hate crime' in the multidisciplinary arena of hate studies. By its very nature, hate studies draws on a wide spectrum of theoretical and conceptual perspectives, which makes the development of robust empirical and methodological frameworks that work across this spectrum challenging. In turn, this makes it very difficult to gain common consensus on what hate crime actually is. The chapter attempts to break this impasse by presenting two novel frameworks, the 'spectrum of hate' and 'proof of hate,' for categorising different perspectives on defining and identifying hateful behaviour. These are then applied to criminalised and non-criminalised incidents discussed in Australian legal documents in order to establish a foundation for future policy, research and practice. The chapter argues this will be beneficial in three ways: by providing a common language and conceptual system for understanding different approaches to defining and measuring both criminalised and non-criminalised hate behaviours; by enabling and supporting more effective dialogue across disciplines and between academia and practitioners, and by clarifying the overlaps between hateful behaviours and other areas of violence and harm prevention.

In the next chapter, Amanda Haynes examines 'Hate Crime and Institutional Bias' (in Volume II), focusing specifically on agents of the criminal justice system (police and courts). The chapter highlights that recognition of and responses to institutional bias are essential to creating effective criminal justice responses to hate crime. In the chapter, this recognition comes through in the examination of different manifestations of institutional bias within the criminal justice system. Haynes also offers responses to this problem in the form of lessons offered by critical and abolitionist scholarship. These insights—such as about the importance of education, the need to address systemic causes, the value of adopting transformative justice approaches, and the need for greater transparency and accountability—have huge value in helping us to recognise the limits of criminal justice responses, and look to reform to try to 'genuinely offer justice to minoritised communities.'

Following this 'Understanding Hate Crime Perpetration: The Causes, Enablers and Motivators of Hate' (in Volume II), by Rachel Keighley, looks at how the perpetration of hate crime requires us to examine the 'complex interplay between wider societal attitudes … and the specific factors that enable and motivate individuals to commit hate crimes.' Noting the barriers to engaging with the perpetrators of hate crime, Keighley argues that understanding experiences of hate crime victimisation can help us to understand hate crime perpetration, and does this using case studies looking at rural racism in England and LGBTQI +

hate online to examine some of the factors which victims have identified as underpinning hate. The chapter begins by exploring the 'learning' of hate and prejudice within families and how this is subsequently reinforced in education. It then looks to how these learnt attitudes are legitimised by socio-cultural, economic and political factors within society, before the final section looks into how this can then lead to the manifestation of that hate as personal insecurities can intertwine with structural inequalities to motivate the perpetration of hate crime.

Esli Chan's 'Toxic Monetization and Amplification in Digital Platform Design: The Case of Online Gendered Hate' (in Volume II) examines hate crime in online spaces. Rather than focusing solely on perpetrators, Chan gives insight into how platform design and so social media platforms themselves are not only allowing space for online hate to flourish, but can reward this. Three key themes—digital capitalism, platform design and user behaviour—are identified and considered as interconnected to create a 'cycle of harm.' This is explored through a series of case studies focusing on different social media platforms: YouTube in the context of networked harassment; TikTok and user manipulation of algorithms to evade content removal in relation to 'tradwife' content; Reddit's decentralised networks and volunteer content moderation as emboldening hate speech; and affective strategies as an aspect of podcasts on Spotify. The chapter finishes by reflecting on the challenges of addressing online hate speech, particularly when deplatforming can create more notoriety for content providers who then simply move onto new—and less regulated—platforms.

Tiana Gaudette and Ryan Scrivens in 'Pathways Out of Hate Groups: Trends in the Empirical Literature and Future Directions' (in Volume II) provide a fascinating insight into hate crime perpetration through their examination of the research that explores the disengagement and deradicalization of individuals leaving hate groups ('formers' or 'former extremists'). They note that although there are some concerns about giving space to those 'formers' there are also valuable insights that can be gained through engagement with formers as 'consultants, peer mentors, interventionists, peace makers and participants in research.' Gaudette and Scrivens evaluate the existing literature on formers, identifying that leaving hate groups is a process comprised of several events, facilitated particularly through self-reflection. They are, however circumspect and acknowledge that many questions on formers remain underexplored within the research: they identify the need to further examine the significance of an individual's role within a group on their disengagement, the influences on relapse, the processes of disengagement and the development of models of disengagement.

Nicole Asquith, Andy Kaladelfos and Geoff Steer look at perpetration of LGBTIQA + hate crime in New South Wales (NSW), Australia in their chapter 'Proving it is the problem: Ice cold cases, hot button issues, and justice seeking for historical homicides against gay men and transgender women' (in Volume II). Setting the context at the start of the chapter, they note the history of policing hate crime in Australia and the process of truth-seeking undertaken by the police and LGBTQIA + organisations in relation to 91 historical homicides committed between 1970 and 2010. The first key discussion in this chapter focuses on the findings of three inquiries into the homicides, examining how and why these inquiries show substantial differences in whether they assigned hate motivation to the individual offences. The authors then move on to look at characteristics of the victims, offences and offending behaviours/ perpetrators, and the outcomes of the investigations. Damningly, they note how one inquiry failed to identify the transwomen within the dataset or deadnamed and assigned them male, reflecting concerns raised earlier in the chapter that police responses reflect transphobia and prejudice. The chapter ends by inviting the reader to use the analysis conducted to think about improvements to practice, particularly around investigation and identification of hate motivation.

Chapter, 'Breaking the Cycle? Learning from the Past to Improve the Present' (in Volume II) provides an opportunity to look at hate crime from the perspective of those who work directly with the perpetrators of hate crime. Mark Rusling (Director of Learning at the UK's National Holocaust Museum in Nottingham) examines how their education programme, 'Breaking the Cycle,' offers an opportunity to use a historical understanding of the Holocaust to challenge preconceptions held by individual hate crime perpetrators; focusing on how a climate of intolerance developed across time to allow critical reflection on behaviours, attitudes and stereotype, this approach has shown a positive effect on the individual perpetrators who have participated. This chapter also offers a thorough critical reflection on some of the problems with this approach. Particularly useful is the discussion around how participants may struggle to see the relevance of the Holocaust their own 'low-level' hate behaviours. However, the chapter also offers an analysis of how the National Holocaust Centre have reflected on and improved their programme to meet these challenges, providing 'eight distinct lessons' that others can draw on to develop their own education programmes.

References

Burch, L. (2021). *Understanding disability and everyday hate*. Palgrave Macmillan.

Campbell, R., & Sanders, T. (2021). *Sex work and hate crime: Innovating policy, practice and theory*. Palgrave.

Cokelaere, H., & Goury-Laffont, V. (2024, July 7). France election results 2024: Who won across the country. *Politico* at, https://www.politico.eu/article/france-election-results-2024-map-constituencies-emmanuel-macron-marine-le-pen-live-new-popular-front-national-rally/. Accessed February 24, 2025

Deo, A., & Malik, M. (2024). *Fear and hope 2024: The case for community resilience*. Hope Not Hate.

Garland, J., & Hodkinson, P. (2014). "F**king Freak! What the hell do you think you look like?" Experiences of targeted victimisation among Goths and developing notions of hate crime. *British Journal of Criminology, 54*(4), 613–631.

Home Office. (2023, March 13). *Police will prioritise freedom of speech under new hate incident guidance* at, https://www.gov.uk/government/news/police-will-prioritise-freedom-of-speech-under-new-hate-incident-guidance. Accessed February 24, 2025

Home Office. (2024, October 10). *Hate crime, England and Wales, year ending March 2024*, https://www.gov.uk/government/statistics/hate-crime-england-and-wales-year-ending-march-2024. Accessed February 24, 2025

Kirby, P. (2025, February 24). Germany's conservatives celebrate, but far right enjoy record result. *BBC News* at https://www.bbc.co.uk/news/articles/cvgenlw94n3o. Accessed February 24, 2025

Lawrence, D., & Davis, G. (2020). *QAnon in the UK: The growth of a movement*. Hope Not Hate.

Mason, G. (2014). The symbolic purpose of hate crime law: Ideal victims and emotion. *Theoretical Criminology, 18*(1), 75–92.

Melley, B. (2024, October 26). Supporters of far-right British figure rally as anti-racism demonstrators mount counter-protest. *Independent* at, https://www.independent.co.uk/news/tommy-robinson-ap-london-british-stand-up-to-racism-b2636230.html. Accessed February 24, 2025

Paterson, J. L., Walters, M. A., Brown, R., & Carrasco, D. (2024). Angry and afraid: Exploring the impact of mixed emotional reactions to hate crimes with LGBT+ and Muslim communities. *Journal of Interpersonal Violence*, 0(0). https://doi.org/10.1177/08862605241286455

Perry, P., & Scrivens, R. (2019). *Right-wing extremism in Canada*. Palgrave Macmillan.

Perry, B. (2001). *In the name of hate: Understanding hate crimes*. Routledge.

Sherwood, H., & Quinn, B. (2024, November 1). 'He's like a gangster': How Tommy Robinson became leader of Britain's far right. *The Guardian* at, 'He's like a gangster': How Tommy Robinson became leader of Britain's far right | Tommy Robinson | *The Guardian*. Accessed February 02, 2025.

Vaizey, E. (2021, January 26). 'Britain's 'war on woke' won't work. *Politico* at, https://www.politico.eu/article/britains-war-on-woke-wont-work-history-statues-monuments/. Accessed February24, 2025.

Walters, M. (2014). *Hate crime and restorative justice: Exploring causes*. Oxford University Press.

Wilkin, D. (2020). *Disability hate crime: Experiences of everyday hostility on public transport*. Palgrave Macmillan.

Williams, D., & Tregidga, J. (2013). *All Wales hate crime research project: Research overview & executive summary*. Race Equality First.

Zempi, I. (2016). Covered in Stigma? Exploring the impacts of Islamophobic hate crime globally. In J. Schweppe & M. Walters (Eds.), *The Globalization of hate: Internationalizing hate crime?* (pp. 111–125). Oxford University Press.

Offender Profiles

Examining the Reoffending of Hate Crime Offenders in England and Wales

Darrick Jolliffe, Jon Garland, and Ian Brunton-Smith

Introduction

In England and Wales, a hate crime is defined as 'any criminal offence which is perceived, by the victim or any other person, to be motivated by hostility or prejudice towards someone based on a personal characteristic' (College of Policing, 2014), and there are currently five nationally monitored strands of hate crime: race or ethnicity, religion or belief, sexual

D. Jolliffe (✉)
Department of Security and Crime Science, University College London, London, UK
e-mail: d.jolliffe@ucl.ac.uk

Present Address:
J. Garland
Department of Sociology, University of Surrey, Guildford, UK
e-mail: j.garland@surrey.ac.uk

I. Brunton-Smith
Department of Sociology, University of Surrey, Guildford, UK

J. Garland et al. (eds.), *Hate Crime Perpetrators: New Perspectives from Theory, Research and Practice, Volume I*, Palgrave Hate Studies,
https://doi.org/10.1007/978-3-031-92666-2_2

orientation, disability and transgender identity. Yet, while this legal definition is relatively clear, hate crime has been referred to as a concept 'fraught with contradictions' (Burch, 2021: 2) because of the challenges associated with identifying, operationalising and therefore measuring this offence. For example (and as detailed in Chapters X, Y, Z), certain hate incidents may not be recognised as such by the victim as the incidents may not be considered sufficiently serious to be reported to authorities, or they may be such a commonly experienced negative occurrence as to become normalised into their everyday lives (Haynes et al., 2023). Similarly, the structural disadvantage that characterises the social position of many victims of hate crime may, perhaps understandably, reduce their confidence in the criminal justice system and therefore their willingness to report such offences. Previous bad experiences of reporting to the police coupled with longstanding wariness of the police due to some minoritised communities feeling over-policed and under-protected may also affect the reporting rates of hate crimes (Chakraborti et al., 2014). Even if the victim does report the offence to the police, if their victimisation occurred based on a form of difference that does not 'fit' with the official recording of hate crime (e.g. homelessness or alternative subcultural status) this may not be recorded as such (Garland et al., 2015). The considerable drop in the number of offences from offences taking place to the official characterisation and identification of these offences is a known and studied 'fact' in wider criminology, but the nature of hate crime may significantly broaden this crime funnel.

Despite these methodological challenges there has been a proliferation of research dedicated to understanding the nature, social causes and importantly, the heightened negative consequences of hate crime victimisation (e.g., Schweppe et al., 2018; Zempi, 2019). For example, Brunton-Smith et al. (2025) used 8 years of nationally representative data to isolate the unique emotional impact of hate-motivated violence and vandalism on the victim. They did this by employing multi-level modelling to control for the influence of a host of variables including the type of hate offence (i.e., race, religion, sexual orientation, age, gender, disability), the age and ethnicity of the victim, their length of residence in the area, the number of experiences of victimisation, where in the series of incidents the hate offence occurred, the seriousness of the offence, the number of perpetrators and the relationship between the perpetrator and the victim (i.e., casual acquaintance, stranger). The results showed that the emotional impact of experiencing many forms of hate crime were more profound than experiencing a similar non-hate-motivated offence. The serious negative emotional impacts of hate crime have been replicated in many other studies (Botcherby et al., 2011; Coleman et al., 2013; Iganski & Lagou, 2014; Nocon et al., 2011; Paterson et al., 2024). It is these profound negative impacts on individuals and the damaging 'ripple' effects of these offences on those within the wider communities of those victimised (e.g., Paterson et al., 2019) that provide the motivation for identifying the causes of this form of offending.

Recent avenues for hate crime scholarship include in-depth explorations of the form and impacts of online expressions of hate (Bliuc et al., 2018), and the link between hate crime victimisation and the risk of self-harm and suicide (Cramer et al., 2018). However, research into the perpetrators of hate crime has not kept pace with the exponential increase in wider hate crime study. This might be because the epistemological orientation of many hate crime scholars tends to be sociological, with perpetrators conceptualised as a construction of the social structural order in which they find themselves. For example, one of the leading voices in this field of research refers to hate crime as a process by which perpetrators both reinforce their status as dominant and remind subordinate groups of their lesser status (Perry, 2001). This approach is important because it directs research to understanding the wider social environment and contexts in which multiple forms of hate crime might be evident, as well as the difficulties that police may have in making sense of hate crime, which is often more of an ongoing series of incidents of victimisation than singular, isolated events (Chakraborti & Garland, 2015).

While likely accurate, this understanding does not explain why only certain individuals commit hate crimes sufficiently serious to evoke a criminal justice response, what features might differentiate hate crime offenders from offenders who commit similarly serious, but non-hate offences, and whether hate crime offenders are more likely to repeat hate offences. If one of the goals of hate crime scholarship is to reduce the perpetration of hate crime, much more research which specifically focusses on perpetrators is required.

Previous Research on Hate Crime Offenders

One of the most widely cited contributions on hate crime perpetrators comes from McDevitt et al. (2002) who used 169 police case files of known suspects or those arrested for hate crime in the US to infer offender motivation and identify hate crime offender typologies. The authors suggested that 66% of the perpetrators were 'thrill' offenders who were young and committed hate crime impulsively while in groups, while 25% were 'defensive' offenders, committing their offences to 'protect' their turf (e.g., neighbourhood) from perceived outsiders. Unfortunately, this study didn't provide a demographic or criminal history profile of these hate crime 'typologies' or illustrate how these offenders might be similar to, or different from, non-hate crime offenders. It is worthwhile noting that impulsiveness is one of the best predictors of later general offending (Jolliffe & Farrington, 2009).

Iganski and Smith (2011) used the police data of those accused of hate crime from Lancashire, London and Northern Ireland to examine the demographic and socioeconomic characteristics of this group. They found that hate crime offenders were predominantly male, of white racial background, were typically unemployed and aged under 30. The suggestion that most racially motivated offenders are male and White was also reported in a study of youth (age 10 and 17) serving community sentences for racially motivated offending in England and Wales (Wilcox et al., 2010).

In the United States, Dunbar et al. (2005) examined the criminal history of 204 hate crime offenders who had been identified and apprehended by the police. They found that most hate crime offenders were male (87%) and had an average age of about 33. Less than half of the arrestees were of Euro-White ethnicity, with those of Latino (26%) and African-American descent (15%) being the next most prevalence ethnic groups. A relatively small proportion of the sample (16%) were classified as members of hate-oriented criminal gangs or groups, but it was not clear how this classification was made. Importantly, a significantly higher proportion of hate crime offenders had previous experience with the criminal justice system, with 45% having previous misdemeanour convictions and 36% having prior felony convictions. Details about the types of previous offences was not available, but an assessment of the severity of the previous offending suggested that hate crime offenders had criminal histories which included both violent and non-violent offending.

The criminal records of 58 hate crime offenders convicted in Los Angeles were reviewed by Dunbar (2003), which was the entire population of those convicted for hate crimes between 1995 and 1997 in Los Angeles. Of these offenders, over 91% were men, and their average age was 24.5 (sd = 8.1, range 16–44). The ethnicity of the hate crime offenders was generally representative of the Los Angeles area (over 43% Latino, 33% European White, 15.5% African-American, 3.4% Asian Pacific). Almost half of the hate crime offenders had previously been convicted for physical assault, with robbery/extortion being the next most prevalent offence (about 25%), followed by property offences (17%). Interestingly, Dunbar (2003) also used the records of hate crime offenders to score a validated risk assessment measure to predict their subsequent offending (HCR-20; Webster et al., 1997). While the reoffending of these offenders was not followed up to assess the predictive validity of this measure with hate crime offenders, this sample of hate offenders were found to be in the low-moderate range in their likelihood of reoffending compared to a group acquitted because of insanity.

In Finland Näsi et al. (2016) used a nationally representative self-reported study of children (aged about 15, 51% female) to explore factors associated with the perpetration of hate-motivated assault and bullying. The results suggested that the factors that predicted hate crime offenders were very similar to those that predicted non-hate offenders. Both groups were more likely than those who did not report committing offences to be male, come from lower socioeconomic backgrounds, have parents who were drunk often, have received poor parental supervision and have low self-control. Hate crime offenders were unique in additionally having parents who fought often.

Jolliffe and Farrington (2020) used administrative data to explore the demographic and criminal histories of the population of hate crime offenders released from prison in England and Wales over one year. A total of 355 (out of 47,775) released offenders or (0.7%) had an index offence for a hate crime offence (83% violence, 13% public order, 4% criminal damage), and these offenders were predominantly White and about age 34. In addition, these hate crime offenders had very prolific criminal careers, with about 87% having a previous conviction for violence and 76% having had a previous public order offence. In fact, the average hate crime offender had committed 8 different types of offences (out of 20 possible) before their current offence, had an average of 42 previous offences in total and had served an average of 7 previous custodial sentences. When hate crime offenders who committed violence were compared to those who had committed a non-hate violent offence, violent hate crime offenders were found to be significantly older with far more prolific and versatile criminal histories, including more previous violent offences and previous incarcerations.

Taken collectively, research on hate crime offenders does not address key questions such as: what factors might increase the likelihood of becoming a hate crime offender, and are these factors unique to hate crime? If, for example, hate crime offenders are simply high-volume offenders who commit their hate crime offence almost at random in a prolific criminal career (e.g., Farrington, 1998), then evidence-based interventions targeted at prolific or persistent offenders would have the greatest impact on reducing later hate crime offences. If, however, the commission of a hate crime is the result of a unique factor or combination of factors (e.g., hate orientation), then interventions specific to addressing the needs of hate crime offenders will be the most effective at reducing later hate crimes (e.g., Walters, 2020).

Current Study

The current study is a prospective examination of the reoffending of all adult males released from short-term incarceration in England and Wales in one year, including a proportion who were originally incarcerated for committing a hate crime. This is the first study of the reoffending of hate crime offenders (HCO) and the first study to evaluate the extent to which the reoffending of hate crime offenders may be distinguishable from non-hate crime offenders (NHCO).

The overarching research questions which guide this research are:

1. Do HCOs released from short-term incarceration differ from NHCOs in their prevalence, frequency or speed of reoffending?
2. To what extent is the prevalence of the reoffending of HCOs and NHCOs in line with their predicted reoffending using an actuarial risk assessment tool?
3. Do HCOs differ from NHCOs in the profile of their type of their reoffence?

Data

The data for this study comes from the Police National Computer database (PNC), which is the national database for offences and convictions held and updated by the police in the UK. This data is commonly made available for the purposes of evaluation or academic study by the Ministry of Justice who have oversight of prisons, courts, probation and attendance centres in England and Wales. An overview of what PNC data comprises, and how it is typically used in research is summarised by Sutherland (2013). Briefly, the anonymised extracts of the PNC provided to researchers contain basic demographic information about the offender (e.g., age at index offence, race, nationality, gender, religion, region where offence occurred) and criminal history information such as the age at first offence and the number and the type of previous offences. The present study is based on a complete population of male offenders aged 18 and over who were released from short-term incarceration in England and Wales. Short term prison sentences are those in which the individual was sentenced to prison for up to one year for their current offence. This data also included information about the type, timing and number of reoffences that were committed 12 months after the individual was released from prison.

The main benefit of this data is that it allows for a prospective assessment of reoffending for a large sample of both HCOs and NHCOs. This allows for an examination of the prevalence, frequency and type of reoffending of HCOs and for the main type of reoffence. The reoffending of HCOs has not yet been addressed in the growing body of hate crime literature. The main limitation of this data is that it only captures the behaviour of a very specific type of HCO, namely those who committed a hate offence of a sufficient severity (and form) to result in a short prison sentence. Those who committed a hate crime offence which was not recognised as such by the victims, not reported to the police, not recorded by the police, who were not convicted or were convicted but received a lesser (e.g., community order) or more serious (e.g., incarceration for longer than a year) sanction are not included. The focus on a specific sample, and the implications of this for the generalisability of the findings of this study for all those who may perpetrate hate crime, need to be borne in mind when interpreting the results.

Results

The demographic and criminal history characteristics of the entire population released from prison can be seen in Table 1. About 83% were of White ethnicity, and over 87% were UK Nationals. Most of the offenders had committed their offences in London, followed by the North West (14.7%) and West Midlands (12.9%), and the average age of those released from prison was 33.0 (sd = 12.3). As would be expected, those released from prison typically had extensive criminal careers, with almost all having many previous offences (95.7%) and court appearances (95.5%) and over three-quarters having previously served a previous prison sentence.

The difference between the offender's average age of first offence (M = 18.1) and average age of index offence (M = 31.1), or the offence that resulted in their current incarceration, was 4772 days (sd = 3465). This

Table 1 Descriptive statistics of the sample

Demographic Information		Previous offending	%
Ethnicity	%	With Previous Offences	95.7
White	82.8	With Previous Court Appearances	95.5
Black	10.2	With Previous Incarcerations	77.3
Asian	5.3	**Frequency**	**M (sd)**
Other	1.7	Av. Age at Index Offence	31.1 (9.9)
		Av. Age at First Offence	18.1 (7.5)
Nationality		Av. No. of Previous Offences	43.6 (43.6)
UK Nationality	87.7	Av. No. Previous Court Appearances	18.7 (17.8)
Region		Av. No. Previous Incarcerations	7.4 (8.2)
East Midlands	8.0	Av No. Different Offences (Versatility, 0 - 20)	8.2 (3.7)
East of England	8.5	Av. OGRS Score (0–100)	55.6 (23)
London	18.8	Av. Sentence Length (days)	127.2 (76.8)
North East	3.9	Av. Time Served (days)	51.6 (85.4)
North West	14.7	Av. Criminal Career Duration (days)	4772 (3465)
South East	10.8		
South West	7.1		
Wales	5.6		
West Midlands	12.9		
Yorkshire and the Humber	9.6		
Age	M (sd)		
Age at Release	33.0 (12.3)		

is equivalent to an average criminal career duration of 4772 days (about 13 years).

Further attesting to the prolific criminal history of this sample, they had on average 44 previous offences, seven previous prison sentences and had committed eight out of a possible 20 types of offences (see Table 2). These offenders had an average Offence Group Reconviction Score (OGRS) of about 55. OGRS is an actuarial risk assessment device that provides a prediction of the likelihood of an individual reoffending (from 0 to 100) one year after release (Howard et al., 2009). This estimate is made based on the offender's gender, age at index offence and a measure of their speed of accruing convictions across their criminal career. This actuarial measure was developed and validated on criminal justice-involved individuals in England and Wales and is used to inform decision making (e.g., level of supervision after release) about that individual (Howard et al., 2009). An OGRS score of 55 means that it would be expected that about 55% of this sample would reoffend within a year.

Table 2 shows the proportion and actual number (n) of offenders released from prison categorised into the twenty Ministry of Justice index offence types. The most prevalent index offences were theft and violence, which together accounted for close to half of all index offence types. There were four categories of hate crime offences that resulted in short-term incarceration in this population: criminal damage, public order,

Table 2 Index offences of population

Offence type	% (n)	Offence type	% (n)
Absconding	3.49 (1348)	Sexual	1.23 (474)
Criminal Damage	2.36 (909)	Sexual Child	0.63 (243)
Domestic Burglary	2.06 (795)	Soliciting/Prostitution	0.09 (33)
Drink Driving	3.87(1494)	Taking and driving away	2.33 (899)
Drugs (import/export/ supply)	0.52 (201)	Theft	23.95 (9240)
Drugs (possession)	2.19 (844)	Theft from Vehicle	1.89 (731)
Fraud/Forgery	3.15 (1217)	Violence	23.77 (9170)
Handling	1.56 (600)	Serious Violence	0.76 (292)
Other	5.59 (2158)	***Hate Criminal Damage***	***0.04 (17)***
Other Burglary	4.28 (1650)	***Hate Public Order***	***0.12 (45)***
Other Motoring	9.98 (3851)	***Hate Violence***	***0.74 (287)***
Public Order	4.89 (1885)	***Hate Serious Violence***	***0.02 (6)***
Robbery	0.49 (190)	**Total**	100 (38,579)

violence and serious violence (the bottom of Table 2). The most prevalent of these was a violent hate crime offence (287 individuals), and the least prevalent was hate serious violence (6 individuals). Hate crime offenders (HCOs) therefore constituted 3.1% of those with an index offence of violence (287/9170), 2.4% of those with a public order offence (45/1885), 2.0% of those with serious violence (6/292), and 1.9% of those with criminal damage (17/909). Overall, those with hate crimes constituted 0.9% of the total population of those released from a short-term incarceration.

Information about reoffending 12 months after the individual was released from prison was available from the Police National Computer administrative records.[1] This included whether the individual was convicted of a proven reoffence and the type of offence committed in the follow-up period. When the index reoffence was committed, the disposal for the most serious offence (e.g., a community sentence or re-incarceration) and the number of reoffences over the follow-up period was also available.

The results showed that of the 355 HCOs released from prison, 219 (61.7%) had a reoffence in the twelve month follow-up period. However, of the 38,224 NHCOs released 23,959 (62.7%) had a reoffence over the same time-period (Table 3). This difference was not statistically significant (chi squared = 0.2, OR = 1.0[2]), suggesting that HCOs and NHCOs had a similar prevalence of reoffending. Interestingly, however, HCOs were significantly less likely to be re-incarcerated for their reoffence. About 23% of HCOs were sentenced to re-incarceration compared to 29.7% of NHCOs (chi squared = 9.3, $p < 0.002$, OR = 0.65). There was no indication that HCO or NHCOs differed in the number of offences that they committed in the follow-up period or in the duration of time that elapsed to committing their first reoffence.

[1] The actual follow-up period was 18 months, but this included 6 months for the offences to be processed and added to the PNC.

[2] The Odds Ratio is a measure of effect centred around 1.0. As a rule of thumb odds ratios around 2.0 (or 0.5) are considered important (Cohen, 1996).

Table 3 Reoffending of Hate Crime Offenders (HCO) and Non-Hate Crime Offenders (NHCO)

	HCO	NHCO		
N	355	38,224		
	% (n)	**% (n)**	**Chi squared**	**OR**
Reoffending	61.7 (219)	62.7 (23,959)	0.15	0.96
Reincarcerated	22.8 (81)	29.7 (11,338)	9.3	0.65*
	M (sd)	**M (sd)**	**t**	**OR**
Number of Offences	5.7 (5.3)	5.4 (5.1)	0.7	1.11
Days to Reoffence	91.0 (94.7)	92.2 (92.0)	0.3	0.98
Days to Reoffence (median)	50	59		

Controlling for Risk of Reoffending

While overall HCOs and NHCOs did not significantly differ in their prevalence or frequency of reoffending this analysis did not control for any differences which may have existed in the likelihood of reoffending of these two groups. A considerable amount of research has established that certain demographic features (e.g., younger age) and criminal history factors (e.g., index offence of violence) increase an individual's likelihood of committing a reoffence (e.g., Howard et al., 2009). As previously mentioned OGRS is a validated risk assessment tool which provides an actuarial assessment of an individual's risk of reoffending one year after release. This risk is codified in a continuous score that ranges from 0 to 100, and although this tool is not without its limitations (Fazel et al., 2012), it has been demonstrated to predict reoffending as well as any risk assessment tool available (Farrington et al., 2008).

In this study, HCOs had an average OGRS score of 50.2 (sd = 20.3) which suggests that about 50% of this group was predicted to reoffend one year after release. In comparison, NHCOs had an average OGRS score of 55.6 (23.3). This was a statistically significant difference ($t = 4.3$, $p < 0.0001$, $OR = 0.66$), suggesting that NHCOs were, on average, more likely to reoffend. It is interesting to note that despite this elevation in the likelihood of reoffending, NCHOs were no more likely to actually reoffend than HCOs (Table 3).

This significant difference in the likelihood of reoffending between HCOs and NHCOs was more closely examined by categorising these groups into ordinal categories based on their OGRS scores. Table 4 shows the comparison between HCOs and NHCOs in the prevalence and frequency of reoffending in four ordinal categories of risk based on their OGRS score. For example, 99 HCOs had an OGRS score between 0 and 39, and of these offenders 39 (or 39.4%) reoffended within one year of release, compared to 2596 out of 9545 (27.2%) NHCOs who were in the same risk category. This difference was statistically significant with an OR = 1.7 (1.1–7.7), which suggests that low risk HCO were significantly more likely to reoffend than low risk NHCO. HCOs who were of medium risk (OGRS score 40–60), medium–high risk (60–74) and high risk (75–100) were no more likely to reoffend than NHCOs.

The righthand side of Table 4 also shows the number of reoffences committed per reoffender for both HCOs and NHCOs in the four ordinal categories of risk. It can be seen that low risk HCOs (0–39) committed an average of 3.5 reoffences in the follow-up period compared to an average of 3.0 reoffences by NHCOs. This difference was not statistically significant. However, there was evidence that HCOs who were of both medium–high and high risk had committed more reoffences than comparable NHCOs.

Table 4 Reoffending controlling for risk of reoffending

		HCO		NHCO			HCO	NHCO	
	OGRS Score	Tot N	% Reoff	Tot N	% Reoff	OR	Av. No. Reoff M (sd)	Av. No. Reoff M (sd)	OR
Low	0–39	99	39.4	9,545	27.2	1.7*	3.5 (3.3)	3.0 (3.0)	1.3
Med	40–60	131	61.1	9,514	58.7	1.1	4.3 (4.5)	4.1 (4.0)	1.1
Med-High	60–74	90	76.7	9,556	75.8	1.0	6.6 (5.1)	5.0 (4.4)	1.9*
High	75–100	35	88.6	9,606	88.9	1.0	9.2 (7.2)	7.2 (6.0)	1.8

Type of Reoffence

Data about the type of the most serious reoffence was available. The top of Table 5 shows the comparison of the primary non-hate related reoffence types between HCOs and HNCOs. For example, of the 219 HCOs who reoffended, the primary reoffence for 8 HCOs (or 3.7%) was absconding. When compared to the 711/23960 (or 3.0%) of the NHCOs who committed this reoffence, this was equivalent to an odds ratio of 1.2, a difference which was not statistically significant. Interestingly, HCOs were significantly more likely to have a reoffence for criminal damage (OR = 1.6), public order offences (OR = 2.8), violence (OR = 1.5) and serious violence (OR = 3.3), while being significantly less likely to reoffend with motoring offences (OR = 0.3) and theft (OR = 0.4).

The bottom of Table 5 shows the comparison between HCOs and NHCOs for reoffences of hate crime. Over the entire population of the 24,179 individuals who reoffended (both HCOs and NHCOs) a total of 186 had a reoffence for a hate crime (0.8%). No HCOs reoffended with hate criminal damage (compared to 9 NHCOs) or hate serious violence (compared to 3 NHCOs). However, HCOs were significantly more likely to reoffend with a hate crime for public order (OR = 4.2) and much more likely to reoffend with hate violence (OR = 12.3) compared to NHCOs.

Overall, a total of 12 (out of 219) HCOs reoffended with a form of hate crime (5.5%), which was a much greater proportion than the 0.7% (174/23960) of the NHCOs (OR = 7.9). Keeping in mind the small number of HCOs repeating a hate crime, these results suggest that HCOs had a statistically significantly higher likelihood of repeating a hate crime compared to NHCOs, particularly with a violent and public order hate crime.

Table 5 Type of reoffending of Hate Crime Offenders (HCO) and Non-Hate Crime Offenders (NHCO)

Offence type	HCO %	NHCO %	Chi squared	OR
Absconding	3.7	3.0	0.35	1.2
Criminal Damage	8.2	5.3	3.9	1.6*
Domestic Burglary	1.4	2.5	1.1	0.5
Drink Driving	0.0	1.3		
Drugs (import/export/supply)	0.5	0.5	0.007	1.0
Drugs (possession)	4.1	5.1	0.42	0.8
Fraud/Forgery	1.4	1.4	0.0	1.0
Handling	1.8	1.5	0.15	1.2
Other	5.0	6.8	1.1	0.7
Other Burglary	2.3	3.5	1.0	0.6
Other Motoring	1.8	5.6	6.0	0.3*
Public Order	23.3	9.7	45.4	2.8*
Robbery	0.0	1.2		
Sexual	1.4	1.0	0.3	1.4
Sexual Child	0.0	0.04		
Soliciting/Prostitution	0.0	0.1		
Taking and driving away	0.9	1.9	1.1	0.5
Theft	17.8	33.4	23.7	0.4*
Theft from Vehicle	0.0	2.0		
Violence	18.7	12.9	6.4	1.5*
Serious Violence	2.3	0.7	7.7	3.3*
Hate Crime Reoffence Types				
Hate Criminal Damage	0.0	0.04		
Hate Public Order	1.4	0.3	6.9	4.2*
Hate Violence	4.1	0.3	81.1	12.3*
Hate Serious Violence	0.0	0.01		
Total (N)	219	23,960		

Discussion

Very little is known about hate crime offenders. In a population of males released from short-term incarceration in England and Wales, hate crime was a relatively infrequent offence. About 0.9% of the males had originally been incarcerated for a hate offence and one year after release the prevalence of hate crime offending was 0.8%. The main purpose of this research was to evaluate whether those who commit hate crime were discernibly different from non-hate crime offenders in the profile of their reoffending.

The results suggested that, overall, HCOs were no more or less likely to reoffend, were not more likely to commit a greater number of reoffences or to reoffend more quickly than NHCOs. However, when this reoffending was investigated more closely, interesting differences between HCOs and NHCOs were noted. When their risk of reoffending was controlled using an actuarial risk assessment tool, HCOs who were classified as low risk were significantly more likely to reoffend than NHCOs. This may indicate that the risk assessment tool predicts reoffending less well for HCOs or that low risk HCOs are in some way different from low risk NHCOs (e.g., Singh et al., 2013).

This 'difference' was even more evident when the profile of the types of reoffending were examined. Surprisingly, HCOs were significantly more likely to reoffend with another hate crime offence and the magnitude of the effect was very large. This analysis was based on a relatively small number of individuals, and therefore requires replication before it can be confidently concluded that hate crime offenders may specialise in hate. It should also be noted that the profile of the reoffending of HCOs may increase the likelihood of them perpetrating hate crime. That is, HCOs were also significantly more likely to reoffend in non-hate crime offence categories that can have hate crime elements (e.g., criminal damage, public order, violence, serious violence) and less likely to commit offences that do not have the capacity for hate elements (e.g., motoring offences, theft). Therefore, while we may tentatively conclude that hate crime offenders are 'different', whether this is a qualitative difference (i.e., hate crime offenders are specialists) or a quantitative difference (i.e., hate crime offenders are prolific and therefore are more likely to commit hate crime) remains unresolved.

There could be multiple reasons why HCOs appeared to be specialists. Quite simply, HCOs may possess entrenched views (i.e., a hate orientation) which increases the likelihood of them repeating hate crime. It is also possible that this finding could reflect a biassed criminal justice system response. Perhaps police, prosecutors and magistrates are more likely to 'see' hate crime amongst those who have already served time in prison for such an offence. Similarly, there is past research from the

US (Messner et al., 2004) and England and Wales (Jolliffe & Farrington, 2020) that has suggested that hate crime offenders might just be more prolific than other similar offenders. This increased frequency and form of offending may accounts for the eventual commission of a hate offence, almost by chance.

Overall HCOs were no more or less likely to reoffend, but they were less likely to be re-incarcerated. This was a counter-intuitive finding, especially in light of the fact that HCOs appeared to, on average, commit more serious reoffence types (violence) and this included repeating hate offending. This somewhat worrying finding may be the result of the fact that HCOs were generally of lower risk, so may have been considered by magistrates or judges as less likely to require prison. It will be important to replicate this study and determine whether this nationally validated risk assessment is appropriate for hate crime offenders or whether a bespoke hate crime offender prediction tool is warranted (e.g. Singh et al., 2013).

Limitations

Given the practical urgency of understanding hate crime as a topic of investigation and the limited research available on hate crime offenders it is crucial that the limitations of this study, and the implications of these limitations, are clear. The data that was available for this study provides a picture of the reoffending of hate crime offenders, which makes a unique contribution to knowledge. However, this was official police data, and official records are often referred to as the 'tip of the iceberg' in terms of the actual offending taking place (e.g., Jolliffe & Farrington, 2015), but this issue is exacerbated in the study of hate crime. While many non-hate offences are not reported to the police, not recorded by the police, have no suspect identified or arrested, and are not convicted and sent to prison, these drop offs in the so-called crime funnel are known to be greater for hate offences (Hall et al., 2015). Therefore, although a population of all hate crime offenders, this is also a highly selective sample where most perpetrating hate offences are likely missed. Exacerbating this, unless the hate crime perpetrated was of the limited forms recorded by the police (i.e., racist, homophobic), this offence could have been recorded as a non-hate offence, resulting in them being treated as a non-hate crime offender in our analyses.

It is also important to note that the reoffending data that we have was recorded in the standard format of PNC data (Sutherland, 2013). This means that the type of the most serious offence was recorded, but the type of the other offences committed were not available. While this may mean that a hate reoffence was missed because this was overshadowed by a more serious non-hate offence, this seems unlikely. This is because hate crime is generally considered more serious, but this is still a possibility.

Conclusion

Considering the general prevalence of hate crime in England and Wales and other Western countries (Keighley, 2024), the serious and severe personal and societal consequences of hate crime victimisation (Paterson et al., 2024) and the growing body of academic research on hate crime, the absence of careful comparative research on hate crime offenders is stark. Relatively little is known about who these offenders are, and less still about what might differentiate hate crime offenders from other those who perpetrate other forms of offending. These are essential questions to address in order to develop the appropriate approaches and interventions needed to reduce the prevalence and frequency of this harmful offence.

While only a single contribution, the results of this research suggest that hate crime offenders may be distinguishable from non-hate crime offenders in the signature of their reoffending. Some practitioners have long suggested that specialist intervention programmes for hate crime offenders are needed (e.g., Davies, 2014), but this is the first large-scale study to provide evidence to support these perceptions. What the current study cannot do is provide much needed insight into the content or key targets of these interventions. This is because while hate crime offenders differed from non-hate crime offenders, it was not possible to disentangle the form of this 'difference'. Hate crime offenders could be qualitatively different (i.e., have a hate orientation), as evidenced by their increased likelihood of reoffending with another hate offence. Alternatively, they could be quantitatively different (i.e., be prolific offenders), evidenced by their increased frequency of reoffending and the fact that they were more likely to reoffend when categorised as low risk and within non-hate offence categories that can have hate elements, such as criminal damage, public order and violence. Future research on those that perpetrate hate crime should focus on understanding this variation so that the profound harm of this form of offending can be mitigated.

References

Bliuc, A. M., Faulkner, N., Jakubowicz, A., & McGarty, C. (2018). Online networks of racial hate: A systematic review of 10 years of research on cyber-racism. *Computers in Human Behavior, 87*, 75–86.

Botcherby, S., Glen, F., Iganski, P., Jochelson, K. & Lagou, S. (2011). *Equality groups' perceptions and experience of crime: Analysis of the British Crime Survey 2007–08, 2008–09 and 2009–10*, Briefing Paper 4. EHRC.

Brunton-Smith, I., Jolliffe, D., & Garland, J. (2025). How does hate hurt more? National evidence for the varying emotional impacts of hate crime. *European Journal of Criminology* (in production).

Burch, L. (2021). *Understanding disability and everyday hate*. Palgrave Macmillan.

Chakraborti, N., Garland, J., & Hardy, S. J. (2014). *The Leicester Hate Crime Project: Findings and Conclusions*. University of Leicester.

Chakraborti, N., & Garland, J. (2015) *Hate Crime: Impact, Causes and Responses* (2nd ed.). Sage

Cohen, P. (1996). Childhood risks for young adult symptoms of personality disorder: Method and substance. *Multivariate Behavioral Research, 31*(1), 121–148.

Coleman, N., Sykes, W., & Walker, A. (2013). *Crime and Disabled People. Baseline statistical analysis of measures for the formal legal inquiry into disability-related harassment.* Research Report 90. Equality and Human Rights Commission.

College of Policing. (2014). *National Policing Hate Crime Strategy*. Available at http://www.college.police.uk/What-wedo/Support/Equality/Documents/National-Policing-Hate-Crimestrategy.pdf#search=hate%20crime

Cramer, R. J., Wright, S., Long, M. M., Kapusta, N. D., Nobles, M. R., Gemberling, T. M., & Wechsler, H. J. (2018). On hate crime victimization: Rates, types, and links with suicide risk among sexual orientation minority special interest group members. *Journal of Trauma & Dissociation, 19*(4), 476–489.

Davis, E. (2014). 'Helping offenders to "think again": A practitioner's perspective on developing an intervention for hate offenders. In N. Hall, Corb, A., P. Giannasi & J. Grieve (Eds.), *The Routledge International Handbook on Hate Crime* (pp. 391–399). Routledge.

Dunbar, E. (2003). Symbolic, relational, and ideological signifiers of bias-motivated perpetrators: Toward a strategy of assessment. *American Journal of Orthopsychiatry, 73*(2), 203–211.

Dunbar, E., Quinones, J., & Crevecoeur, D. A. (2005). Assessment of hate crime perpetrators: The role of bias intent in examining violence risk. *Journal of Forensic Psychology Practice, 5*(1), 1–19.

Farrington, D. P., Jolliffe, D., & Johnstone, L. (2008). *Assessing violence risk: A framework for practice*. Cambridge University, Cambridge.

Fazel, S., Singh, J. P., Doll, H., & Grann, M. (2012). Use of risk assessment instruments to predict violence and antisocial behaviour in 73 samples involving 24 827 people: Systematic review and meta-analysis. *British Medical Journal*, *345*.

Garland, J., Chakraborti, N., & Hardy, S. (2015). "It felt like a little war": Reflections on violence against alternative subcultures. *Sociology, 49*(6), 1065–1080.

Hall, N., Corb, A., Giannasi, P., & Grieve, J. (Eds.). (2015). *The Routledge international handbook on hate crime*. Routledge.

Haynes, A., Schweppe, J., & Garland, J. (2023). The production of hate crime victim status: Discourses of normalisation and the experiences of LGBT community members. *Criminology***.

Howard, P., Francis, B., Soothill, K., & Humphreys, L. (2009). OGRS 3: The revised offender group reconviction scale. *Research Summary, 7*(09), 1–6.

Iganski, P., & Lagou, S. (2014). The personal injuries of "hate crime". In N. Hall, Corb, A., P. Giannasi & J. Grieve (Eds.), *The Routledge International Handbook on Hate Crime* (pp. 34–46). Routledge.

Iganski, P., & Smith, D. (2011). *Rehabilitation of hate crime perpetrators—Research report*. Equality and Human Rights Commission.

Jolliffe, D., & Farrington, D. P. (2009). A systematic review of the relationship between childhood impulsiveness and later violence. In M. McMurran &

R. Howard (Eds.), *Personality, Personality Disorder and Violence* (pp. 40–61). Wiley.
Jolliffe, D., Farrington, D. P. (2015). Self-reported offending: Reliability and validity. In G. Bruinsma, & D. Weisburd (Eds.), *Encyclopedia of Criminology and Criminal Justice*. Springer. https://doi.org/10.1007/978-1-4614-5690-2_648
Jolliffe, D., & Farrington, D. P. (2020). The criminal careers of those imprisoned for hate crime in the UK. *European Journal of Criminology, 17*(6), 936–955.
Keighley, R. (2024). *Researching hate as an activist: Exploring LGBTQ+ online hate, its impacts, and our responsibility towards equality*. Palgrave Macmillan.
McDevitt, J., Levin, J., & Bennett, S. (2002). Hate crime offenders: An expanded typology. *Journal of Social Issues, 58*(2), 303–317.
Messner, S. F., McHugh, S., & Felson, R. B. (2004). Distinctive characteristics of assaults motivated by bias. *Criminology, 42*(3), 585–618.
Näsi, M., Aaltonen, M., & Kivivuori, J. (2016). Youth hate crime offending: The role of strain, social control and self-control theories. *Journal of Scandinavian Studies in Criminology and Crime Prevention., 17*(2), 177–184.
Nocon, A., Iganski, P., & Lagou, S. (2011). *Disabled people's experiences and concerns about crime: Analysis of the British Crime Survey 2007–08, 2008–09 and 2009–10*, Briefing Paper 3. Equality and Human Rights Commission.
Paterson, J. L., Brown, R., & Walters, M. A. (2019). Feeling for and as a group member: Understanding LGBT victimization via group-based empathy and intergroup emotions. *British Journal of Social Psychology., 58*(1), 211–224.
Paterson, J. L., Walters, M. A., Brown, R., & Carrasco, D. (2024). Angry and afraid: Exploring the impact of mixed emotional reactions to hate crimes with LGBT+ and Muslim communities. *Journal of Interpersonal Violence*, 0(0). https://doi.org/10.1177/08862605241286455
Perry, B. (2001). *In the name of hate: Understanding hate crimes*. Routledge.
Pezzella, F. S., Fetzer, M. D., & Keller, T. (2019). The dark figure of hate crime underreporting. *American Behavioral Scientist*. https://doi.org/10.1177/0002764218823844
Schweppe, J., Haynes, A., & Walters, M. A. (2018). *Life cycle of a hate crime—Comparative report.* Irish Council for Civil Liberties.
Singh, J. P. (2013). Predictive validity performance indicators in violence risk assessment: A methodological primer. *Behavioral Sciences & the Law., 31*(1), 8–22.
Sutherland, A. (2013). A methodology for reconviction studies using Police National Computer (PNC) data. *Available at SSRN 2378345*.

Walters, M. (2020). Developments in the use of restorative justice for hate crime. *International Journal of Restorative Justice., 3*, 446–457.

Webster, C. D., Douglas, K. S., Eaves, D., & Hart, S. D. (1997). HCR-20. *Assessing the risk of violence*. Version, 2.

Wilcox, A., Smithson, H., Christmann, K., & Wong, K. (2010). *Racially motivated offending and targeted interventions*. Youth Justice Board. Available http://dera.ioe.ac.uk/2200/1/Racially%20Motivated%20Offending%20and%20Targeted%20Interventions.pdf

Zempi, I. (2019). Veiled Muslim women's views on law banning the wearing of the niqab (face veil) in public. *Ethnic and Racial Studies., 42*(15), 2585–2602. https://doi.org/10.1080/01419870.2019.1588985

Who Are the Perpetrators of Online Hate? A Case Study of Islamophobia

Imran Awan

Introduction

Trigger events such as the Brexit vote, the Southport riots in the UK as well as terrorist attacks both in the UK and internationally, have led to a spate of hate crimes committed against Muslim communities, both in the offline and the online world. In particular, these incidents include Muslim women being targeted for wearing the headscarf and mosques being vandalised. For example, the Al Brahma community centre in Muswell Hill in North London was burnt down soon after the murder of British soldier Lee Rigby by Michael Adebolajo and Michael Adebowale in Woolwich in May 2013 (BBC News, 2013a). Other examples of hate incidents include graffiti being scrawled against mosque walls and petrol bombs being left outside mosques (Saul, 2013). There has also

I. Awan (✉)
Department of Criminology and Sociology, Birmingham City University, Birmingham, UK
e-mail: Imran.Awan@bcu.ac.uk

J. Garland et al. (eds.), *Hate Crime Perpetrators: New Perspectives from Theory, Research and Practice, Volume I*, Palgrave Hate Studies,
https://doi.org/10.1007/978-3-031-92666-2_3

been a spike in racist and Islamophobic hate crime, following the tragic murder of three children in Southport on 29 July 2024. The far-right riots across England and in Northern Ireland have been fuelled by false claims circulated online that the perpetrator was Muslim.

All these incidents have led to a heightened atmosphere for British Muslims, fearful of reprisal attacks against them because of incidents such as Southport and the Woolwich attack. However, whilst street level Islamophobia, remains an important area of investigation, a more equally disturbing picture is emerging with the actions of perpetrators of online anti-Muslim hatred (Tell MAMA, 2024). This chapter explores a case study conducted by the author which examined 500 separate tweets, to try and find out how Muslims are being viewed and targeted by perpetrators of online abuse who are using social media sites such as X (formerly Twitter) to espouse anti-Muslim prejudice. The study used three hashtags, namely; #Woolwich, #Muslims and #Islam, to note and look at patterns emerging regarding online Islamophobia via the X search engine. The chapter provides a typology of perpetrator characteristics, made up of people who are committing the online abuse and argues that online Islamophobia must be given the same level of attention as street level Islamophobia. Although this specific case study uses Woolwich as an example, the chapter makes the case that this typology can be applied to other similar events such as the online hate targeted at Muslims after the tragic murders of the three girls in Southport, and can be transferable to all other forms of hate and abuse online.

Woolwich and Terror

In May 2013, Michael Adebowale and Michael Adebolajo murdered British soldier Lee Rigby in Woolwich, south-east London. The men ran him over in a car before using knives and a meat cleaver to attack and murder him. Adebowale and Adebolajo were convicted of the murder of Lee Rigby in December 2013. At the time, the incident provoked strong public anger and outrage by politicians, policymakers and the media. British Prime Minister David Cameron at the time, argued that the Woolwich attack would not 'divide us' but instead make us 'stronger' in the fight against global and home-grown terrorism. However, the events of that day also led to a series of attacks against Muslims, mosques and Islamic institutions which amounted to a sharp increase in Islamophobic related incidents. Indeed, a number of police forces saw a dramatic surge in the number of reported hate crimes against Muslims, with the Metropolitan police recording 500 Islamophobic crimes (*The Guardian*, 2013). Whilst a number of these incidents took place offline (i.e. with the use of direct physical force) there were also perpetrators who used social media sites to either vent their anger or to make actual death threats against Muslim communities (BBC News, 2013b). Clearly, major trigger events such as the Woolwich attack can provoke public outrage, anger and can lead to stereotyping of all Muslim communities as being violent extremists (Larsson, 2007). Indeed, the Internet and social media sites such as X (formerly Twitter), have become a popular arena for online hate, partly due to their accessibility and the anonymity they offer for offenders who use it to intimidate, harass and bully others (Christopherson, 2007). Moreover, following trigger events such as Brexit, we also witnessed how X was used by offenders who were promoting this type of online Islamophobic hate, which was loaded with tactics of harassment and threats of reprisal attacks (BBC News, 2013b). Below is a selection of some of the tweets that appeared post the Woolwich attack (Fig. 1).

Clearly, online hate is not restricted to online Islamophobia, however this chapter aims to shed light on this phenomenon, which following trigger events has become the prime focus for the British police force and other similar agencies that had to investigate online hate crime. Indeed, this is reinforced by statistics from the police and organisations such as Tell MAMA (Measuring Anti-Muslim Attacks) who reported a significant increase in the amount of people reporting online anti-Muslim abuse to them (Tell MAMA, 2013). Feldman et al. (2013, p. 21) found that: 'The majority of the incidents of Muslim hate crime reported to Tell MAMA are online incidents and 300-69 per cent - of these online cases reported a link to the far right.' Moreover, Feldman et al. (2013) found that from the 74% of online hate incidents reported to Tell MAMA that some online incidents did also include threats made about offline action. They also found that most of the online hate was committed by males,

Fig. 1 Selection of Tweets following the Woolwich Attack, which can also be accessed via http://publicshaming.tumblr.com/search/woolwich

and 70% of online incidents had a link to the Far Right, specifically to the English Defence League (EDL) and the British National Party (BNP). The EDL is a UK-based far-right organisation that has at its core the aim to tackle 'militant Islam,' and the BNP is a far-right UK political party.

These facts are not isolated, as the UK's Association of Chief Police Officers (ACPO), also revealed a similar trend that saw them receive 136 complaints of online anti-Muslim abuse, which did coincide with the immediate aftermath of the Woolwich attack and were reported through its 'True Vision website' which deals with hate crimes following the death of Lee Rigby (ACPO, 2013). True Vision is the UK police's main cyber tool in tackling online hate. It examines illegal content that threatens or harasses a person or group of persons because of hostility towards their race, religion, sexual orientation, disability or transgender identity. It notes, however that: 'Most hateful or violent website content is not illegal' and gives victims of online hate three options in dealing with the incident. These include reporting the material to the police, or reporting the material to a hosting company, or contacting the website administrator to remove the material (True Vision, 2013).

This study analysed and examined 500 separate tweets, to try and find out how Muslims were being viewed and the way in which perpetrators of online abuse were targeting them through social media sites such as X. All of the tweets were analysed between January 2013 and April 2014, and are available and accessible in the open public domain. The overwhelming number of tweets were written and posted by people who were living in the UK, although there were some tweets from users who were based in Australia and the United States. From the data collected, the majority of tweets were posted by males (72%) in comparison to females that accounted for (28%). The study used three hashtags, namely; #Woolwich, #Muslim and #Islam, to note and look at patterns emerging regarding online Islamophobia on X. The reason those hashtags were used was because they had appeared on the X search engine as words that had been recently 'Trending' in the United Kingdom. Trending words on X is when the most mentioned words are posted on X and are considered to be important or 'hot' topics that people are discussing. For example, on September 11, 2013, the hashtag #FuckMuslims was trending (see Fig. 2 with examples of the tweets that were trending that day). Following this, the chapter provides a typology of perpetrator characteristics. This chapter therefore makes an important contribution to helping us understand the role of perpetrators of online hate.

Clearly, the above 'hate' comments made online can have a negative impact on the victims who are targeted and can be very upsetting and unsettling for them and their families (Bunglawala, 2012). Evidence from Feldman et al. (2013) also suggests that post Woolwich, the Internet and social networking sites have been used by far-right groups such as the EDL to promote online cyber hate attacks against Muslim communities. This type of prejudice follows a 'drip-drip' effect, which has intensified (Feldman et al., 2013) post Woolwich. Another problem when dealing with online abuse seems to be the laissez-faire attitude from some of the social media sites such as X (formerly Twitter) who

Fig. 2 A selection of trending tweets on September 11, 2013

simply ask the victim either to block someone or close their account. In response to the criticisms by Stan Collymore, X stated that: 'We cannot stop people from saying offensive, hurtful things on the internet or on X. But we take action when content is reported to us that breaks our rules or is illegal' (BBC News, 2014).

Cyberspace can become a safe environment for some perpetrators, but equally internal and external mechanisms are required to support victims of online hate (Sayyed & Vakil, 2011). The above examples of online anti-Muslim abuse also show that a number of the cyber hate incidents that have occurred online have done so via social networking sites, such as X. These incidents can be categorised as being 'cyber harassment,' 'cyber bullying,' 'cyber abuse,' 'cyber incitement/threats' and 'cyber hate' (Wall, 2001). Many of the comments posted online through social networking sites, like X consist of an extremist and incendiary undertone. Moreover, they are not confined to social networking sites and include sites dedicated to blogging, online chat rooms and other virtual platforms that promote online cyber hate and online Islamophobia (Allen, 2014). Many of these prejudicial statements are often used by perpetrators to target a particular group or person. This is often personified by racist jokes and stereotypical 'banter' (Weaver, 2013). If these incidents go unchecked physical attacks can also take place and could culminate from extreme online prejudice and discrimination which are intertwined together (Allport, 1954). Indeed, this type of negativity can also lead to an escalation of online abuse and the normalisation of such behaviour. For example, a number of sites such as the http://anti--islam.blogspot.co.uk/ and http://www.jihadwatch.org/, all aim to tackle what they call the 'anti-civilization of Islam.' Whilst many of these blogs and websites use the cloak of freedom of expression to perpetuate an anti-Muslim rhetoric, it does inevitably attract perpetrators who are quick to post comments on pieces that have a deeply embedded anti-Muslim narrative (JihadWatch, 2013). This chapter argues that online anti-Muslim hate therefore requires a multi-faceted and international approach from different agencies, including the police, social networking sites and a government-led approach that tackles online Islamophobia as a separate phenomenon.

Background and Context

Threatening and abusive comments, whether it be by visual images, fake profiles, Facebook messages, online YouTube videos and tweets such as the above, can have a detrimental effect on the victims who are targeted, and their families (Waddington, 2010). What the above preceding examples demonstrate is that online behaviour can be normalised by perpetrators, which allows a perpetrator to use in many cases anonymity, manipulation and social control to target their victims (Douglas et al., 2005). However, whilst this form of cyber hate often remains invisible, sometimes due to offenders deleting tweets and also because the perpetrator can hide their identity, the threat remains very real for the victims it targets (Hall, 2005). Indeed, trying to ascertain all the potential threats and risks posed online does pose a major challenge for the security services, the police and the government. Cyber hate within the policing context therefore requires due diligence and an investigation that determines potential online perpetrators, offensive tweets and those they believe can be prosecuted alongside the UK's Crown Prosecution Service (CPS) rules.

Communications via social media sites, like X, can be a criminal offence. The CPS guidelines state that there must be either: a credible threat of violence; communications which specifically target an individual or group of people; communications which amount to a breach of a court order; or communications which may be considered grossly offensive, indecent, obscene or false (CPS Guidelines, 2014). In many of these cases people can be charged for comments made via social networking sites under 'racially motivated' or 'religiously motivated' crimes through the Crime and Disorder Act 1998, the Malicious Communications Act 1988, the Communications Act 2003 and the Public Order Act 1986 (Coliandris, 2012). Overall, policing X and people's activity via social media sites remains difficult, and the Leveson Inquiry (2012) in the UK, set up by the British government to investigate the culture, practices and ethics of the Press also acknowledges that it is problematic to regulate.

Despite this, following trigger events such as terrorist attacks like Woolwich or the Brexit vote, a number of arrests were made where people had posted comments on X and Facebook that were deemed to incite racial hatred or violence. In one case, a person was convicted under the Malicious Communications Act 1988, after an offensive message was posted on Facebook (Urquhart, 2013). Cyber hate regulation therefore requires the police and other agencies to act quickly and more effectively in relation to online Islamophobic abuse. At the moment, it appears social media sites such as X resemble a virtual minefield of hate and therefore policing it requires a new process of educating people of the dangers of online abuse and providing victims with support from perpetrators (Chan, 2007).

What Is Cyber Hate?

There is no universal definition of a hate crime; instead we have a myriad of interpretations, which include statements or terms aimed at targeting a person or person(s) because of their particular religion, gender, race, sexual orientation, physical or mental disability and ethnicity. Cyber hate, therefore is the nexus of those communications and concepts where a perpetrator utilises electronic technology and the convergence of space, movement and behaviour in a 'safe' virtual environment to 'control' and target 'opponents' considered to be a threat (Awan & Blakemore, 2012). This type of control allows the perpetrator to act in a dominant way against groups they deem to be subordinate; often in the case of Muslims, attacking their faith and ethnicity (Perry, 2001).

It also allows perpetrators to use the online world and other social networking platforms to target individuals they deem to be 'different' from them both in an ideological, political and religious sense (Taras, 2012). As noted above, cyber hate is a complex phenomenon and is used to promote a particular ideology that promotes racial hatred, religious intolerance and also allows 'lone wolves' and 'hate groups' to exert cyber power and social control in a systematic and targeted manner that has no respect for a victim's rights (Perry, 2001). Academics looking at the psychology of online offenders have also argued that such people form an individual identity crisis whereby their use of the Internet becomes a safe haven for them and creates a sense of anonymity, allowing them to use and exploit social and political beliefs as an ideology that has no respect for the individuals or groups it targets. This can therefore result in them trying to use online methods as a means of self-protectionism and false patriotism for groups like the far right, which fuel anti-Muslim hate and abuse (Cole & Cole, 2009). This can also often be played out by abusive, threatening and coordinated tweets or through the use of sites like X to send messages of hate, including the use of visual images to target particular individuals (Whine, 2003). Clearly, it should be noted that cyberspace can also be an extremely valuable tool in helping detect and tackle online cyber crime, and increasingly is being used by the police to help engage with communities. Blakemore (2013), for example, argues that the use of social networking sites by the police can have an important impact on people's level of 'fear of cyber-crime' and also can help assist them report such incidents to the police.

The Runnymede Trust (1997) has identified eight components that they define as being Islamophobia. They include where people view: (1) Islam as a faith that is unresponsive to change; (2) where the values of Islam appear not to be compatible with other cultures and faiths; (3) Islam is viewed as being a religion that is barbaric and sexist; (4) Islam is also seen as being a religion that is both violent and aggressive; (5) Islam is viewed as a political ideology; (6) Islam and criticisms made about the faith are unwarranted; (7) discriminatory practices are used to justify exclusion of Muslim communities; and (8) anti-Muslim crime is seen as normal.

Interestingly, very little discussion is made of the perpetrators of online Islamophobia. They argue that Islamophobic views is shaped by a 'closed set' of narrow views on Islam and Muslims, which has helped contribute to the 'othering' of Muslim communities through discriminative practices and affects (Awan, 2012). The Forum against Islamophobia and Racism (FAIR) (2013) argues that Islamophobia constitutes fear and hostility against Muslim communities. However, like the above interpretations, they confine Islamophobia to physical attacks such as abuse and targeted violence against Muslim communities, mosques, cemeteries and discrimination in places of education (Allen, 2001). Whilst these definitions remain limited in scope with regards the online dimension of Islamophobia, they do, however, give us a starting point for further discussion and discourse in this area about the methods required for policing perpetrators of online hate.

Methodology and Findings

This chapter aims to examine how Muslims are being viewed via one main social media platform, namely X. In doing so, this research, involved the analysis of 500 tweets and looked for patterns that were emerging about the perpetrators of online hatred. A lot of the data collected as we shall see, was used by perpetrators to promote online hate and targeted abuse against Muslims. As a result, some of the research questions explored in this chapter include:

- How is X being used to view Muslims?
- What content is being used via X to demonise and stereotype Muslims?
- What physical and non-physical threats are being used against Muslims via X?

This study used a mixed-methodology which was part of a wider content analysis that utilised qualitative and quantitative data gathering techniques that was embedded within grounded theory. As noted previously, the overwhelming number of tweets were written and posted by people in the UK, although there were some tweets from users who were based in Australia and the United States. From the data collected, the majority of tweets were posted by males (72%) in comparison to females that accounted for (28%). The article used three hashtags, namely; #Woolwich, #Muslim and #Islam, to note and look at patterns emerging regarding online Islamophobia on X. Following this, the author examined the tweets to try and find out how Muslims were being viewed and targeted by perpetrators of online anti-Muslim abuse. Some of the most common reappearing words used to describe Muslims in a derogatory were also examined. This allows for further research in this area and help collect further patterns and trends about the perpetrators of online anti-Muslim hate. Clearly, there are drawbacks to using and analysing data via social media sites such as X, with the obvious limit in the actual word frequency. However, this was overcome by using hashtags and taking a random sample of 500 tweets and then collating and identifying tweets, correlations and patterns that emerged. Indeed, tweets were examined to try and understand how Muslims were being targeted by perpetrators of online abuse. Some of the most common reappearing words used to describe Muslims in a derogatory way included the words #Muslimpigs, #Muzrats, #MuslimPaedos, #Muslimterrorists, #Muslimscum and #Pisslam (see Fig. 3 for a breakdown of the most common words used). Interestingly, Tell MAMA, which measures anti-Muslim hate attacks also examined the use of words on social media to describe Muslims from January 2013 to December 2013 and used a software system to collate high-frequency words that were directly related to anti-Muslim hate and prejudice. Similarly to the current project, they also found the words 'Ninja,' 'Muzrats' and 'Paedo' were being used against Muslims (Tell MAMA, 2014).

After examining the separate tweets, and looking at the use of language to depict Muslims in a negative light this chapter proposes a typology consisting of eight different people who the author identified as online cyber trolls; i.e. people who are using social networking sites such as X

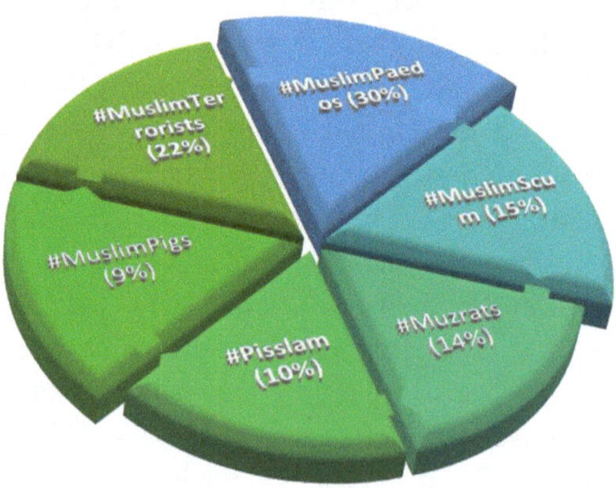

Fig. 3 Common reappearing words used to describe Muslims via X

to produce a sustained campaign of hate against Muslim communities. Some of the examples of those tweets are grouped in Fig. 4.

A Typology of Online Perpetrators

Over 75% of the tweets examined (above) indicated and showed a strong and Islamophobic feeling which was used to stereotype and blame all Muslims on a particular issue which was used to justify the abuse. For example, @ensine and @seafarer1847 were open about their anger and hatred for Muslims as a result of recent cases surrounding Asian men convicted of grooming underage girls. Both those accounts used and showed related publications which were exploited in order to send out tweets that defamed and caricatured Muslims as dangerous paedophiles. Indeed, the word 'MuslimPaedos' does reflect and coincide with recent cases of Muslim men convicted of grooming offences (Greenwood, 2013).

However, in other cases people simply used X as a means to antagonise and create hostility which @ShellyMonsoon and @DeSoosider did by referring to Muslims as 'Muzrats' which is a demeaning word to describe Muslims as bacteria or a type of disease. Both people showed a sustained level of anti-Muslim abuse which was depicted through language that was hostile and offensive to Muslims. For example, @ShellyMonsoon noted how #Islamkills and whites will become a minority unless the Muzrats are stopped. Interestingly, the word #Muslim terrorists also appeared high on the list of frequent words used. In particular, it became part of the September 11 trending words across X where Muslims were being depicted through pictures and videos as extremists and terrorists. On the face of it, a number of perpetrators shared similar characteristics but were uniquely different in their approaches to targeting Muslim communities online. Using an online content behavioural offender typology, this chapter grouped the tweets together in different categories and created a typology based on the following. These are; **the trawler** (a person who has gone through other people's X accounts to specifically target people with a Muslim connection); **the apprentice** (someone who is fairly new to X but nonetheless has begun to target people with the

Fig. 4 A brief selection of tweets examined within the article

help of more experienced online abusers); **the disseminator** (someone who has tweeted about and retweeted messages, pictures and documents of online hate that are specifically targeting Muslims); **the impersonator** (a person who is using a fake profile, account and images to target individuals); **the accessory** (a person who is joining in with other peoples conversations via X to target vulnerable people); **the reactive** (a person who following a major incident, such as Brexit, or issues on immigration, will begin an online campaign targeting that specific group and individual); **the mover** (someone who regularly changes their X account in order to continue targeting someone from a different profile) and finally, **the professional** (a person who has a huge following on X and regardless of consequences has and will launch a major campaign of hate against an individual or group of people because they are Muslim. This person will also likely to have multiple X accounts all aimed at targeting Muslim communities). See Table 1 which has grouped the profile of the offender behaviour and characteristics which includes the number of cases that I found within the tweets examined.

At the heart of each of these different categories, it became clear that the perpetrators involved had similar motivations. Some of those were based on seeking authority and power as shown by the tweets from @RestoreAust who used his X account to collect and maximise influence. In such a case, this affords some people the motivation to commit the online abuse and as a result, they are able to target specific people (Iganski, 2012). Figure 5 shows a cycle demonstrating those key characteristics of such perpetrators.

Challenges Around Online Hate

As noted previously, online hate is under researched both at a policy level and an academic level, and this chapter argues that a new cyber hate policy is much needed both at government level and policing level which would be timely considering the spike of online anti-Muslim abuse which has led to ACPO receiving over 136 separate incidents following Woolwich (ACPO, 2013). However, these challenges remain the same at the time of writing this chapter in 2025 with issues that persist today

Table 1 Typology of offender characteristics

Type	Characteristics	No of cases
The trawler	Someone who has gone through other people's twitter accounts to specifically target people with a Muslim connection	57
The apprentice	A person who is fairly new to Twitter but nonetheless has began to target people with the help of more experienced online abusers	39
The disseminator	Someone who has tweeted about and retweeted messages, pictures and documents of online hate that are specifically targeting Muslims	75
The impersonator	A person who is using a fake profile, account and images to target individuals	76
The accessory	A person who is joining in with other peoples conversations via Twitter to target vulnerable people	82
The reactive	A person who following a major incident, such as Woolwich, or issues on immigration, will begin an online campaign targeting that specific group and individual	95
The mover	Someone who regularly changes their Twitter account in order to continue targeting someone from a different profile	46
The professional	A person who has a huge following on Twitter and regardless of consequences has and will launch a major campaign of hate against an individual or group of people because they are Muslim. This person will also have multiple Twitter accounts all aimed at targeting Muslim communities	30

such as the Southport riots. Interestingly, cyber hate has been used by the far right and White supremacists who have used it to inflame religious and racial tensions. For example, a study for the British-based think-tank group Demos (2011) found that far-right populist movements are gaining in support across Europe and playing upon a small perception of public disenfranchisement within society to promote an agenda of protecting national identity as a method to whip up online anti-Muslim hate. The Demos study (2011) is interesting because their findings would seem to suggest that the EDL have become a web-based far-right group that is using social networking sites such as Facebook and X where it has gained a core group of online sympathisers to target Muslim communities (Awan & Blakemore, 2012). The Online Hate

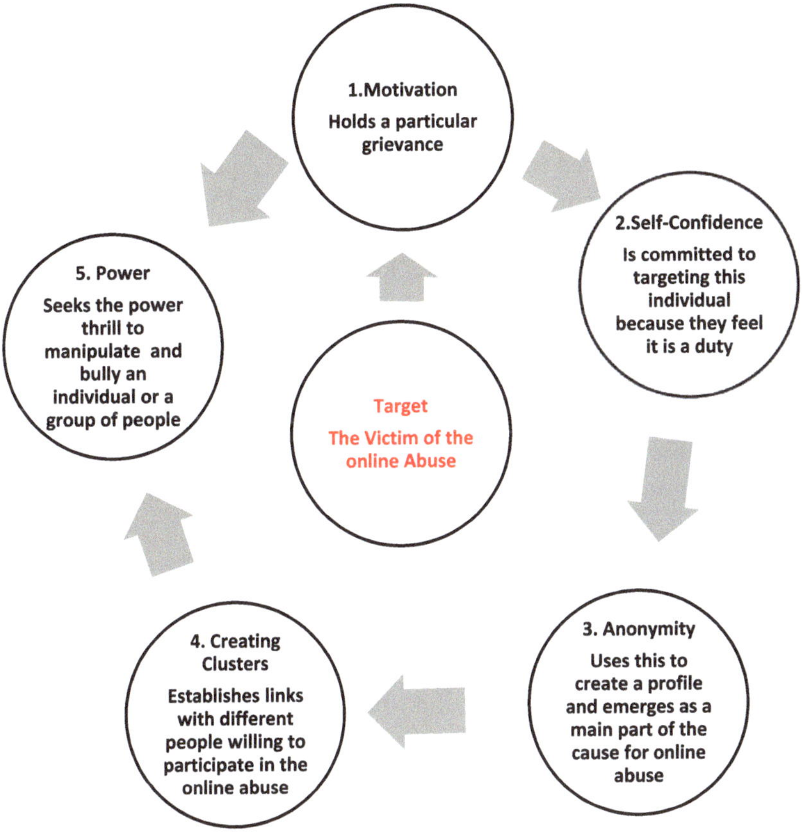

Fig. 5 The cyber troll: a cycle of online abuse

Prevention Institute report (2013) into online Islamophobia searched over 50 different Facebook pages and found a clear correlation of hate speeches online that were targeted towards Muslims. Overall, they found 349 separate instances of online hate speeches directed against Muslims. Indeed, they also included a number of those Facebook pages that were created in order to specifically target Muslim communities. For example, they found a number of group pages that had a number of people who had visited and 'liked' the page. As noted above, policing cyberspace is difficult. Accordingly, Feldman et al. (2013) found that 74% of anti-Muslim prejudice occurred online, in comparison to 26% of offline incidents. Worryingly, critics argue that the difficult nature of policing cyberspace has therefore led to Muslim communities being failed by their local police forces in the UK (BBC News, 2013c).

Another problem for the police appears to be the way in which data is recorded and collected by local police forces. The problem for the police therefore is helping root out far-right groups and lone wolf extremists who are using social networking sites like X to post malicious statements (Esposito & Kalin, 2011). This realm of cyber activism used by groups like the EDL and others who are promoting online hate means the police require more people to report what they see and what they read so that they can take the necessary actions required to either remove the online hate material or in some cases arrest and charge people. At the moment those perpetrators who use online hate to disguise themselves in a cloak of anonymity remain at large because they understand that unless someone reports them they can remain anonymous.

Feldman et al. (2013, p. 23) state that a number of online incidents reported included direct threats from burning down mosques to killing Muslim babies. They state that: 'Racist remarks were, in turn, mainly anti-Pakistani comments and references to dirt and filth. More generally there were comments accusing Muslims of rape; paedophilia; incest; interbreeding; being terrorists; and killing Jews.' Below the chapter will examine the issue of reporting online abuse from Muslim communities and why issues of a lack of trust with the police and Muslim community, may also have an impact on reporting perpetrators.

Reporting Online Islamophobia

One of the major issues of online anti-Muslim hate is the role of the police in dealing with an increasingly complex arena that allows many people to remain anonymous. Tell MAMA (2024) for example actively encourages people to report these incidents. Apart from these problems, the role of the police in dealing with hate incidents offline will also have an impact on how incidents are reported online. For example, public perception of the police in tackling offline hate crime has had a significant impact upon police and Muslim community relations (BBC

News, 2013c). Historically, the policing of ethnic minorities have often been tainted by allegations of policing by stereotypes that include racial prejudice and racial discrimination of black and Asian men (Bowling, 1999). Following the 9/11 attacks the risk is that those stereotypes have re-emerged with 'over policing' of Muslim communities, who are increasingly viewed with suspicion (Awan, 2012). This intensified with cases such as Rizwaan Sabir. Sabir, a student at the University of Nottingham, was arrested by the police for downloading an al-Qaeda training manual but released without charge. After winning damages of £20,000 from Nottinghamshire police, for false imprisonment, Sabir said: 'I was very, very lucky in the sense that I was released without charge because I was innocent in the first place…' (cited by Jones in *The Guardian*, 2011).

The Sabir case highlights how, post-9/11, the police need to be very careful about how they deal with counter-terrorism cases because old stereotypes may re-emerge and may have an impact upon how Muslim communities report online abuse. The study by Awan et al. (2013) regarding policing and Muslim community relations found that often participants would describe the police as either being 'racist,' 'heavy-handed,' 'unprofessional' and having a 'lack of communication and community skills.' This in turn resulted in the Muslim community not reporting crime to the police because they felt a sense of mistrust.

Indeed, core issues such as a lack of trust in the police service were also discussed by participants in the Awan et al. (2013) study, suggesting that individual experiences with the police may be a reason why the community lost trust in the police, and why some communities may not feel comfortable in reporting online abuse to the police. Counter-terrorism policing operations also appeared to have a significant impact on the Muslim community's perception of the police service. For example, in Birmingham, the local community and area had been making headline news in the wake of controversial counter-terrorism arrests. Project Champion and the installation of secret CCTV cameras to effectively ring-fence the Muslim community in predominately Muslim areas in Birmingham and monitor their movements was an additional reason why the community were distrustful of the police (Awan, 2012).

Moreover, the problem regarding the low level of people reporting perpetrators of online abuse may be because people are not aware when an online offence has been committed. Furthermore, even if such cases are reported to the police, it is acknowledged that they have limited resources, and in many cases tracking this crime can have many problems from both a jurisdictional point of view with Internet Service Providers, to the role of free speech and the issue of online anonymity. Thus, for the police it can be like 'finding a needle in a virtual haystack' (Awan & Blakemore, 2012). The police therefore must look to adopt different policing models, ranging from community-led policing to intelligence-led policing, in helping tackle the problem.

Conclusion

Tracking perpetrators of cyber hate remains a complex problem and with the emerging rise of online anti-Muslim hate, prejudice, discrimination and threats, there is an urgent need to look at this area in more depth. This chapter provided a brief snapshot of the problem of online anti-Muslim abuse by examining the typology of offenders of online Islamophobia. As a result, a new international and national online cyber hate strategy should be adopted, that highlights the manner in which online anti-Muslim abuse occurs and ways in which the police can deal with such incidents. Perhaps a further strengthening of cyber hate regulation and protocols could also be used to tackle online threats made against people of all backgrounds, including anti-Muslim abuse, and at the same time ensuring free speech is protected. Accordingly, the UK Government and police service must examine all online threats and the links with actual offline violence as this could help agencies have a better understanding of what they are dealing with. The reporting of online anti-Muslim abuse must also be taken seriously; improved relations between the police and Muslim community may help to achieve that. A more robust and clearer definition of what is online Islamophobia should also be adopted.

The typology which was subsequently, created of online abusers shows that perpetrators presented some key characteristics, and motivations behind their actions. The tweets examined also revealed a dark picture emerging regarding online Islamophobia on X, and shows that we need to begin a process of evidence-based research that helps create a safer online space for users. I hope that this study can be used to help examine how online hate is determined and look at more innovative ways that policymakers, the police, third sector organisations and social networking sites (such as X and Facebook) examine how best to respond to online anti-Muslim hate crime. This can than result in an improved dialogue between the different stakeholders and ensure that online anti-Muslim hate incidents are taken more seriously. In particular, X has been criticised for the lack of real action towards online hate and I am hopeful this study can shed light on some important changes they and the police can make to ensure online hate crime can be dealt with in a more efficient and proactive manner.

References

Allen, C. (2001). *Islamophobia in the media since September 11th, forum against Islamophobia and racism* [Online]. http://www.fairuk.org/docs/islamophobia-in-the-media-since-911-christopherallen.pdf

Allen, C. (2014). *Findings from a pilot study on opposing Dudley Mosque using Facebook groups as both site and method for research* [Online]. Sage Open. http://sgo.sagepub.com/content/4/1/2158244014522074.full-text.pdf+html

Allport, G. W. (1954). *The nature of prejudice*. Addison-Wesley.

Association of Chief Police Officers. (2013). *True vision records* [Online]. http://www.report-it.org.uk/true_vision_records_a_significant_weekly_reduct

Awan, I. (2012). The impact of policing British Muslims: A qualitative exploration. *Journal of Policing, Intelligence and Counter-Terrorism, 7*(1), 22–35.

Awan, I., & Blakemore, B. (2012). *Policing cyber hate, cyber threats and cyber terrorism*. Ashgate.

Awan, I., Blakemore, B., & Simpson, K. (2013, September). Muslim communities attitudes towards and recruitment into the British police service. *International Journal of Law, Crime and Justice*, 1–17. https://doi.org/10.1016/j.ijlcj.2013.08.004

BBC News. (2013a). Al-Rahma Islamic Centre destroyed in 'hate crime' fire [Online].
BBC News. (2013b). *632 anti-Muslim hate incidents recorded by Tell Mama* [Online]. http://www.bbc.co.uk/news/uk-21712826
BBC News. (2013c). *Police 'failing' to investigate anti-Muslim abuse* [Online]. Available at: http://www.bbc.co.uk/news/uk-25057246
BBC News. (2014). *Ex-footballer Collymore accuses Twitter over abusive messages* [Online]. http://www.bbc.co.uk/news/uk-25838114
Blakemore, B. (2013). Extremist groups and organisations. In I. Awan & B. Blakemore (Eds.), *Extremism, counter-terrorism and policing* (pp. 87–102). Ashgate.
Bowling, B. (1999). Revised Edition. *Violent racism: Victimisation, policing and social context*. Oxford University Press.
Bunglawala, I. (2012). Online racist abuse: We've all suffered it. *The Guardian* [Online]. http://www.theguardian.com/commentisfree/2012/jul/11/online-racist-abuse-writers-face
Cole, J., & Cole, B. (2009). *Martyrdom: Radicalisation and terrorist violence among British Muslims*. Pennant Books.
Chan, J. B. L. (2007). Police and new technologies. In T. Newburn (Ed.), *Handbook of policing*. Willan Publishing
Christopherson, K. (2007). The positive and negative implications of anonymity in internet, nobody knows you're a dog. *Computers in Human Behavior, 23*, 3038–3056.
Coliandris, G. (2012). Hate in a cyber age. In I. Awan & B. Blakemore (Eds.), *Policing cyber hate, cyber threats and cyber terrorism* (pp. 75–94). Ashgate.
Crown Prosecution Service. (2014). *Guidelines on prosecuting cases involving communications sent via social media* [Online]. http://www.cps.gov.uk/legal/a_to_c/communications_sent_via_social_media/
DEMOS Report. (2011). *The rise of populism in Europe can be traced through online behaviour* [Online]. http://www.demos.co.uk/files/Demos_OSIPOP_Book-web_03.pdf?1320601634
Douglas, K., McGarty, C., Bliuc, A. M., & Lala, G. (2005). Understanding cyberhate: Social competition and social creativity in online white supremacist groups. *Social Science Computer Review, 23*(1), 68–76.
Esposito, L. J., & Kalin, I. (2011). *Islamophobia: The challenge of pluralism in the 21st century*. Oxford University Press.
Forum Against Islamophobia and Racism. (2013). [Online] http://www.fairuk.org/introduction.htm

Feldman, M., Littler, M., Dack, J., & Copsey, N. (2013). *Anti-Muslim hate crime and the far right*. Teeside University [Online]. http://tellmamauk.org/wp-content/uploads/2013/07/antimuslim2.pdf

Greenwood, C. (2013). *Stop tip-toeing around race of grooming gangs, say MPs: Committee says police and prosecutors must be able to raise issue without being accused of racism*. Mail Online [Online]. http://www.dailymail.co.uk/news/article-2338640/Stop-tip-toeing-race-grooming-gangs-say-MPs-Committee-says-police-prosecutors-able-raise-issue-accused-racism.html

Hall, N. (2005). *Hate crime*. Willan Publishing.

Iganski, P. (2012). *Hate crime: Taking stock: Programmes for offenders of hate*. Northern Ireland Association for the Care and Resettlement of Offenders, Belfast.

JihadWatch. (2013). [Online]. http://www.jihadwatch.org/

Jones, S. (2011). Student in Al Qaida raid paid £20,000 by police. *The Guardian* [Online]. http://www.theguardian.com/uk/2011/sep/14/police-pay-student-damages-al-qaida

Larsson, G. (2007). Cyber-islamophobia? The case of WikiIslam. *Contemporary Islam, 1*(1), 53–67.

Leveson Inquiry. (2012). *Culture, practice and ethics of the press* [Online]. http://www.levesoninquiry.org.uk/about/the-report/

Online Hate Prevention Centre. (2013). *Islamophobia on the internet: The growth of online hate targeting Muslims* [Online]. http://ohpi.org.au/islamophobia-on-the-internet-the-growth-of-online-hate-targeting-muslims/

Perry, B. (2001). *In the name of hate: Understanding hate crimes*. Routledge.

Sayyed, S., & Vakil, A. (2011). *Thinking through islamophobia: Global perspectives*. Hurst and Co

Saul, H. (2013). Police call home-made bomb outside Walsall's Ashia Mosque a 'hate crime' and draft in counter-terror police. *The Independent* [Online]. http://www.independent.co.uk/news/uk/crime/police-call-homemade-bomb-outside-walsalls-ashia-mosque-a-hate-crime-and-draft-in-counterterror-police-8670548.html

Taras, R. (2012). *Xenophobia and islamophobia in Europe*. Edinburgh University Press.

Tell MAMA. (2013). *Anti-Muslim hate crime* [Online]. http://tellmamauk.org/

Tell MAMA. (2014). *Analysing the Lexicon of Anti-Muslim prejudice* [Online]. http://tellmamauk.org/analysing-the-lexicon-of-anti-muslim-prejudice/

Tell MAMA. (2024). *Anti-Muslim hate crime* [Online]. http://tellmamauk.org/

The Guardian. (2013). *UK Anti-Muslim hate crime soars, police figures show* [Online]. Available at: http://www.theguardian.com/society/2013/dec/27/uk-anti-muslim-hate-crime-soars
The Runnymede Trust. (1997). *Islamophobia a challenge for us all* [Online]. http://www.runnymedetrust.org/uploads/publications/pdfs/islamophobia.pdf
True Vision. (2013). *Internet hate crime* [Online]. http://www.report-it.org.uk/reporting_internet_hate_crime
Urquhart, C. (2013). Attacks on Muslims soar in wake of Woolwich murder. *The Guardian* [Online]. http://www.theguardian.com/uk/2013/may/25/woolwich-murder-attacks-on-muslims
Waddington, P. A. J. (2010, April 23). An examination of hate crime. *Police Review, 118*(6077), 14–15.
Wall, D. (Ed.). (2001). *Crime and the internet*. Routledge.
Weaver, S. (2013). A rhetorical discourse analysis of online anti-Muslim and anti-Semitic jokes. *Ethnic and Racial Studies., 36*(3), 483–499.
Whine, M. (2003). Far right extremists on the internet. In D. Thomas & B. Loader (Eds.), *Cyber crime: Law enforcement, security and surveillance in the information age*. Routledge.

Towards a New Typology of Disablist Hate Crime Offenders: A Contextual Analysis

Valerie Houghton and Jane Healy

Introduction

Disabled people have long lived lives in segregation and institutionalisation, excluded from society, experiencing neglect and abuse (Goffman, 1961; Sobsey, 1994). Data from 2022/2023 shows there were an estimated 16.1 million disabled people in the UK (Kirk-Wade et al., 2024), which amounts to 24% of the population. In the UK, the Equality Act (2010) and hate crime legislation were introduced to provide some protection from harm for disabled people (Schuelke et al., 2021). This chapter uses the term *disablist (hate) crime* to describe such harms,

V. Houghton (✉)
Edinburgh Napier University, Edinburgh, UK
e-mail: v.houghton@napier.ac.uk

J. Healy
Department of Social Science and Social Work, Bournemouth University, Bournemouth, UK

J. Garland et al. (eds.), *Hate Crime Perpetrators: New Perspectives from Theory, Research and Practice, Volume I*, Palgrave Hate Studies,
https://doi.org/10.1007/978-3-031-92666-2_4

acknowledging the social, structural and cultural elements of discriminatory and oppressive behaviour evidenced within them (Goodley & Runswick Cole, 2011). The social model of disability is advocated as a useful lens through which to view disablist hate crime, as wider societal factors are considered (Taylor, 2022). Disabled people are acknowledged as individuals who are living with an impairment[2] which affects their day-to-day lives. This position recognises disability as a positive identity, thus rejecting notions of passivity, tragedy, pity and the label of inherent vulnerability often assigned to victims.

Hate crime emerged as a framework for recognising the harms created by acts of prejudice, hostility and discrimination that present significant challenges for social and criminal justice. The term was intended to recognise the targeted victimisation of a minority group, or members of a minority group, where prejudice, hatred or hostility were the motive or intent (Jacobs & Potter, 1998). Initial hate crime law was introduced following activism in civil rights and other social movements in the 1960–1970s and the consequent emergence of identity-based politics to protect individuals from racially and religiously motivated targeting. To recognise the historic and ongoing targeting and abuse of disabled people (Hollomotz, 2013; Quarmby, 2011), the Criminal Justice Act (2003), (superseded by the Sentencing Act, 2020), allowed the Courts to increase (or uplift) the sentencing for perpetrators convicted of an offence where evidence of hostility or prejudice is presented.[3] Latest figures indicate there were over 11,000 disability-motivated hate crimes recorded by the police in England and Wales (Home Office, 2024), 48 in Northern Ireland (NISRA, 2024), and 552 by Police Scotland (Scottish Government, 2023).

Theoretically, this chapter aligns with Perry (2001) in maintaining that hate crimes are a means for power and control through a process of subordination. Thus, hate crimes are 'acts of violence and intimidation, usually directed towards already stigmatised and marginalised groups' and 'intended to reaffirm the precarious hierarchies that characterize a given social order' (Perry, 2001, p. 10). Drawing on West and Zimmerman's (1987) 'doing gender', Perry describes hate crime perpetrators as 'doing difference', by recognising and subordinating those perceived as having less value to society through processes of interaction.

Recent academic debate however suggests hate crime is driven less by entrenched prejudice than a momentary lapse of control, a weakness or a rejection of socially expected behaviour due to stress, anger or inebriation. Chakraborti (2015) contends that 'many hate crimes tend to be committed by relatively "ordinary" people in the context of their 'ordinary' day-to-day lives' (p. 18). This suggests that the capacity to act out of hostility or prejudice exists in everyone in society, irrespective of social hierarchies, to which this chapter will return later.

The chapter develops a conceptual profile of perpetrators of disablist crimes by interrogating existing datasets. The next section examines the extent of disablist hate crimes and evaluates existing hate crime perpetrator typologies. It then presents an overview and critical analysis of the datasets, comprising victim self-reports, police records, safeguarding practitioner accounts and publicly available reports. Common factors are presented and compared to existing typologies: interactions and/or relationships between victim and perpetrator; processes of exploitation and/or dehumanisation; escalations of abuse; and underlying motivations of perpetrators. Explicit differences between disablist hate crime perpetrators and other types of hate crime offenders are identified; and patterns of exploitation, dehumanisation, intimidation and threats, leading to coercion and /or increased violence, illustrate the daily challenges of many disabled people. Combined, these contribute to the development of a framework of disablist hate crime perpetrators.

Prevalence of Disablist Hate Crime

Few disablist hate crimes are thought to be reported to the police or hate crime reporting centres (Sin, 2014b; Williams & Tregidga, 2014), and only a small minority of reports are prosecuted (Healy, 2018). Thus, it is useful to combine data from victim self-reported studies, to produce a (more) reliable picture of the extent of disablist hate crimes, such as data gathered through the Crime Survey for England and Wales (CSEW). Given different legislation applies across the UK, this section considers England and Wales statistics only. The CSEW is a bi-annual survey of sample of households which collects data on many different types of offences, including hate crimes. The survey also presents police recorded figures of crimes and, not surprisingly, suggests a large 'dark figure' of crime between those reported to and recorded by police, and those experienced by victims. The police recorded 11, 719 disability-motivated hate crimes in England and Wales (Home Office, 2024) during the year ending March 2024. Although this is far higher than when records began it shows a concerning 18% reduction year on year, which may be down to changes in recording methods. Previously, the period between 2021 and 2022 saw disablist hate crimes increase by 43%, which the Home Office (2023) claimed was a consequence of improved police responses to reported crime. Yet the CSEW estimates there are approximately 50,000 disablist hate crimes or incidents per year, second only to racially motivated offending (Home Office, 2020). In terms of prosecutions, however, for 2023/2024, there were only 338 prosecutions, and 256 successful convictions, with only 76% of those achieving sentence uplifts, reflecting a high attrition rate [4] (CPS, 2024). The disparity between self-reporting and successful outcome figures is described as the 'justice gap' (Walters et al., 2018) and potentially indicative not only of the lack of confidence victims of hate crime have in achieving justice, but also the credibility afforded to some victims when faced with prosecutions. Aldridge-Waddon (2020) for example suggests that people with learning disabilities or communication difficulties are often seen as 'unreliable' witnesses, which further problematises the evidence gap for researchers of disablist hate crimes.

Additionally, there are unique elements to some forms of disablist hate crime that do not occur with other forms of hate, such as those involving grooming or establishing 'false' friendships in order to gain advantage over or exploit disabled people. This can be done either through taking over the disabled person's home for drug-dealing and/or criminal networking (known as 'cuckooing'; Macdonald et al., 2024) or to benefit financially, sexually or personally (often referred to as 'mate crime'; Landman, 2014).

Data on convicted disablist hate crime perpetrators is particularly difficult to gather, given that they are not subject to specific aggravated offences, like race and religious hatred offences.[5] Walters et al. (2017) articulate concerns that CPS prosecutors, judges and magistrates found it difficult to successfully prosecute disablist hate crimes without clear evidence of demonstration of hostility, often in the form of verbal or physical abuse. Indeed, even when such evidence is available, it may not be considered when sentencing. For example, in the Winterbourne View scandal, the CPS identified a regime of 'appalling and systematically brutal abuse', motivated by 'hostility ignorance, prejudice, and hate' (Pring, 2012), yet there is no record that the sentencing judge took these motivations into account when sentencing the perpetrators.

Additional evidence on the extent of disablist hate crimes is available through hate crime victim surveys. In Leicester, Chakraborti et al. (2014) included disabled people ($n = 271$) in their hate crime research and found that 90% had experienced verbal abuse, 50% had experienced violent crime and 22% were victims of sexual violence. In Wales, Williams and Tregidga (2014) found that 48% of disablist hate crime victims ($n = 247$) were repeatedly victimised, resulting in significantly high levels of negative psychological impacts including feelings of isolation and lack of support. In North-East England, Macdonald (2015) suggested that low figures of disability hate crimes were related to the complex nature of such acts. Their study also found that whilst people with learning disabilities were at increased risk of victimisation, there did not seem to be any correlation between the type of impairment and the type of victimisation experienced.

Combined, the evidence suggests there is widespread targeted victimisation of disabled people and a gap in prosecutions and sentencing uplifts in response to these. The next section considers the motivations for such actions.

Understanding Hate Crime Perpetrators

Extensive academic and policy research have tended to prioritise racial and religious hatred studies, leaving disability-motivated offending on the margins of research and practice (Healy, 2018; Tyson et al., 2015). Notwithstanding, there has been a growth in disablist hate crime research in recent years (*cf*. Houghton, 2022; Taylor, 2022; Wilkin, 2020) which demonstrates the significant impact and extent of disablist offending.

Despite this improvement, most of the research has focussed on victims' experiences, resulting in a lack of empirical evidence on perpetrators (Hall, 2015; Jolliffe & Farrington, 2020). Thus, there remains a significant knowledge gap in understanding disablist motivations. This section briefly considers theoretical conceptualisations of hate crime perpetrators before moving on to specific frameworks addressing disablist hate.

Early academic research by McDevitt et al. (2002) identified key characteristics of hate (bias) crime as involving excessive brutality, an inter-changeable victim, usually associated with random stranger-based violence, and often perpetrated by more than one offender. Their analysis suggested that whilst primarily motivated by bigotry, internal and external factors also drive hate crime perpetrators. The majority (three quarters) of hate crimes cases that they analysed were committed by groups of young offenders, mostly teens and young adults looking for excitement and thrills. A further quarter were defensive crimes, conducted by teens and young adults who believed they were 'defending their turf'. Another 10% were considered retaliatory crimes, again committed by teens and young adults in retaliation for crimes committed against them or others they shared identity with. Finally, less than one per cent were conducted by those perceived as being on a mission, usually involving a goal to annihilate an entire category of people with a shared identity (McDevitt et al., 2002). Whilst making a significant contribution to our understanding of hate crime motivations, disablist crimes were not then included in legal statutes in the US and hence were not part of their analysis. Levin (2013) later used case studies and newspaper reports to apply the typology to disablist offenders, but there remains limited literature in this field.

In 74% of McDevitt et al.'s (2002) cases, there was no 'victim-offender history' recorded by the police (see also Levin & McDevitt, 1993), thus they concluded that that the typical hate crime perpetrator was a stranger. Both Iganski et al. (2005) and Phillips (2009) tested McDevitt's typology in bias crimes in London (Antisemitic hate) and New Jersey (ethnicity, race, religion or sexual orientation hate), using cases which had been identified by the police as prosecuted as hate/bias crimes. Whilst Iganski et al. (2005) expanded the typology to include situational factors such as opportunistic and aggravated crimes, Phillips (2009) found that in

30% of cases, the typology was difficult to apply, due to overlap between and across categories, and an inability to categorise some forms of hate: particularly where bias was identified as a secondary motivation. Phillips (2009) concludes that the typology is most useful in identifying those crimes which are completely motivated by hate or bias. This supports Mason's (2005) concept of the circularity of definition, in that crimes identified by the police as hate crimes using certain criteria were more likely to include conclusive evidence of such and thus more likely to reinforce the proposed criteria.

Using different data sources can offer a complex, possibly more nuanced perspective. For example, recognising the importance of context to the construction of hate crime, Sibbitt's (1997) analysis of racial and homophobic harassment sought the voices of the perpetrator's community and considered additional situational factors. She found that most hate crime perpetrators were not the typical young men or teenage stereotype, instead constructing five distinct perpetrator groups (in some cases whole families), responsible for different acts, with different modus operandi. The image of a stranger suggested by Levin and McDevitt (1993) was further challenged by Mason (2005), researching racist and homophobic hate crime perpetrators, who found that perpetrators were predominantly young males 'known' to the victim, acting alone or with others, targeting an individual, close to the victim's home, where incidents are ongoing rather than isolated. More recently, there is evidence that almost half of hate crime victims were targeted by strangers, though a quarter of perpetrators were uncategorised, with victims of disablist hate crime more likely to identify perpetrators as neighbours (13%), work colleagues (9%), acquaintances (8%), friends (6%), or family members (5%) (Chakraborti et al., 2014). Fundamentally, extensive research suggests disabled people are more likely to be targeted by people they know (cf. Burch, 2021; Healy, 2018, Sin, 2015, Williams & Tregidga, 2014), suggesting distinct patterns of perpetrators for disablist crimes.

An important early contribution to the academic hate crime discourse came from Bowling's research on racist violence in east London (1998). His analysis of a range of data sources suggested the context of incidents are important to our understanding of hate crimes, constructing violent racism as a dynamic process rather than static event, one which involves several different actors. Hate crime processes are thus context dependent, with the time and location in which they occur being important, along with: the roles of the actors involved, the community in which the crime is situated, the police and others responsible for reacting to the incident, and the media in their portrayal of the event(s). It is only within this context, argues Bowling (1998), that the actions of individual perpetrators can then be considered, drawing parallels with work by Kelly (1987) on domestic violence, reflected through a continuum of violence towards women. This perspective helps to account for repeated victimisation, which is often a feature of violent racism, and better captures the impact this has on the victim. It may also capture the nature of repeat victimisation which it has been identified as a feature of disablist hate crimes (EHRC, 2011; MacDonald et al., 2017; Williams & Tregidga, 2014).

Disablist hate crimes range from non-violent incidents such as name calling and verbal abuse, to serious and extreme physical violence and harm, sometimes culminating in the death of those targeted (see Houghton & Muller, 2025). Hollomotz (2013) attempted to conceptualise the breadth of hate crime offending as sitting along a continuum of disability, oppression and violence, arguing that the concept of a non-hierarchical continuum allows for processes of both oppression and violence to co-occur and reflecting macro-level and micro-level factors, which combine to produce long-lasting harm, reinforced and deeply engrained within society (see also Perry, 2002). Similarly, Sin (2014a) advocates for a 'layers of influence' approach to researching disablist hate crime victimisation, which considers not simply the immediate environment surrounding a targeted event, but also interactions with outer 'layers' such as the police, social care, housing and wider society. Sin (2014a) describes 'social layers' that are interactive and interdependent, reflecting the immediate circumstances of the disabled person being targeted but also the organisations and institutions surrounding them, within wider social environments. Thus, the perceived vulnerability of disablist hate crime victims is a consequence of their social or physical environment, reproduced via attitudes and environments that are sustaining the structures maintaining violence and subordination. Although Sin's (2014a) model does not explicitly consider potential perpetrators, he does acknowledge the unequal power within relationships which drives perpetrator behaviour, similar to Perry's (2001) work cited earlier.

Sin's (2014a) model relates to a multi-factorial model theorising hate crime victimisation presented in the USA by Sobsey and Calder (1999), incorporating characteristics of victims, and offenders, and considers the interacting and interdependent relational and environmental factors as increasing the risk of targeted victimisation. The model embeds relationships between a disabled person and any potential perpetrator within wider environmental and cultural contexts, in interaction with agents of social control. Although the research drew heavily upon care environments, it emphasised that socially and culturally accepted messages around disabled people can contribute to justifications of targeted abuse, and the depersonalisation of disabled victims which trivialises their experiences.

Henceforth, this chapter draws upon these different conceptualisations in relation to disabled hate crime victimisation (Hollomotz, 2013; Sin, 2014a; Sobsey & Calder, 1999) and established hate crime offender typologies (Bowling, 1998; Iganski et al., 2005; McDevitt et al., 2002; Sibbitt, 1997) to interpret the perpetrator data collated by this chapter's authors. Being mindful that the motivation for one type of hate crime strand may not be broadly applicable to others (Roulstone et al., 2011), the next section investigates whether those typologies presented above are appropriate and applicable to disablist hate crimes.

Research Process

The data presented below was collected by both authors as part of their PhD studies. Houghton (2022) applied grounded theory methods of sensitising concepts and theoretical sampling to analyse disablist hate crime cases (n = 100) collected in the UK between 2016 and 2021. Sources included police files (case logs, witness statements, perpetrator interviews, action boards and offender history), safeguarding practitioner accounts, Serious Case Reviews, Independent Office for Police Conduct Inquiries and newspaper and media reports. In most cases a perpetrator was identified, and contextual information gathered to explore the relationship between victims and offenders; and the actions and reactions of victims, offenders and others including criminal justice actors.

Healy (2018) conducted a mixed methods study of disablist hate crime victimisation in the UK, which included survey self-report data, focus groups and interviews with disabled people and key informants. Data was collected between 2011 and 2014. Each element asked participants explicitly about perpetrators and given the sparsity of literature in this field this data is still deemed relevant. Healy's (2018) research directly engaged with disabled people's stories of victimisation, and the majority of participants identified as having been victims of disablist hate crime. The data were interrogated for all references to perpetrators and then combined with Houghton's (2022) into a separate dataset. This included as much perpetrator detail as possible, though this varied depending on method of data collection.

Of the combined dataset available for analysis, Houghton contributed 100 cases and Healy added 56 reports of hate crime victimisation where specific perpetrator details were available. These were thematically analysed using open coding. Codes included description of victim, description of perpetrator/s, number of perpetrators involved, location of offence/s, relationship (if any), repetition or incidental event, police involvement, potential alignment to McDevitt et al.'s typology, and any other relevant evidence from the case itself. Each case was populated individually and then results compared and categorised according to the dominant themes identified and presented below.

Analysis: Understanding Disablist Hate Crime Perpetrators

The analysis supports previous findings that disablist hate crime can be viewed as a dynamic process, one which begins with perpetrators 'othering' the disabled person, defining them as 'different', as 'vulnerable prey' and a target for humiliation, intimidation, exploitation, dehumanisation and brutalisation (Healy, 2018; Houghton & Muller, 2025). Some victims were identified as having more than one protected characteristic, such as identifying as LGBT+ and disabled, highlighting the intersectional nature of hate crime (Healy, 2019; MacDonald et al., 2021; Mason-Bish, 2015). The focus herein is on disablist offending specifically.

To contribute to a contextualised account of disablist hate crime offenders, four intersecting and overlapping findings are addressed below. Firstly, the situated actions and reactions occurring between victims and perpetrators are presented. Next, constructions of exploitation and dehumanisation explicit to disablist offending are considered. Following this, distinctive patterns of escalation of harm and abuse are explored. Finally, the processes involved in the targeting of disabled people are interrogated, and potential underlying motivations are tentatively considered. These findings are compared to the typologies presented above. Before doing so however, we briefly consider the demographic make-up of perpetrators from the data.

Who Are the Perpetrators?

Analysis of the combined dataset (n = 156) indicated that 19.7% of perpetrators were complete strangers to their victims, and an additional 7.7% were described as 'familiar strangers' (what Mason, 2005, refers to as 'known' strangers). Perpetrators also included neighbours (12.4%); friends (11.5%); local youths (10.7%); relatives/family (9.8%); carers (9.4%); medical/social care professionals (7.7%); co-workers (3%); partners (2.1%); fellow students (2.1%) and the police (1.7%) (see Table 1). A very small minority were categorised as 'other' (2.1%) which included two transport employees, a DWP employee, the Government, and 'someone I met once' (no further detail was given).

Whilst these figures are broadly in line with other perpetrator profiles (high numbers of strangers, teens, neighbours), closer analysis revealed differences between the data sets. Many more of the victim-reported cases identified their perpetrators as strangers (n = 36 out of 56 reported

Table 1 Combined disablist hate crime data

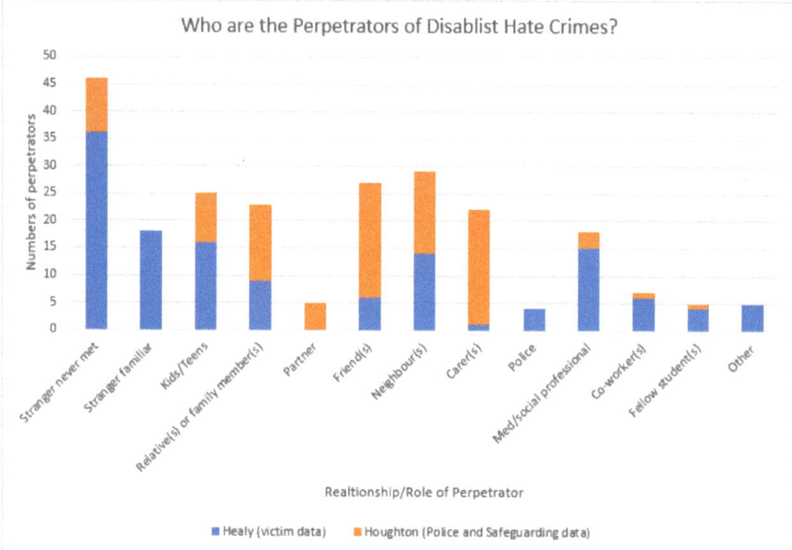

victimisation by known or unknown strangers), than was evidenced in the police and safeguarding practitioners' cases ($n = 10$ unknown strangers, out of 100). Victims also reported higher numbers of perpetrators as medical or social care professionals ($n = 15$ out of 56, compared to 3/100). In contrast, the police/safeguarding case analyses revealed more friends (21) and carers (21) as perpetrators, than did the victim reports (6 and 1, respectively). This suggests self-reported victim reports are less likely to involve friends and carers, and more likely to involve strangers, than case analyses, perhaps indicative of the successful prosecution of cases involving identified perpetrators.

Situated Interactions Between Perpetrator and Victim

Considering the relationships between victim and perpetrator in more depth, 27% of perpetrators were strangers (of some form), which is fewer in number than other studies, such as the Leicester Hate Crime Project findings mentioned above; instead, a greater proportion were neighbours, friends, relatives or carers. Perpetrators were also identified as medical and/or social care professionals, something that is not seen in other forms of hate crimes. Only 11% of perpetrators were described as teenagers or young people ($n = 25$), which directly contradicts the framework proposed by McDevitt et al. (2002). Rather, the data suggests that disablist perpetrators are of all ages and all walks of life.

The location and type of hate crime or incident victims reported were also interrogated. Most of the incidents of intimidation were in public spaces, but almost all exploitative incidents (such as intimidating or manipulating a disabled person for any form of gain: money, property, labour or sex) happened in private spaces, including homes and care facilities. This feature of disablist hate crime (or 'mate' crime) is distinct from other forms of hate crime. Brutalisation was almost exclusively within the victim's home, suggesting that the home or private space is a particularly high-risk location for disabled people, from some types of perpetrators.

Another important finding was that, in almost half of the cases analysed, the perpetrator was in some form of relationship with the targeted person. When the compiled data was further interrogated, perpetrator differences were identified. For example, in *isolated cases of intimidation*, most perpetrators were 'unknown' (and these occurred more likely in public), however perpetrators of *repeated intimidation* were relational, often friends, carers and partners.[6]

Most perpetrators of exploitation were male, possibly due to the high proportion of sexual exploitation incidents being perpetrated by men. Almost all of the perpetrators of exploitation were known to victims. The most harrowing crimes, which included sustained and violent acts involved brutalisation, including sexual assaults. These perpetrators were all known to their victims, they were all adults, mostly men.

Patterns of Exploitation and Dehumanisation

An important feature of many disablist acts was the dehumanising behaviour of perpetrators, seen in brief, isolated incidents and in sustained victimisation. Dehumanisation is evident in other research on disablist hate crimes (Ralph et al., 2016), but here was both the result of, and a precursor to, later stages in the process of disablist hate crime. It happened in public (on the streets) and in private (in care homes and private homes). An example of this is presented in the catalogue of disturbing and dehumanising incidents by female staff in a care facility, which included putting a person's dementia doll[7] in the washing machine, throwing stones at an elderly frail person, and openly mocking distressed victims, then posting videos on social media (Fitzgerald, 2016).

The dangers of dehumanising behaviour are highlighted by Wolfensberger (2002), who suggested that groups of people devalued in all societies include those not conforming to norms of attractiveness, good health, physical fitness, economic productivity and 'usefulness'. The consequences of this devaluation are a series of wounding experiences: segregation from society, distancing, congregation, scapegoating, othering and being seen as less than human. This can lead to experiences of 'brutalisation, killing thoughts and deathmaking' (Wolfensberger, 2002, p. 11). Disablist hate crime can be thus considered an extreme consequence of this process. When the perpetrator no longer sees the disabled person as human, they are more likely to brutalise the victim, by imprisonment, rape, torture, assault or neglect, and justify often extreme and sustained violence, something which is 'more common in murders of disabled people than other murders' (EHRC, 2011, p. 22). The distressing murder of Brent Martin illustrates this process:

Brent was murdered in Sunderland in 2007 by three young men, aged 22, 16 and 17 years. Brent was 23 years old, with mental health issues and learning disabilities, and was living alone on a housing estate when he was a target of 'mate' crime. He had £3000 in cash but was befriended and exploited by several local youths, until only £5 remained. His murderers carried out a dehumanising, degrading and sadistic attack, chasing him for a mile and a half around the estate. Two of the perpetrators were trained boxers; Brent was punched, kicked, head-butted, stamped on and thrown against a car. As Brent lay dying from head injuries sustained during his ordeal, the perpetrators pulled down his trousers and posed for photographs. This dehumanisation can be seen not only in their actions but in how they spoke of Brent at the murder trial, one offender saying: 'I'm not going down for a muppet' (Case 87). This is a common term of abuse for people with learning and physical disabilities, yet the sentence did not acknowledge or reflect that this was a disablist hate crime.

Escalation of Harm and Abuse

The evidence from the datasets indicates patterns of escalating abuse, echoing existing literature which found high levels of repeat victimisations being commonplace in disablist crimes (e.g. Balderston, 2013). Many cases describe years of repeated targeting and abuse, from perpetrators known to them.

Some perpetrators engaged in power struggles with the targeted person to keep control over them or their social situation, evident in public and private settings. On occasions the victim retaliated and/or sought help, but many endured the abuse, either because they valued the relationship or were coerced into believing they had little choice or feared making things worse. For example, a disabled man targeted a young disabled co-tenant in a care facility, masturbated in front of her, followed her into her bedroom and pushed her onto the bed. When she resisted, he became increasingly violent. She told police:

> I pushed (perpetrator) off me and ran downstairs...he grabbed hold of me...pulling me off the ground, shouting at me...I screamed for (staff)...he started to damage the kitchen, was totally uncontrollable. [Case 37]

This is a common pattern, in that attempts to stop the assaults and regain control can lead to rapid deterioration. In another example, a group of local youths repeatedly targeted a disabled man in his home, damaging his property. During a chance meeting on the street, one of the perpetrators began taunting him. He tried to retaliate, asking to be left alone, but the situation quickly escalated, with the perpetrator becoming increasingly violent. The victim reported:

> he says he's going to kill me, cut my head off, I'm a cripple, a knobhead, I wanna fight you, come on fight me...he was throwing everything, broke trees, branches, a branch hit me... [Case 1]

This incident was one of the few prosecuted as disablist hate crime, due to the disablist terms used by the perpetrator.

Some victims tried to stop incidents by reporting them to the police, or other professionals, again with little impact. For example, when a disabled woman was repeatedly targeted by a group of young people, reporting the perpetrators to the police led to one being given an anti-social behaviour order. He continued to harass the disabled woman from the ASBO dictated distance, thus maintaining his control over the situation and the victim [Case 4].

Not all targeted people felt able to challenge their situation. For some disabled people the threat of removing the relationship stopped them seeking help, as the justification for maintaining an exploitative relationship can be that any relationship is better than none (Landman, 2014). However, without an intervention the perpetrator, as family member, friend or carer, can continue to exploit and abuse the relationship with the victim, leading to greater risk of harm and sometimes even death.

Interrogating Perpetrator Motivations

It must be acknowledged that the datasets contain limited perpetrator self-reported motivations for hate crime offending, as analysis of the data is based on investigations and interpretations of victim reports, safeguarding and police records. Nevertheless, the evidence above suggests there are distinct patterns to disablist hate crime perpetrators that are not evident in other forms of hate crime research.

As with Levin and McDevitt's (1993) typology of perpetrator motivations, which suggests that hate crime attacks are most likely done for fun and amusement, this analysis found groups of young people targeted disabled women in particular, for example:

> they get in like a group or a gang and they're quite young people, and they do take the mickey out of people that have got a disability. (Ciara, interview)
> this same bunch of kids kept on harassing me, they'd throw snowballs in the winter at me windows, stones at me door, like great big stones... they'd jump on me flat roof... (Gemma, interview)

Whilst these acts may seem innocuous events, they are acts of social degradation, humiliation and shaming, which can escalate quickly and cause significant harm and impact. In this escalation the disabled person is no longer seen as a person who deserves to be treated with respect. Two disabled women recalled:

> this man...said I was a nuisance he said I should have been killed at birth and as I wasn't he was gonna kill me there and then. (Amy, interview)
> [he said] "you're abnormal, you're a freak... I should be exterminated along with the rest of them" (Sarah, interview)

Furthermore, the gendered nature of sexually violent hate crimes is notable in many cases including those where perpetrators committed violent and aggressive attacks on disabled women. The combined motivations of control, sexual and violent impulses led to many women experiencing long-term trauma as well as physical harm. This supports the suggestion by Sherry (2013) that disablist hate crimes are particularly sadistic, high harm and hyper violent and links disablist crimes to domestic abuse (Healy, 2021; Kelly, 1987).

Some perpetrators used less physical violence but controlled disabled people by coercion, manipulation and grooming. Some relationships were created or developed by perpetrators exploiting a casual acquaintance or an opportunity, deliberately grooming, gaslighting and isolating the targeted person. The process of grooming may take days, months or years. To gain trust, the perpetrator may try to appear vulnerable or in need of help. Recognising the processes of increasing manipulation can be difficult for some disabled people, as was evident in Landman's (2014) work on 'false' friends and 'mate' crime.

Figure 1 demonstrates how our framework can be applied to disablist hate crimes. To summarise, whilst McDevitt et al. (2002) perpetrator typology is undoubtably significant in terms of hate crime advances, it does not apply to all forms of hate crime offending. The majority of perpetrators in this combined data set were *not* strangers, but there was some evidence of 'thrill seekers' in some of the cases examined, particularly those involving young people. Iganski et al.'s (2005) expanded typology, including situational factors such as opportunism, does fit with some of the cases examined. Additionally, the work by Bowling (1998), Sin (2014a), and Sibbitt (1997) mentioned above, with their emphasis on the dynamic processes involved in relational crimes, within social structures, can be applied to the cases here. The disablist hate crimes explored were sometimes opportunistic, sometimes considered, context dependent and time and location sensitive. Relationships between victim and perpetrator were a strong factor in whether the harm continued over long periods of time or occurred in one-off places and spaces (see also Clayton et al., 2022). The gender of the victim was a significant factor in many cases in the types of harm inflicted. Thus, the findings draw instead upon Perry's (2001) theory of doing 'difference' as a method of othering, dehumanising and subordinating disabled people from mainstream society.

Hollomotz's (2013) continuum of disability, oppression and violence is also shown to have merit when applied to disablist offenders' motivations, in that violence and subordination are co-occurring and reinforcing processes, which are embedded within the actions of many in our society.

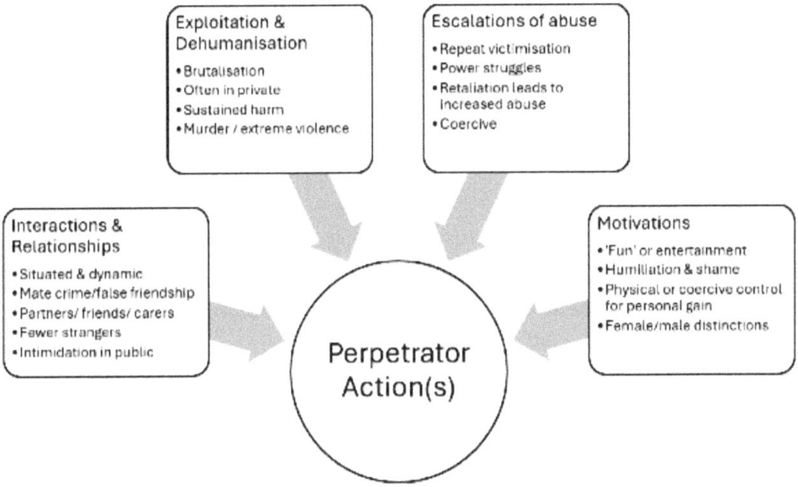

Fig. 1 Framework for conceptualising disablist hate crime

Conclusion

Patterns in the types and experiences of disablist hate crimes were identified in the scrutiny of the combined dataset. In most police and safeguarding cases analysed, perpetrators were known to their victims. Those who self-reported their experiences were more likely to share stories of targeting by strangers and family members or carers, resulting in fewer reports to the police. This underlines how official figures on disablist hate crimes under-represent the nature and extent of the problem.

Both Houghton and Healy's original research suggested that disablist hate crime is a dynamic process. This involves a process of othering, in which the victim is seen as different, vulnerable 'prey' and a target for intimidation, exploitation and brutalisation. Targeting may include direct subjugation, grooming and gaslighting of the victim who may resist, often leading to increased threat, coercion or violence. This process is described in more detail in Houghton and Muller (2025) but is evident in Fig. 4.1.

The categories in the framework presented above are not mutually exclusive; dehumanisation tends to start with intimidation and exploitation; exploitation starts often with intimidation; sexual violence and abuse can run concurrently to other forms of targeted violence. Cases of intimidation, exploitation and brutalisation often involved different types of perpetrators who may be motivated by more than one impulse. These motivations were difficult to identify. However, all the cases analysed were conceptualised as disablist hate crime: the person was targeted because they were (or were perceived to be) disabled.

The research acknowledges that any hate crime framework must be mindful to recognise the diversity *within* groups, as the dynamics of particular elements of subgroups can be lost (Sherry, 2013). This is particularly relevant when examining cases of disablist hate crimes that may involve a variety of different impairments and conditions, both seen and unseen, and lived experiences may intersect with other categories of identity.

Undoubtedly, it was difficult to identify with absolute certainty the motivational impulses of many offenders from the case histories and stories considered here; as Iganski et al. (2005) indicate, this can only be confirmed when the perpetrator states it explicitly. This chapter therefore adds to calls for greater research into disablist hate crime offenders and disablist motivations. The tentative typology needs further exploration and empirical research to test for its validity and applicability across a larger dataset and, ideally, working with disablist perpetrators directly. Nevertheless, it is proposed as a starting point in the hope it may prove useful for understanding how and why disabled people are victimised to such an extent, and on such a repeated cycle, in contemporary society. It further positions the perpetrator act(s) as central, rather than any victim vulnerability. Further research is encouraged, to focus disablist hate as a priority for research and practice.

Notes

2. The term impairment is a value free term referring to physical or learning disabilities or mental health needs.

3. This differs significantly from racial or religious hate crimes where specific aggravated offences exist for prosecutions, with higher sentencing tariffs as a result.
4. CPS has changed reporting statistics and now produces quarterly figures which does not break down by type of hate crime; see: https://www.cps.gov.uk/publication/cps-quarterly-data-summaries.
5. The Hate Crime and Public Order (Scotland) Act 2021 include new offences of stirring up hatred for other protected characteristics including disability.
6. Neither project looked specifically at cases of domestic abuse though the data indicates that there were some cases given the perpetrators selected/described. It is not possible to tell from the data how long or frequently that abuse occurred.
7. Dementia dolls are used therapeutically in some dementia care facilities. The dolls are given to people with dementia who develop an attachment to the doll, caring for it as if it was a real baby.

References

Aldridge-Waddon, M. (2020). Vulnerable witnesses in police investigative interviews in England and Wales. In M. Coulthard, A. May, & R. Sousa-Silva (Eds.), (2021), *The Routledge handbook of forensic linguistics*. Routledge.

Balderston, S. (2013). Victimized again? Intersectionality and injustice in disabled women's lives after hate crime and rape. In M. Texler Segal & V. Demos (Eds.), *Gendered perspectives on conflict and violence: Part A (Advances in Gender Research, Volume 18A)* (pp. 17–51). Emerald Group Publishing Limited.

Bowling, B. (1998). *Violent racism victimization, policing and social context*. Clarendon Press.

Burch, L. (2021). *Understanding disability and everyday hate*. Palgrave Macmillan.

Crown Prosecution Service (CPS). (2019). *Hate Crime Report 2018–19*. Available online: https://www.cps.gov.uk/publication/hate-crime-report-2018-2019. Accessed 24 May 2024.

Crown Prosecution Service (CPS). (2024). Quarterly Data Summary Quarter 1 2024–2025 available online: CPS data summary Quarter 1 2024–2025 Accessed 20 October 2024.

Chakraborti, N., et al. (2015). Framing the boundaries of hate crime. In N. Hall (Ed.), *The Routledge international handbook on hate crime* (pp. 13–23). Routledge.

Chakraborti, N., Garland, J., & Hardy, S.-J. (2014). *The Leicester hate crime project: Briefing Paper1: Disablist hate crime: Victims' perspectives.* University of Leicester [online]. Accessed 18 August 2016. https://www2.le.ac.uk/departments/criminology/hate/documents/bp1-disablist-hate-crime/view

Chapman, L. (2020). Still getting away with murder: Disability hate crime in England. *Inclusion London.*

Clayton, J., Donovan, C., & Macdonald, S. J. (2022). Living with hate relationships: Familiar encounters, enduring racisms and geographies of entrapment. *Society and Space, 40*(1), 60–90.

Equalities and Human Rights Commission. (2011). *Hidden in plain sight: Inquiry into disability related harassment* (Final Report). London: EHRC.

Fitzgerald, T. (2016, November 21). Careworkers in 'dementia doll' abuse storm at nursing home are jailed. *Manchester Evening News Online.*

Goffman, E. (1961). *Asylums: Essays on the social situation of mental patients and other inmates.* Aldine Transaction.

Goodley, D., & Runswick Cole, K. (2011). The violence of disablism. *Sociology of Health & Illness, 33*(4), 602–617. ISSN 0141-9889 https://doi.org/10.1111/j.1467-9566.2010.01302

Hall, N. (2015). Understanding hate crimes: Sociological and criminological perspectives. In N. Hall, A. Corb, P. Giannasi, & J. G. D. Grieve (Eds.), *The Routledge international handbook on hate crime* (pp. 69–80). Routledge.

Healy, J. C. (2018). *On the periphery of hate crime: Disability at the intersections of marginalisation, vulnerability and difference* (PhD thesis). Middlesex University.

Healy, J. (2019). Thinking outside the box: Intersectionality as a hate crime research framework *Papers from the British Criminology Conference, 19*, 60–83. https://www.britsoccrim.org/pbcc2019/

Healy, J. C. (2021). An exposition of sexual violence as a method of disablist hate crime. In I. Zempi & J. Smith (Eds.), *Misogyny as hate crime.* Routledge.

Houghton, V., & Lancaster University. Theses. Law School. (2022). Defining disablist hate crime: acts, mis/constructions, and the process of othering [Lancaster University]. https://doi.org/10.17635/lancaster/thesis/1903

Houghton, V. & Muller, T. (2025). 'I Feel Persecuted. It's So Distressing and Upsetting, It Is All Too Much'. A disablist hate crime typology: Intimidation, exploitation and brutalization. *The British Journal of Criminology*, azaf014. https://doi.org/10.1093/bjc/azaf014

Hollomotz, A. (2013). Disability and the continuum of violence. In A. Roulstone & H. Mason-Bish (Eds.), *Disability* (pp. 52–63). Routledge.

Home Office. (2020). *Hate crime, England and Wales 2019/20. Statistical Bulletin 29/20*. https://www.gov.uk/government/statistics/hate-crime-england-and-wales-2019-to-2020

Home Office. (2023). *Hate crime, England and Wales, 2022/2023*. https://www.gov.uk/government/statistics/hate-crime-england-and-wales-2022-to-2023/hate-crime-england-and-wales-2022-to-2023

Home Office. (2024). *Hate crime, England and Wales, year ending March 2024*. https://www.gov.uk/government/statistics/hate-crime-england-and-wales-year-ending-march-2024/hate-crime-england-and-wales-year-ending-march-2024

Iganski, P., Kielinger, V., & Paterson, S. (2005). *Hate crimes against London's Jews: An analysis of incidents recorded by the Metropolitan Police Service 2001–2003*. Institute for Jewish Policy Research and the Metropolitan Police Service.

Jacobs, J. B., & Potter, K. (1998). *Hate crimes: Criminal law & identity politics*. OUP.

Jolliffe, D., & Farrington, D. P. (2020). The criminal careers of those imprisoned for hate crime in the UK. *European Journal of Criminology, 17*(6), 936–955. https://doi.org/10.1177/1477370819839598

Kelly, L. (1987). The continuum of sexual violence. In J. Hanmer & M. Maynard (Eds.), *Women, violence and social control* (pp. 46–60). Palgrave Macmillan UK. https://doi.org/10.1007/978-1-349-18592-4_4

Kirk-Wade, E, Stiebahl, S., & Wong, H. (2024) Research Briefing: no. 09602. UK Disability statistics: Prevalence and life experiences. House of Commons Library.

Landman, R. A. (2014). "A counterfeit friendship": Mate crime and people with learning disabilities. *Journal of Adult Protection, 16*(6), 355–366.

Levin, J. (2013) Disablist violence in the US: Unacknowledged hate crime. In A. Roulstone & H. Mason-Bish (Eds.), *Disability, hate crime and violence* (pp. 95–105). Routledge.

Levin, J., & McDevitt, J. (1993). *Hate crimes: The rising tide of bigotry and bloodshed*. Plenum.

Macdonald, S. (2015). 'Community fear and harassment': Learning difficulties and hate crime incidents in the north-east of England. *Disability & Society, 30*(3), 353–367.
Macdonald, S., Donovan, C., & Clayton, J. (2017). The disability bias: Understanding the context of hate in comparison with other minority populations. *Disability and Society, 12*(4), 483–499.
Macdonald, S. J., Donovan, C., & Clayton, J. (2021). 'I may be left with no choice but to end my torment': Disability and intersectionalities of hate crime. *Disability & Society, 38*(1), 127–147. https://doi.org/10.1080/09687599.2021.1928480
Macdonald, S. J., Donovan, C., Clayton, J., & Husband, M. (2024). Becoming cuckooed: Conceptualising the relationship between disability, home takeovers and criminal exploitation. *Disability & Society, 39*(2), 485–505.
Mason, G. (2005). Being hated: Stranger or familiar? *Social & Legal Studies, 14*(4), 585–605.
Mason-Bish, H. (2015). Beyond the silo: Rethinking hate crime and intersectionality. In N. Hall, A. Corb, P. Giannasi & J. G. D. Grieve (Eds.), *The Routledge international handbook on hate crime* (pp. 24–33). Routledge.
McDevitt, J., Levin, J., & Bennett, S. (2002). Hate crime offenders: An expanded typology. *Journal of Social Issues, 58*(2), 303–317.
Northern Ireland Statistics and Research Agency. (2024). *Incidents and crimes with a hate motivation recorded by the Police in Northern Ireland.* https://www.psni.police.uk/system/files/2024-08/1050879717/Hate%20Motivations%20Bulletin%20Period%20ending%2030th%20June%202024.pdf
Office for National Statistics. (2018). *Disability and Crime, UK*. Office for National Statistics.
Perry, B. (2001). *In the name of hate: Understanding hate crimes.* Routledge.
Perry, B. (2002). Hate crime and identity politics. *Theoretical Criminology, 6*(4), 485–491.
Phillips, N. D. (2009). The prosecution of hate crimes: The limitations of the hate crime typology. *Journal of Interpersonal Violence, 24*(5), 883–905.
Pring, J. (2012, November 8). *Anger over judge's 'appalling' Winterbourne View hate crime failure.* Disability News Service.
Quarmby, K. (2011). *Scapegoat: How we are failing disabled people*. Portobello Press.
Ralph, S., Capewell, C., & Bonnett, E. (2016). Disability hate crime: Persecuted for difference. *British Journal of Special Education/ NASEN, 43*(3), 215–232.

Roulstone, A., Thomas, P., & Balderston, S. (2011). Between hate and vulnerability: Unpacking the British criminal justice system's construction of disablist hate crime. *Disability & Society, 26*(3), 351–364.

Schuelke, L., Munford, L., & Morciano, M. (2021). Estimating the additional costs of living with a disability in the United Kingdom between 2013 and 2016. *The European Journal of Health Economics, 23*, 313–327.

Scottish Government. (2023). *An updated study into the characteristics of police recorded hate crime in Scotland.* Justice Analytical Services. https://www.gov.scot/binaries/content/documents/govscot/publications/research-and-analysis/2023/01/updated-study-characteristics-police-recorded-hate-crime-scotland/documents/updated-study-characteristics-police-recorded-hate-crime-scotland/updated-study-characteristics-police-recorded-hate-crime-scotland/govscot%3Adocument/updated-study-characteristics-police-recorded-hate-crime-scotland.pdf

Sherry, M. (2013). International perspectives on disability hate crime. In A. Roulstone & H. Mason-Bish (Eds.), *Disability, hate crime and violence* (pp. 80–91). Routledge.

Sibbitt, R. (1997). *The perpetrators of racial harassment and racial violence. Research Study 176.* Home Office

Sin, C. H. (2014a). Using a 'layers of influence' model to understand the interaction of research, policy and practice in relation to disablist hate crime. In N. Chakraborti & J. Garland (Eds.), *Responding to hate crime: The case for connecting policy and research*(pp. 99–112). Policy Press.

Sin, C. H. (2014b). Hate crime against people with disabilities. In N. Hall, A. Corb, P. Giannasi, & J. G. D. Grieve (Eds.), (2015) *The Routledge international handbook on hate crime* (pp. 193–206). Routledge.

Sin, C. H. (2015). Hate crime against people with disabilities. In N. Hall, A. Corb, P. Giannasi & J. G. D. Grieve (Eds.), *The Routledge international handbook on hate crime* (pp. 193–206). Routledge.

Sobsey, D. (1994) *Violence and abuse in the lives of people with disabilities: The end of silent acceptance?* Brooks

Sobsey, D., & Calder, P. (1999). *Violence against people with disabilities: A conceptual analysis.* National Research Council.

Taylor, S. (2022). *Hate crime policy and disability: From vulnerability to ableism.* Bristol University Press. https://muse.jhu.edu/book/102971/

Tyson, J., Giannasi, P., & Hall, N. (2015). Johnny come lately? The international and domestic policy context of disability hate crime. In R. Shah & P. Giannasi (Eds.), *Tackling disability discrimination and disability hate crime* (pp. 20–35). Jessica Kingsley.

Walters, M., Owusu-Bempah, A., & Wiedlitzka, S. (2018). Hate crime and the "justice gap": The case for law reform. *Criminal Law Review, 12*, 961–986.
Walters, M., Wiedlitzka, S., & Owusu-Bempah, A. (2017). *Hate crime and the legal process: Options for law reform* (Final Report October 2017). Sussex: University of Sussex.
West, C., & Zimmerman, D. (1987). Doing gender. *Gender & Society, 1*, 125–151.
Williams, M. L., & Tregidga, J. (2014). Hate crime victimization in Wales: Psychological and physical impacts across seven hate crime victim types. *British Journal of Criminology, 54*(5), 946–967.
Wilkin, D. (2020). *Disability hate crime: Experiences of everyday hostility on public transport*. Palgrave Macmillan. https://search.ebscohost.com/login.aspx?direct=true&scope=site&db=nlebk&db=nlabk&AN=2293372
Wolfensberger, W. (2002). *The new genocide of handicapped and afflicted people* (3rd ed.). Author.

Familiar Faces: Hate Relationships and the Everyday-ness of Hate Perpetration

John Clayton, Stephen J. Macdonald, and Catherine Donovan

Introduction

This chapter contributes to a body of work that explores the character and actions of those who perpetrate hate towards 'othered' people in the course of their everyday lives (Iganski, 2008; Mason, 2005; McDevitt et al., 2002). It does so by focussing on victim-perpetrator relations that involve degrees of familiarity and residential proximity. To do this we draw upon research examining repeat reports of hate perpetrated by neighbours that form a cumulative pattern of harm, what we refer to

J. Clayton (✉)
Department of Geography and Environmental Sciences, Northumbria University, Newcastle, UK
e-mail: john.clayton@northumbria.ac.uk

S. J. Macdonald
Criminology and Disability Studies at Durham University, Durham, UK

C. Donovan
Department of Sociology, Durham University, Durham, UK

J. Garland et al. (eds.), *Hate Crime Perpetrators: New Perspectives from Theory, Research and Practice, Volume I*, Palgrave Hate Studies,
https://doi.org/10.1007/978-3-031-92666-2_5

as ‘hate relationships’ (hereafter HRs) (Donovan et al., 2021). Working with a hate crime advocacy service in North East England, we analysed anonymised case notes of advocacy clients experiencing ongoing, often long-term victimisation, that provide us with a partial, yet important understanding of the everyday-ness of hate perpetration.

HRs not only involve explicitly violent and criminal acts, but are more often constituted by abuse, obstruction, intimidation, surveillance and noise that are less easily evidenced and which can take hold over long periods of time. Elsewhere we have argued that HRs are akin to coercive control in domestic abuse (Donovan et al., 2023) in terms of the domestic concentration of harm; targeting of perceived and ‘othered’ identities; entitlement of perpetrators to act; repeat reporting; and cumulative health related impacts that are exacerbated by (in)actions of help providers. The other key parallel of particular interest here is that perpetrators and victims are familiar to each other and live close by, sometimes as next-door neighbours. This level of familiarity, as work on domestic abuse and intimacy has shown (Pain, 2014), means that violent relations manifest in distinctive ways including temporal regularity, spatial concentration, entrapment and emotional control which often goes under the radar of responding agencies (Clayton et al., 2022a). Whilst established literature on everyday harmful encounters highlights the significance of hate, and particularly racism, that is evident in public spaces and perpetrated by strangers (Hopkins et al., 2020; Listerborn, 2015; Nayak, 2017), we highlight intersectional hateful relationships in situations where degrees of familiarity matter.

Here we tread that difficult line between a recognition of the serious and harmful impacts of these behaviours, whilst departing from psychological, individualised and generic understandings of hate (Hall et al., 2022). Through an examination of the character and dynamics of perpetration in HRs, we make three main points. Firstly, that perpetrators in HRs are not isolated individuals. There is a danger of seeing perpetrators as not one of us, when in fact the experiences we discuss here, whilst morally unacceptable, are situated within the challenges and tensions of contemporary society and dominant political discourse. Perpetrators also operate with others in different kinds of ways within those contexts—in the recruitment of other perpetrators, in the context of peer pressure and friendship groups and in the intergenerational transmission of practices of 'othering'. Secondly, as others have argued in relation to hate crime more generally (Iganski, 2008), perpetrators of HRs are not just extremists and not necessarily 'offenders' in the sense of having been prosecuted for criminal acts. We are then less concerned with motivation as some internal psychological profile that sets people apart as hate offenders. Instead, we are concerned with multiscalar contexts which produce spaces for the actions of 'ordinary' perpetrators and the consequences of this action for those harmed, but also for the re-legitimisation of these acts. Our third point is that perpetrators in HRs are not just strangers. This matters because they are known to those targeted through everyday residential proximities and the regularity of harmful encounters that become overwhelming, damaging to health and very difficult to escape (Clayton et al., 2022a). It also matters because relationships can be messy and complex and, in some situations, hate may be preceded by or co-exist with other affective relations. It also helps us to appreciate that hate emerges from existing tensions where neighbours share spaces in settings of division, scarce resource and social change that is framed as threatening.

We begin by situating the actions of perpetrators of HRs within established work, highlighting the ordinariness of hate perpetration and identifying a need to nuance this with an appreciation of the dynamics that familiarity brings. We then clarify the concept of HRs to show how these are experienced as frequent, unpredictable and sometimes inescapable, before introducing our data source and our approach to analysis that recognises the case notes provide an important but partial understanding. In our analysis and discussion, we explore the diverse character of perpetrators including the role of young people, their families as well as older residents and wider social networks in making life unbearable for those victimised. Attention is drawn to the group-based nature of many HRs, the transmission of offending behaviours beyond individual lead perpetrators and the contexts through which these emerge. Whilst we emphasise how dominant and intersectional power relations (in terms of 'race', faith, disability, sexuality and transgender) give relative control over neighbourhood relations and spaces to perpetrators, we acknowledge both the complexity of some relationships and that perpetrators are, in different ways also often marginalised, alienated and disempowered.

Ordinary Perpetrators, Everyday Encounters

There exists a rich body of work which attempts to understand what drives individuals and groups to commit hateful acts towards those identified as 'Other' and thus re-produce hierarchical relationships (Schweppe & Perry, 2022). This is increasingly characterised by attempts to move beyond individualised psychological understandings of motivation (Perry, 2009). Approaches which emphasise the socio-political context of (and for) hate are many and varied. This includes critical approaches that for example view hate as a manifestation of neoliberal harms where needs and desires are not realised (James & McBride, 2022) or emphasise how material oppression works alongside cultural constructions of 'otherness' (Young, 1988). Building upon this, Perry (2009) suggests the perpetration of hate, is one means through which dominant identities are re-asserted in socially manufactured contexts of threat by 'doing difference'. Chakraborti and Garland (2012) focus less on the threats posed by those victimised in the eyes of perpetrators than on the perceived vulnerability of victims that goes beyond, in their view, restrictive identity-based motivations. Chakraborti (2015, p. 1747) argues this complicates 'motivations' as solely a process of subordination, but also an 'act arising from more banal motivations, be it boredom, jealousy or unfamiliarity with "difference"'. Geographically informed approaches such as the socio-ecological approach set out by Hall (2022), speak to the multiple scales and spaces of everyday life which facilitate the enactment of (and responses to) hate. Other geographical work highlights the defence of spaces seen as encroached upon by problematised embodiments and expressions of social difference (Clayton et al., 2022b; Nayak, 2017). In a different way, Ahmed (2001) detaches perpetration from individuals by emphasising the affective and circulating nature of hate which becomes stuck to specific bodies amidst divisive and devaluing political rhetoric. In various guises therefore, interdisciplinary approaches have considered the relation of those enacting hate to broader socio-political contexts, everyday environments and the charged encounters that constitute those spaces (Clayton, 2009). Beyond more general theories of perpetration, there is a need for greater attention to the dynamics of hate enacted through specific spaces and places—in this case the spaces of the neighbourhood and home in North East England.

Aside from work which looks to understand hate perpetration, there is also a body of research that attends to the profile and characteristics of perpetrators. Some of this, for example Jolliffe and Farrington (2020), is quantitative and focuses on analysis of hate crimes recorded through police data. The emphasis is on acts identified as criminal and prosecutable. Perpetrators are thus conceptualised as 'offenders'—those guilty and prosecuted for committing such illegal acts. Joliffe and Farrington (2020) pay particular attention to violent hate crime offenders, arguing such offenders are found to have prolific criminal careers. One of the conclusions from the review of available studies on hate crime offenders (Joliffe and Farrington, 2020, drawing on the work of DeLisi & Piquero, 2011) is that such offenders are 'generalist' offenders, that is they are not just hate crime offenders. Other work also drawing on police data (from the US) that includes but goes beyond violent hate crime offenders such as McDevitt et al. (2002), draws contrasting conclusions. For example, they show that over half of perpetrators examined are young offenders, operating in groups and often motivated by the 'thrill' of these acts. This is differentiated from those (a quarter of offences examined) who are motivated by the protection of their 'turf' from those seen as outsiders (McDevitt et al., 2002). In their work Iganski et al. (2011) also highlight the key social characteristics in the overall profile of hate crime offenders in the UK context as young, male, white and unemployed.

Collectively, such work highlights that the data type examined and the 'kind' of offences we are interested in, are crucial to the conclusions drawn regarding the character of perpetrators. In the work of Hall (2019) for example, who explores daily harassment experienced by disabled people as 'micro-aggressions', the profile of perpetrator and the nature of those acts are very different to those explored in police data mentioned above. Indeed, Iganski (2008) argues our understanding of hate crime perpetration is skewed by a fascination with police data and only those who come into contact with the criminal justice system—an argument that feels pertinent to our research where such contact can be partial and often unsatisfactory. It is also clear that the perpetration of hate is not the preserve of extremists and highly motivated, pre-meditated bigots. Chakraborti (2015), Hall et al. (2022) and Iganksi (2008) all emphasise the importance of recognising hate is most often committed by ordinary people in the contexts of their everyday lives, that for Chakraborti (2015, p. 19) includes a recognition that '… hate crimes are not committed exclusively by obvious "haters"'.

Within work that does go beyond analysis of police data to explore everyday hateful encounters (Hopkins et al., 2020; Listerborn, 2015; Nayak, 2017), ordinary perpetrators are most often seen as strangers; those encountered on a fleeting basis (Wilson, 2017) and often in public spaces of the street, transport, commercial spaces or the night time economy where diverse lives can intersect and sometimes clash (Iganski, 2008). Whilst such a focus is crucial to understanding broader 'landscapes of hate' (Hall et al., 2022), it often means the nature of the relationships between victims and perpetrators remains under-explored (Mason, 2005), with the exception of work highlighting racist offending against 'acquaintances' formed through, for example, neighbourhood based commercial spaces (Nayak, 2010). Where familiarity is raised, it can be associated with more positive social interactions. Hall and Bates (2019, p. 108) for example, rightly argue in relation to the experiences of disabled people navigating everyday urban spaces, that familiar faces in a range of settings can 'provide a set of relations to support them as they spend time in the city'. However, if we pay attention to the spaces of the home and neighbourhood, being known *and* being seen as 'Other' can be used as the basis for exclusion, abjection and harm. Through the lens of HRs, we shift attention to harms enacted in and around domestic spaces, emphasising both the ordinariness of perpetration, but also, the temporality, spatiality and sociality that familiarity brings.

Hate Relationships and Methodology

HRs emerged from our research (Donovan et al., 2023) as a way of capturing experiences of hate characterised by repeat incidents, often over an extended period of time, perpetrated by those living in close proximity to the victim. We discuss in detail elsewhere the parallels of these experiences with victims of domestic abuse, particularly elements of coercive control and health-related impacts (Donovan et al., 2021). Incidents that constitute a hate relationship can at various moments be overtly violent, but also include abuse and intimidation that are not so clearly criminal or are very difficult to evidence as such. This includes the blocking of pathways, loud music at un-social hours, banging on walls, vexatious counterclaims against those victimised, surveillance, hanging around the perimeter of homes and other acts which make life incredibly difficult for residents (Donovan et al., 2021). Viewed in isolation these may be seen as 'low-level' or mis-characterised as anti-social behaviour or neighbourhood disputes, but when seen cumulatively as an attack on *already marginalised* individuals and their families, the harm can be life-changing (Donovan et al., 2021, 2024). Such minimisation and misrecognition by responding agencies including the police, housing and local authorities also often results in hate relationship being drawn out, in some cases, for years.

Building upon previous work with the same organisation (Donovan et al., 2021), we collaborated with a regional advocacy organisation in North East England who run a Hate Crime Advocacy Service (HCAS). We thematically analysed 168 anonymised and redacted case notes (44% of 384 referrals received by the HCAS) within the period 1/4/2019–31/3/2022 that met our criteria for HRs (perpetrated by the same perpetrator(s); by those who live close by; with impacts akin to coercive control). The notes include records of interactions between advocates and clients including details of incidents, actions, problems and communication with responding agencies. It is worth noting this period coincided with the COVID-19 pandemic and national lockdowns, which exacerbated negative experiences of help-seeking for advocacy clients, and in many cases allowed perpetrators to act with greater impunity (Donovan et al., 2024). The notes inevitably tell us more about the experience of the victim and the actions of the advocates than they do about perpetrators. Whilst we therefore recognise limitations, we have also been able to glean significant insights into the influence of degrees of familiarity and proximity, the profile and role of perpetrators, the social nature of targeting and challenges faced by perpetrators. These themes are explored below with reference to relevant anonymised case note excerpts.

Perpetrators as Familiar and Proximate

> It is fair to say that throughout my life I have had the odd comment directed at me, however this has always been in jest, or some idiot when I had been out with friends, but nothing like this within an environment that is meant to be my safe space, being my home. (Case recorded as homophobic hate) [E-mail from client to advocate]

As this e-mail excerpt indicates, in HRs perpetrators are not strangers and this has a direct bearing on the form and intensity of hate experienced. Such perpetrators are local, often co-residents of the neighbourhood, sometimes next-door neighbours and in some rarer cases might even be seen by clients as former friends or acquaintances. Being a neighbour, especially in housing environments where neighbours are immediately proximate, means encounters are regular and lives bleed into each other with more force (Stokoe, 2006). However, we distinguish HRs from neighbourhood disputes by emphasising how conflict involves the targeting of already marginalised identities, defined legally as 'protected characteristics'. Such residential intimacies means responding agencies can mis-recognise HRs as 'neighbourhood disputes' (Cheshire et al., 2021) or anti-social behaviour (ASB), thus removing consideration of power relations (Donovan et al., 2024). The following case illustrates this distinction, but also highlights how being neighbours can intensify hate. The perpetrator here continues to complain about 'normal' behaviours, in a way which is clearly racialised.

> ...the neighbour has been complaining about her children playing out in the street. He has shouted and sworn at the children (telling them to 'fuck off') and complained to the council. He has also complained about the only other black children who play out. He never complains about the white children, so she firmly believes that his behaviour is racially motivated. He has also complained about them playing even in their own home, when they are simply causing the normal noises the children make. (Case recorded as racist hate) [Email to social housing from advocate]

Familiarity and proximity are crucial in that HRs can be immediate, frequent (but also unpredictable), enduring, overwhelming and inescapable (Clayton et al., 2022a). The excerpt below captures this immediacy and entrapment where perpetrators use proximity as the basis for their actions (an 'undesirable' family in the flat above) as well as enhancing the degrees of harm felt. The targeted family are viewed by perpetrators as what Puwar (2004) calls 'space invaders', bodies out of place, for whom life is made unbearable. Perpetrators construct these individuals and families as legitimate targets for ongoing violence, often as a means of purging them from the neighbourhood (Nayak, 2017). This can be seen through both the neighbours' actions, but also by their landlord who served an eviction because of complaints regarding noises caused by their autistic child.

> They also believe that the downstairs neighbours are now deliberately harassing them by playing loud music day and night, and using offensive language when they ask them to turn the noise down so that the children can sleep, in an attempt to force them out. They believe that the neighbours are acting in this way because of their race and their son's disability. (Case recorded as racist and disablist hate) [Email from advocate to local authority]

Familiarity here is experienced as a means of controlling lives, mobilities and emotional states. The use of sound and noise (Stokoe & Hepburn, 2005) is significant in that this can easily travel through terraced housing and flats—both common housing arrangements in our data. HRs therefore take place through multiple encounters that rely on the proximity of the perpetrator to those targeted. These include physical violence, face to face abuse, harm mediated through sound through the walls of the home, memories and reminders of past incidents and the potential for future harm through the threatening presence of perpetrators around the perimeter of the home. The following excerpt speaks to these kinds of feared encounters and the impact on clients' health.

> Please could you write a letter for my client [client] of [address], to recommend that he is rehoused due to the racial harassment he has experienced on numerous occasions from his neighbour ... [Housing association] have spoken to the perpetrator in the past but the harassment continues. [client] has complex mental health problems and is under the care of [doctor]. His depression, anxiety and paranoid delusions have considerably worsened because of the hate crime incidents. He is fearful of leaving the house in case he encounters the neighbours and cannot use his garden when the neighbours are in. (Case recorded as racist hate) [Letter from advocate to Police]

The spatiality of HRs also means perpetrators have access to the personal property of the victim and in some situations are able to undermine the safety of their home through incursions and disruptions to that most intimate of social spaces (Mallett, 2004). Knowing perpetrators are close and may be monitoring their behaviour, has an impact upon how clients conduct themselves:

> She has had ongoing issues with her upstairs neighbour. Over a period of 8 months she has had items in her garden moved around, her key in the inner lock of the door pushed out from outside, plants put in front of her door and a piece of rope in her garden turned into a noose. She believes this has been her neighbour and that they have been doing this to scare her. Her husband has been working away over this period and she has been home alone. She has not reported previous incidents. She is frightened to talk on the phone in the flat for fear of her conversation being overheard and is currently selling her flat due to the issues. (Hate category unspecified) [Advocate notes]

Perpetrators can also use familiarity and proximity to their own advantage. This is often seen through counter accusations against those targeted, even when these are fabricated, exaggerated or come as a reaction to initial actions towards clients. In many such cases, the aim appears to be to shift perceptions of guilt for responding agencies such as the Police, aligning with an often-held practitioner perspective in our research, that all parties are 'as bad as each other' and engaged in tit-for-that anti-social behaviour. We note how the claim of victim status can be a tactic employed to prevent prosecution as the police have to legally deal with both as perpetrators.

> Last night [police] came round and said that [neighbour] has accused him and [partner] of harassing her. [Client] was very upset as it seemed to him that [police] were assuming that [neighbour] was in the right and they were in the wrong despite having no evidence, whereas he never accepts any evidence when they present it of the neighbours harassing them. He was adamant that neither of them have done any harassing. (Case recorded as homophobic hate) [Advocate notes]

Who Are Perpetrators of Hate Relationships?

Besides the fact most perpetrators of HRs are neighbours and (in our data) mostly reside in deprived neighbourhoods where tensions are most keenly felt (Lloyd et al., 2021), what else can we say about their profile? In line with our argument that socio-spatial conditions and the purchase of divisive ideas and affects, rather than psychological profiles, best help us understand these behaviours, we suggest it is difficult to generalise. Whilst the majority are men, women are also involved—sometimes as primary perpetrators, but more often as partners or friends of those that appear to initiate behaviours. In some cases, perpetrators have past involvement with the criminal justice system, whilst for others there seems to be no apparent evidence of criminal records or interactions with the authorities. Therefore, in some cases the perpetration of HRs comes on the back of other forms of violent or anti-social behaviour (that may or may not include other hate offences), aligning with work on the 'prolific' criminal careers of hate crime offenders (Joliffe and Farrington,

2020). Yet, where the evidence permits us to comment, these kinds of biographies are the exception.

Whilst our data is imperfect in terms of consistency of detail, the age range of perpetrators varies from children of various ages through to those in their 90s. In those cases where children are involved, this often involves groups of children gathered near to clients' homes but can also include following those targeted on regular routines to the shops and school for example. In the following case a woman and her daughter experienced ongoing racist harassment, over 2 years, by the same group that includes children:

> [client] moved into her property 2 and a half years ago and has had ongoing harassment from a group of people throwing eggs and stones at the house and at her and her son. [client] has reported incidents to the police. The most recent incident was reported to the police one month ago + one of the boys who threw things at them was spoken to. (Case recorded as racist hate) [Advocate notes]

In another case, a family who have been granted asylum in the UK after fleeing from Syria via a refugee camp also illustrate how groups of children have made their home feel like a prison, so much so that the father of the family (with four young children) suggested they would rather return to the camp than stay under these conditions. The collective, daily racist targeting indicates the cumulative harm caused when groups of children focus their energies in this way.

> [client] informs me that he suffers from harassment and racist abuse on a daily basis, including local children throwing stones and rubbish into their yard, leaving rubbish on the doorstep, shouting abuse, knocking on the door and running away, throwing water bombs and using racist language. Incidents happen every day (Case recorded as racist hate) [Advocate e-mail to social housing]

Whilst children do feature in some HRs, there is also evidence that they are often empowered to do this by adults in their life. Indeed, the excerpt above hints that it is not *just* children involved. There are limited options for dealing with children and young people as offenders, which inevitably requires the involvement of parent/guardians. This may clearly present difficulties if the parents themselves are also engaged in the HR. In the following example of disability hate, which constitutes a lengthy 20 years-long campaign involving many residents in the neighbourhood, the encouragement of children's participation in the targeting of this client, even very young children, is clear:

> Details of a number of neighbours engaging in abuse towards him - including children encouraged by parents: woman with black hair scrunched back in ponytail pushing pushchair up street encourages her small child to yell ""minger!"" then after each time, ""louder!"" she says and the kid obeys until as they pass mine she laughs a little, content at trying to, no doubt, wake me. (Case recorded as disablist hate) [Advocate notes including direct quotes from client]

In other cases, there is further evidence of lead perpetrators recruiting other local residents beyond their immediate family, including young people and encouraging them to engage in harassment and violence. In such cases, we might consider the way in which such young people, whilst engaged in and responsible for harmful behaviour are also subjected to forms of exploitation that may well protect those adults involved.

> [advocate] to call re. previous anti-social behaviour incidents. 4 year history of incidents. [client] believes that the neighbours at [house number] are involved in organising teenagers and other people to throw bricks and damage other people's property. [client] said police speak to the neighbours at [house number] but have not been taking statements from her. (Case recorded as racist hate) [Advocate notes]

Motivation is hard to read, and we have to be open to the idea that for many, especially perhaps younger people, there are a range of motivations and drivers sitting alongside and intersecting with discourses of hate as a form of subordination (Frost, 2008). As research has shown these may well include affective states of thrill, danger, excitement and peer pressure to perform such behaviours in front of friends as a means of achieving groups status and capital (McDevitt et al., 2002). In the case of disablist hate above, the mother of the child finds some amusement and satisfaction in mocking the client. Yet the impacts of these behaviours, regardless of motivation are clear. What was more apparent in our data, where perpetrator articulations were recorded, was a desire to defend and/or purge the neighbourhood, and as Nayak (2017) argues, the nation, of those seen as 'space invaders' (Puwar, 2004) in a political context where the profile of those 'outsiders' is already constructed. This is apparent in the following case of homophobic hate, where the client details encounters with his neighbour.

> ...he encountered me in the driveway to the xxxx complex and said, "hey bum boy thought I had told you to move out of here." I said I did not have to experience comments from him, but he just laughed, spat at me saying I was "a dirty faggot and that fags are not welcome in [city] be warned I will get you out one way or another ... From that day his comments escalated in frequency and often from his flat below mine, so I could hear his voice ... Every time thereafter he would make comments relating to my moving out (Case recorded as homophobic hate) [E-mail to advocate from client]

There can be a complexity to HRs due to the familiarity and proximities involved that also sheds light on questions of motivation. Although not common in this current data set, in previous work using the same data source from an earlier period (Donovan et al., 2021), one HR involved co-habiting partners experiencing domestic violence and racist hate. Not only does such an example speak to the intersectionality of hate motivation (Chakraborti, 2015) it relates to the complexities of intimate relationships that involve a range of affective relations that includes, but is not just restricted to hate. This is also seen in some (albeit a limited number of) cases which speak to relationships that may not have started as hateful, but through various circumstances, have soured, and over time hate has been implicated. In one such case, resentment and revenge for the behaviours of a friend have evolved into homophobic hate: '*They were originally all planning a holiday because they all used to get on. They then turned on [client] and his partner after [friend] assaulted their friend*' [Advocate notes].

Social Character of Hate Relationships

We have seen above that HRs can be experienced as targeting, not just by individuals, but by groups and through wider recruitment. This group dynamic, whether involving children and young people and/or adults effects the character of these experiences through a sense of being pushed out of places by what might seem like the entire community. Whilst often led by a key individual, perpetrators can also be relatively inter-changeable, especially when others in the area begin to be recruited in the targeting. Other cases also speak to multi-generational HRs, where behaviours are seen as learnt from and passed down from older members of the families. This, of course, is not to say that all those within the neighbourhoods in question engage in these behaviours and clearly some neighbours do not accept this treatment. However, in the case below, acquaintances of the lead perpetrator appear to join in with racist abuse. As we know from the work of Ahmed (2001) hate does not reside within the minds of specific people, but rather travels, with or without the direct recruitment of individuals.

> There have been racist comments from outside as well as inside the property. For example, an incident when the neighbours' friends were shouting racist abuse from the gate, and [client] had to phone the police ... Harassment downstairs but also reports from upstairs neighbours and others: A further incident which was reported on 15 May 2019. This involved another neighbour (Case recorded as racist hate) [Advocates notes]

In other cases, the group nature of these behaviours stands out through collective harassment of individuals and families where the group forms an intimidating presence outside clients' homes. In this following case of racist hate, the inter-changeability of perpetrators is also apparent, where other family members take over the harassment when the initial perpetrator is arrested and put on bail conditions.

> [client] is suffering due to a torrent of racial abuse from her neighbours. Every time she or her children leave the house she is racially abused or threatened. A neighbour at xxxx was arrested and released with bail conditions, however she has since got other family members to make threats.

> Groups have often kicked her door and demanded she came outside to fight, [client] lives on her own with her children and is terrified. She lives in fear that they will set fire to her property and is unable to feel safe (Case recorded as racist hate) [Advocate notes]

However, attempts at drawing in a wider circle of individuals hostile towards those being targeted is not always successful. This shows that not all neighbours are complicit. Whilst fear may prevent some from overtly resisting, there is also evidence that some neighbours maintain good relations with those targeted and refuse to become part of the problem—but perhaps not always part of the solution. In the following case, described by the client as 'complete terror', such failed attempts at recruitment are suggested.

> Every time I would ignore, and move away quickly or have friends with me, or could engage with another of my neighbours to get away from this. It was clear that he had noted that I had a decent relationship with my other neighbours, and as a result began directing false claims against me to neighbours, in a clear attempt to affect my relationship with these people. Throughout the summer of 2019 he spoke to neighbours accusing me of throwing things from my windows and dragging furniture across my floors at night. (Case recorded as homophobic hate) [Email from client to advocate]

Perpetrators and Their Challenges

Whilst we do not condone behaviours of perpetrators and foreground the harm caused (Donovan et al., 2021), we also look to understand such harms - not as the result of essentialised deviance, but as the complex multiscalar product of intersecting contexts, affects and marginalities. Consideration of the social character of HRs therefore goes beyond just those individuals implicated to also consider wider contexts and specific scenarios in which these behaviours take hold. This is especially the case for HRs, concentrated as they are in some of the most deprived neighbourhoods in the region. From this perspective, resolutions have to be underpinned by a recognition of the conditions under which both those victimised and those targeting individuals are often living in a way that does not absolve perpetrators of responsibility and is cognisant of the power relations involved. Whilst our evidence is limited in terms of what it reveals about the longer lives of perpetrators, we identify material and emotional challenges that feed into intimidatory, and manipulative behaviours directed towards those who become a legitimatised focus for a range of difficulties, frustrations and fears. In the following excerpts experiences of alcohol and/or drug addiction are prominent, alongside other markers of structural vulnerability including social isolation, additional support needs and relationships between perpetrators which raise questions regarding their safety.

> Neighbour assaulted her last February, ongoing issues, he is an alcoholic, causing her huge amounts of distress ... [client] feels harassed and intimidated by [perpetrator's] behaviour, and is also very concerned that he is not able to control his drinking and look after himself properly. (Case recorded as transphobic hate) [Advocate notes]
> He has been having trouble with his neighbours for the past 16 months; a 19-year-old woman and her 53-year-old partner who are 'constantly off their heads' (Case recorded as racist hate) [Advocate notes]
> [client]: couldn't give any out and out examples of racist language - they are often drunk and she can't actually make out what they're saying although it's clear it's abusive. She believes they are behaving in this way because of racism though, and that they know her son is disabled and are still intentionally behaving in this way to distress him. (Case recorded as racist hate) [Advocate notes]

Further evidence includes perpetrators experiencing homelessness, poor living conditions, as well as having caring responsibilities. In response to the first case of transphobic hate listed above, the police representative claimed this to be a tenancy enforcement issue rather than a criminal matter, suggesting 'getting together with [perpetrator] social worker or other services'. After a 'quieter' period, it was suggested by the advocate that 'If [the perpetrator's] housing is part of a care package ... then there might be other people who are involved with him and could be approached'. This is a rare mention of social services in the case notes more generally and there is no further mention of these meetings to deal with the perpetrator behaviour in this case spanning four and half years. Rather interventions were much more likely to focus on those victimised. In this case, the client was offered 10 weekly 1-hour sessions with a support worker for supporting tenancies. Towards the end of the case, there are changes in the behaviour of the perpetrator noted, but these do not seem to come as a direct result of any formal intervention:

> no recent issues w/neighbour, 'behaving himself'. Walks his son's dog and this seems to have a positive impact on him - she thinks [housing] should give him a dog. She said it goes round in cycles like this though where he is fine for a while then it 'kicks off'.

Chakraborti (2015) makes the point that the line between victim and offender may not always be a straightforward dichotomy. These situations, whilst not universal, disrupt an image of an 'ideal perpetrator' (Christie, 1986) and speak to structural vulnerabilities that trouble the victim/perpetrator binary. Any forms of progressive intervention must then recognise how conditions for HRs are fertilised by poverty, poor mental health, addiction and the absence of support systems for those in need. At the same time, we refute the idea that in HRs, the victim and perpetrators are 'both as bad as each other'. Indeed, the absence in our research of clear systems of support (beyond advocacy) to problematise and address HRs outside of the criminal justice system are concerning and creates the sense of help providers actively re-producing HRs through interventions ranging from ineffectual to collusion with perpetrators.

Conclusions

Drawing upon research exploring experiences of HRs in North East England, this chapter has emphasised the distinct forms of hate involving familiarity and proximity between victims and perpetrators. Whilst our data is limited, we are able to reflect on perpetrator profiles, roles and actions towards those targeted. We thus challenge the idea that hate should always be seen as perpetrated by strangers who hold extreme views and interact with victims infrequently in public spaces. Through the lens of HRs, we shine a light on the unique dynamics of victim-perpetrator relations that emerge over time in and around domestic spaces and residential neighbourhoods.

In doing so we make three main arguments. Firstly, perpetrators in HRs are not isolated individuals. Perpetrators also operate with, indeed rely on, at worst the explicit and at best the tacit, encouragement of others in different kinds of ways—in the recruitment of other perpetrators, in the context of peer pressure and friendship groups and in the transmission of ideas and practices of 'othering'. This also speaks to the diversity of the profile of perpetrators in terms of age and gender, and the manner in which multiple people can be drawn into HRs, especially when they become campaigns of hate. Secondly, perpetrators of HRs are not just extremists and not necessarily 'offenders' in the sense of having been prosecuted for criminal acts. Whilst some perpetrators in our data have been in trouble with the authorities, this is not comprehensive. This draws our attention to the contexts which produce the spaces for such actions, often in residential contexts of dis-investment and heightened tensions. Third, perpetrators in HRs are 'ordinary', but they are not ordinary strangers, in the sense they are known to victims. When it comes to HRs, we must pay attention to the everyday temporality, spatiality and sociality of these experiences. They become routinised yet unpredictable in and around the home in ways that make living under those conditions feel unsafe and overwhelming. Those targeted through everyday residential proximities and repeated harmful encounters feel despair and a sense of entrapment (Donovan et al., 2023) which is damaging to health and very difficult to escape (Clayton et al., 2022a). Whilst we emphasise the embeddedness of hate into the fabric of contemporary society, we also highlight how HRs are a specific manifestation of hate by those who are familiar and live locally to those victimised.

For many of those victimised by HRs, their primary objective in continuing to problematise these behaviours is to stop the relationship and avoid moving, not necessarily to criminalise perpetrators. In any case, many of the acts constituting HRs are either seen as below the criminal threshold or are very difficult to evidence as a crime. Our other points regarding the social nature of HRs also makes it harder for us to identify perpetrators outside of the spaces and contexts in which such acts are perpetrated. When we combine this knowledge with insight that both victims and perpetrators in marginalised communities face multiple challenges, a criminal justice model of resolution can appear much less appropriate. What is required, yet often absent (certainly before advocates intervene) is a multi-agency response where for example, housing, adult services, community and voluntary organisations and the police work together to support victims, work with perpetrators and de-escalate tensions. The other relevant observation from our wider research project, that also involved speaking with practitioners, is that perpetrators are missing from the broader conversation (Donovan et al., 2024). To address this gap is of course difficult but our research shows that whilst CJS responses are appropriate in some situations, there needs to be more attention to non-CJS responses that facilitate the living together of diverse communities in contexts of divisive politics, change and marginalisation. This may well include forms of restorative justice, but also more community orientated/led approaches that hold behaviours to account and refuse to accept their everyday-ness. We see hints in our data of the ways in which some places and spaces can be experienced as both dangerous and violent, but also supportive and the latter needs to be harnessed.

References

Ahmed, S. (2001). The organisation of hate. *Law and Critique, 12*, 345–365. https://doi.org/10.1023/A:1013728103073

Chakraborti, N. (2015). Re-thinking hate crime: Fresh challenges for policy and practice. *Journal of Interpersonal Violence, 30*(10), 1738–1754. https://doi.org/10.1177/0886260514548581

Chakraborti, N., & Garland, J. (2012). Reconceptualizing hate crime victimization through the lens of vulnerability and 'difference'. *Theoretical Criminology, 16*(4), 499–514.

Cheshire, L., Easthope, H., & Ten Have, C. (2021). Unneighbourliness and the unmaking of home housing. *Theory and Society, 38*(2), 133–151. https://doi.org/10.1080/14036096.2019.1705384
Christie, N. (1986). The ideal victim. In E. A. Fattah (Ed.), *From crime policy to victim policy: Reorienting the justice system* (pp. 17–30). Macmillan.
Clayton, J. (2009). Thinking spatially: Towards an everyday understanding of inter-ethnic relations. *Social & Cultural Geography, 10*(4), 481–498. https://doi.org/10.1080/14649360902853288
Clayton, J., Donovan, C., & Macdonald, S. J. (2022a). Living with hate relationships: Familiar encounters, enduring racisms and geographies of entrapment. *Environment and Planning D: Society and Space, 40*(1), 60–79. https://doi.org/10.1177/02637758211049808
Clayton, J., Donovan, C., & Macdonald, S. J. (2022b). Becoming visible, becoming vulnerable? Bodies, material spaces, and affective economies of hate. In E. Hall, J. Clayton & C. Donovan (Eds.), *Landscapes of hate: Spaces, relations and responses*. Bristol University Press.
DeLisi, M. & Piquero, A. R. (2011). New frontiers in criminal careers research 2000–2011: A state-of-the-art review. *Journal of Criminal Justice, 39*(4), 289–301. https://doi.org/10.1016/j.jcrimjus.2011.05.001
Donovan, C., Clayton, J., Macdonald, S. J., Ungureanu, C., & Knight, M. (2021). *Exploring'hate relationships' through connected voice's hate crime advocacy service: Final project report*. Durham University.
Donovan, C., Macdonald, S., & Clayton, J. (2023). Re-conceptualising repeat reports of hate crime/incidents as hate relationships based on coercive control and space for action. *Sociological Research Online, 28*(2), 502–517. https://doi.org/10.1177/13607804211065052
Donovan, C., Clayton, J., Macdonald, S. J., Long, C., Dutt, A., Jain, V., & Rabe, J. (2024). *Improving responses to HRs: Final report*. Durham University.
Frost, D. (2008). Islamophobia: Examining causal links between the state and "race hate" from "below." *International Journal of Sociology & Social Policy, 28*(11/12), 546–563. https://doi.org/doi.org/10.1108/01443330810915242
Hall, E. (2019). A critical geography of disability hate crime. *Area, 51*(2), 249–256. https://doi.org/10.1111/2019.51.2-10.1111/12455
Hall, E. (2022). Rethinking responses to hate: Towards a socio-ecological approach. In E. Hall, J. Clayton & C. Donovan (Eds.), *Landscapes of hate: Spaces, relations and responses* (pp. 217–237). Bristol University Press.

Hall, E., & Bates, E. (2019). Hatescape? A relational geography of disability hate crime, exclusion and belonging in the city. *Geoforum, 101*, 100–110. https://doi.org/10.1016/j.geoforum.2019.02.024

Hall, E., Clayton, J., & Donovan, C. (Eds.). (2022). *Landscapes of hate: Tracing spaces, relations and responses*. Policy Press.

Hopkins, P., Clayton, J., & Tell MAMA. (2020). *Islamophobia and anti-Muslim hatred in North East England*. Newcastle University.

Iganski, P., Smith, D., Dixon, L., Kielinger, V., Mason, G., McDevitt, J., Perry, B., Stelman, A. Bargen, J., Lagou, S., & Pfeffer, R. (2011). Rehabilitation of hate crime offenders: Research report. *Scotland: Equality and Human Rights Commission.*

Iganski. P. (2008). *'Hate crime' and the city*. Bristol University Press.

James, Z., & McBride, K. (2022). Examining the contours of hate: A critical hate studies analysis. In E. Hall, J. Clayton & C. Donovan (Eds.), *Landscapes of hate: Spaces, relations and responses* (pp. 22–37). Bristol University Press.

Jolliffe, D., & Farrington, D. P. (2020). The criminal careers of those imprisoned for hate crime in the UK. *European Journal of Criminology, 17*(6), 936–955. https://doi.org/10.1177/1477370819839598

Listerborn, C. (2015). Geographies of the veil: Violent encounters in urban public spaces in Malmö, Sweden. *Social & Cultural Geography, 16*(1), 95–115. https://doi.org/10.1080/14649365.2014.950690

Lloyd, A., Devanney, C., Wattis, L., & Bell, V. (2021). "Just tensions left, right and centre": Assessing the social impact of international migration on deindustrialized locale. *Ethnic and Racial Studies, 44*(15), 2794–2815. https://doi.org/10.1080/01419870.2020.1854813

Mallett, S. (2004). Understanding home: A critical review of the literature. *The Sociological Review, 52*(1), 62–89. https://doi.org/10.1111/j.1467-954X.2004.00442.x

Mason, G. (2005). Hate crime and the image of the stranger. *British Journal of Criminology, 45*(6), 837–859. https://doi.org/10.1093/bjc/azi016

McDevitt, J., Levin, J., & Bennett, S. (2002). Hate crime offenders: An expanded typology. *Journal of Social Issues, 58*(2), 303–317. https://doi.org/10.1111/1540-4560.00262

Nayak, A. (2010). Race, affect, and emotion: Young people, racism, and graffiti in the postcolonial English suburbs. *Environment and Planning A, 42*(10), 2370–2392. https://doi.org/10.1068/a42177

Nayak, A. (2017). Purging the nation: Race, conviviality and embodied encounters in the lives of British Bangladeshi Muslim young women. *Transactions of the Institute of British Geographers, 42*(2), 289–302. https://doi.org/10.1111/tran.12168

Pain, R. (2014). Gendered violence: Rotating intimacy. *Area, 46*(4), 351–353.

Perry, B. (2009). The sociology of hate: Theoretical approaches. In B. Perry, B. Levin, P. Iganski, R. Blazak & F. M. Lawrence (Eds.), *Hate crimes* (Vol. 1, pp. 55–76). Greenwood Publishing Group.

Puwar, N. (2004). *Space Invaders: Race, gender and bodies out of place.* Cambridge University Press.

Schweppe, J., & Perry, B. (2022). A continuum of hate: Delimiting the field of hate studies. *Crime, Law and Social Change, 77*(5), 503–528. https://doi.org/10.1007/s10611-021-09978-7

Stokoe, E. (2006). Public intimacy in neighbour relationships and complaints. *Sociological Research Online, 11*(3), 137–157. https://doi.org/10.5153/sro.1383

Stokoe, E., & Hepburn, A. (2005). "You can hear a lot through the walls": Noise formulations in neighbour complaints. *Discourse & Society, 16*(5), 647–673. https://doi.org/10.1177/0957926505054940

Wilson, H. F. (2017). On geography and encounter: Bodies, borders, and difference. *Progress in Human Geography, 41*(4), 451–471. https://doi.org/10.1177/0309132516645958

Young, I. M. (1988). Five faces of oppression. *Philosophical Forum, 19*(4), 270–290.

Perpetrators of Transphobic Hate Crime

James Pickles and Ben Colliver

Introduction

Violence against transgender people has become an emerging concern for criminologists and hate scholars over the past 15 years. In that time, shifts in legislation, policy, and scholarship have been significant. Notably, criminal justice agencies now recognise the importance of recording and reporting mechanisms, which help provide data on the frequency and extent to which people perpetrate violence against trans[1] people. The most recent Home Office (2020) statistics showed an 11% increase

J. Pickles
School of Humanities and Social Science, University of Brighton, Brighton, UK
e-mail: j.pickles@brighton.ac.uk

B. Colliver (✉)
Department of Criminology and Sociology, Birmingham City University, Birmingham, UK
e-mail: Ben.colliver@bcu.ac.uk

J. Garland et al. (eds.), *Hate Crime Perpetrators: New Perspectives from Theory, Research and Practice, Volume I*, Palgrave Hate Studies,
https://doi.org/10.1007/978-3-031-92666-2_6

in reported hate crimes against transgender people, at 4,732 recorded crimes. Generalised increases in hate crimes are largely thought to be due to improved prioritisation of reporting mechanisms by the police. It is therefore difficult to assume that official statistics provide accurate indicators of trends in hate crime prevalence. However, taken in conjunction with other data, such as social attitude surveys and self-reports from the Crime Survey of England and Wales, we have compelling evidence that hostility towards transgender people is on the rise.

According to the 2023 British Social Attitudes Survey, there has been a marked decrease in public support for trans people since 2019 (see Clery, 2023). The National Centre for Social Research (2021) who conducted the survey argue that 'over the last 40 years, Britain has become more liberal in its attitudes towards non-traditional family forms, sexual relationships and abortion…however, the same cannot be said of attitudes towards transgender people'. The BSA survey (Clery, 2023) showed that opinions over whether someone who is transgender should be allowed to change the sex on their birth certificate has fallen by 23 percentage points, from 53 to 30%. In addition, 'the proportion who characterise themselves as "not at all prejudiced" against people who are transgender has fallen from 82 to 64% since 2019'. This coincides with rising anti-trans activism across the UK (see Pearce et al., 2020) and significant increases in news media coverage of trans people and trans related issues (Mediatique, 2020).

Despite the decrease in positive attitudes towards trans people, in conjunction with the rise in anti-trans rhetoric and overall increases in hate incidents, much of this evidence is, justifiably, victim-centric, leaving little commentary on perpetrators. This chapter, therefore, scrutinises the available data and assesses the current scholarly knowledge base on anti-trans hostility. The authors take a holistic approach and examine the wide spectrum of transphobic hate, arguing that the social landscape—such as anti-trans rhetoric, hostile political discourse, discrimination, and non-criminal behaviours such as stereotyping, mocking, and prejudicial disdain—provides a cultural context where criminal behaviour against trans people can increase and flourish.

In the absence of data on perpetrators, the authors examine the nature of transphobic hate discourse and rhetoric, to contextualise the wider transphobia facing trans and queer[2] individuals. We examine the historical and political context of anti-trans rhetoric to help explain the notable rise in anti-trans recorded hate crimes and the wider increase in negative attitudes towards trans people within the public sphere. This is central, as existing research from hate scholars demonstrates that prejudicial political rhetoric influences the perpetration of hate crime, often by legitimising exclusionary and prejudicial attitudes (Murphy, 2021). Until recently, anti-trans rhetoric and (political) discourse was largely confined within academic contributions to certain feminist schools of thought and has a fractious and contentious history within these broad political and activist circles. Largely grouped under the moniker 'TERF' to describe trans exclusionary radical feminists, this activist position has recently achieved mainstream prominence, and has morphed into what is now termed gender critical feminism or 'women's rights' activism; although the latter is contested by trans inclusive women's rights organisations and activists. We scrutinise the history of this activism and analyse the paradigm shifts within anti-trans positions, including the terminology adopted by these groups.

By way of opening, we firstly contextualise hate crimes against trans people by providing a background to gender and gender diversity generally in order to situate our discussion within the historical analyses on gender structures and those who do not conform to the preferences dictated within these structures. This provides a useful conceptual backdrop for the following discussion around the rise of 'gender-critical' discourse which contributes to a hostile social culture for trans people. We then provide an overview of the perpetration of violence and hostility against trans people addressing the most extreme manifestations of transphobia globally and more subtle, insidious forms of prejudice. We close this chapter with a discussion of legislative responses to the perpetration of transphobic hostility. In doing so, we argue that disparity in punishment of hate crime perpetrators contributes to a hostile structural system that devalues the lives of trans people.

Understanding Gender and Gender Diversity

Feminist analyses of the social world have a strong history of calling into question the nature of gender, gendered structures, prescribed and proscribed gendered behaviours, and the extent to which individuals can challenge dominant narratives of gender scripts dictated by the society in which they are delivered and enacted. Broadly, there are two central perspectives for understanding gender: gender essentialism and social constructivism. Gender essentialist approaches argue that gendered behaviours are an intrinsic part of the self through physical body distinctions. Hines (2020, p. 700) argues that historically 'the bodily differences of men and women not only set them apart physically, they determined disparities in personality trait, behavioural characteristic and social role'. As such, gender essentialist perspectives suggest that biological 'sex'—assumed largely to be determined by differences in genitals—dictates more than bodily differences and shapes sex roles. This perspective has been critiqued for holding 'common-sense' assumptions over sex and gender distinctions as a natural phenomenon within the social world and further contributing to the naturalisation of gender inequality; for example, by advocating for differing roles in the division of labour between men and women due to morphological sex differences. Despite adherents of gender essentialism maintaining a 'fact' based, scientistic position to understanding sex and gender, critics argue that gender essentialist values are historically rooted in religious interpretations of gender roles, which have been substituted for scientific values (although there is a lack of scientific consensus over binary sex characteristics in humans, e.g. Dubois & Shattuck-Heidorn, 2021) in order to maintain men's dominance over women (Bem, 1993).

Central to second wave feminist thought, the assumed differences between sex and gender were called into question. In contrast to gender essentialism, early feminist thinkers acknowledged that biological and social or cultural understandings of gender were not inherently related as gender has material, social, historical, cultural, economic, racial, medical, and legal dimensions. Thus, reducing gender to sexed bodily distinctions arguably ignores other ways in which a person is sexed and gendered within their social context. This perspective is largely referred to as anti-essentialist or social constructivist. Adopting a social constructivist approach is not to minimise the significance of the physical body, rather, it acknowledges that physical differences are made relevant because of the social and symbolic meaning attached to them.

Butler (1990) provides a key lens through which we can understand gender as both socially constructed and performative. Butler argues that gender constitutes a range of factors including dress, mannerisms, and patterns of organisation, which contribute to an entrenched, seemingly natural, gender division through repetition of the gendered expectations dictated to us by hegemonic gendered scripts. Indeed, Butler further challenges the biological essentialism associated with sex, arguing that 'when the constructed status of gender is theorised as radically independent of sex, gender itself becomes a free-floating artifice, with the consequence that man and masculine might just as easily signify a female body as a male one, and woman and feminine a male body as easily as a female one' (1990, p. 6). Butler's position marked a significant shift in the analysis of gender and gender-diverse people, by disentangling the categories of sex and gender. The result of this critique was an acknowledgement that gender was potentially plural, and that the binary of male and female may be restrictive, and in fact a fallacy in and of itself, to how gender is assigned and experienced.

Social constructivists have therefore shaped our understanding of gender diversity and have become the theoretical foundation to understanding transgender identities. Rather than adopting a narrow, binary definition, the term transgender is commonly applied in ways that are inclusive of gendered expressions, identities and experiences that fall outside of assumed gender binaries (Davidson, 2007). Hines (2010, p. 1) argues that the term "'transgender' includes gender identities that have, more traditionally, been described as 'transsexual', and a diversity of genders that call into question an assumed relationship between gender identity and presentation and the 'sexed' body". The term 'transgender' is a modern term that has generally been a welcome shift away from previously used terms (like transsexual) which had strong medical connotations and carried the risk of pathologizing people whose gender differed from that assigned at birth (Pearce et al., 2018). However, calling into question an assumed relationship between the sexed body and gender identity can be destabilising to societies in which rigid gendered binaries influence all aspects of social life. This disruption of the naturalised, normative way in which gender is 'supposed to be', and thus the behaviours which are simultaneously permitted and prohibited within certain social contexts contributes to violence and opprobrium towards those who embody challenges to these normative preferences of how gender should be presented and performed. Browne (2004, p. 332) conceptualises this process as 'genderism', that is, 'a hostile reading of gender ambiguous bodies', which provides a particularly useful lens through which to examine transphobia.

Assumptions and expectations around appropriate gendered presentations and behaviours permeate all levels of society but may be more prominent in particular spaces. Within a restrictive gendered society, Doan (2010) argues that people experience the 'tyranny of gender' when these expectations are not met. Young boys may be shamed, for instance, at an early age for not being masculine enough in their social behaviour. Transphobia and hostility towards transgender people may therefore act as a form of social control, an attempt to reaffirm rigid gender expectations, and sanction those who are perceived as violating appropriate gendered presentations. Indeed, comparative analyses of news headlines across Europe show that countries which featured more positive news representations of transgender and gender-diverse people also had higher levels of legal protections and social acceptance (Bracco et al., 2024). The rise in anti-trans activism (Pearce et al., 2020) shapes the cultural narrative and contributes to this socio-cultural hostility towards trans and gender-diverse people.

Activism centred on transgender exclusion and hostility towards trans people has a varied scholarly and political history. We turn to interrogate trans hostile discourse and trans exclusionary activism to contextualise the current mainstream backlash against trans rights and protections, the shift in public opinion and concern, and the social context in which transgender hate crimes are occurring.

Anti-Trans Activism: TERF Histories and the Emergence of Gender Critical

Over the past six years, dedicated activism against trans people, trans rights, and so called 'gender ideology' or 'transgender ideology' has achieved mainstream discourse on many public news channels and entertainment discussion shows. Rallies have been organised in key cities across the UK with the aim of platforming people, largely cisgender women, who want to advocate various anti-trans and trans exclusionary positions, beliefs, and politics (Elliards, 2023). Trans exclusionary politics is not a new position. However, scholars who have traced the history of trans exclusionary politics maintain that the popularisation of trans debates and discourse, the frequent platforming of anti-trans positions within legacy media, and trans exclusionary organisations and activism becoming established as a dedicated position across social media are relatively new phenomena, which need to be interrogated to situate the current climate of (hostile) discourse about and against trans people.

Trans exclusionary politics has its scholarly and intellectual roots in radical feminist debates between a minority of writers and thinkers. Janice Raymond's text *The Transsexual Empire* (1979) is often cited as one of the first major scholarly works within radical feminist discourse. Adopting an explicit trans exclusionary position, Raymond framed trans women as the appropriators of women's bodies who infiltrate women's spaces for the purpose of enacting male violence against women. British radical feminists like Sheila Jeffreys also adopted trans exclusionary positions in their analyses, most notably in her paper *Transgender activism: a lesbian perspective*, which argued that transgender activism is 'deeply problematic from a feminist perspective and that transsexualism should be seen as a violation of human rights' (Jeffreys, 1997, p. 55). Jeffreys cites *The Transsexual Empire* as a foundational text to her framework, and argues that lesbians are at significant risk of 'transsexing' (*sic*), that sex reassignment surgery is a form of surgical and self-mutilation, and that transsexualism generally is 'dangerous politically to women's chances of freedom as it maintains the idea of gender dichotomy which forms the very foundation of male supremacy' (ibid.: 71). Although it can often be assumed the lesbians are the leading figures of trans exclusionary movements, and indeed there is evidence to suggest there are anti-trans rhetoric and perspectives amongst some cis lesbians (see Worthen, 2022), several studies problematise this assumption and find that the majority of cis lesbians do not hold these beliefs and advocate for trans inclusive modalities and positions (e.g. Rogers, 2024; Tate & Pearson, 2016; Worthen, 2022). Nevertheless, there is a significant tension between some feminist and lesbian activism, and trans inclusionary politics.

Reflecting on the earliest anti-trans feminist positions, MacDonald (1998) remarks that Raymond's text is one of the few and exclusive works on transsexualism; however, MacDonald chooses to adopt an exploratory and curious position rather than a hostile or exclusionary one, remaining open to what trans experiences can add and contribute to understanding the oppression of women and of gender experience. Further, other prolific scholars at the time such as Kessler and McKenna (1978) also interrogated 'transsexualism', but, rather than be hostile, wanted to understand what trans experiences and perspectives could offer in understanding the performative aspects of gender, and how this could enhance understandings of gender power relations, and specifically women's oppression and liberation. Scholars charting this history of feminist discourse have noted that trans exclusionary positions, until very recently, have been incredibly niche as 'mainstream feminist thought has generally seen the relationship between feminism and trans phenomena as a locus for enquiry into the construction and manifestation of gender relations and systems' (Pearce et al., 2020, p. 683).

Scholars who chart the new mainstreaming of gender hostile, anti-trans, or gender critical concerns trace it to a public consultation called by the then Prime Minister Theresa May on potential changes and proposals to the 2004 Gender Recognition Act (see Bassi & LaFleur, 2022; Billard, 2023; Hines, 2020; Pearce et al., 2020). The GRA is a largely administrative piece of legislation that allows trans people to change their assigned sex marker on their birth certificates. However, the process to engage with this has been criticised for being invasive, expensive, and too bureaucratic (Hines, 2013) due to requirements that trans people have to 'live in' their gender for two years and be medically diagnosed with gender dysphoria. The public consultation in 2018 was founded on proposals to streamline the administrative process of changing one's sex markers through self-identification rather than medical diagnosis. Although this was welcomed by LGBTQ organisations, a growing backlash grew against the proposals, and organisations such as *A Woman's Place UK*, *Standing for Women*, *Fair Play for Women*, and later, the *LGB Alliance* formed across the UK, establishing a new trans exclusionary activist movement with a large presence online within digital platforms. Counter activists largely referred to these as TERF organisations, a shorthand 'which has travelled globally through online spaces: highly visible TERFs like the theorist Sheila Jeffreys, the journalist Julie Bindel, and the ~~popular~~ writer J. K. Rowling articulate the movement's brand of transphobia by claiming that trans womanhood is a patriarchal invention aimed at infiltrating women's spaces and undermining feminist movement building from within' (Bassi & Lafleur, 2022, p. 314). The moniker TERF is often rejected by the trans hostile or gender critical movement and is regarded as a slur. The term TERF has also been critiqued as a largely erroneous and loose term; many trans exclusionary activists do not identify as radical feminists, for example, and indeed largely disengage from radical feminist scholarship (Fahs, 2024).

Rejecting the TERF acronym and radical feminist frameworks generally, proponents of the movement have largely identified themselves as holding 'gender critical' beliefs and discourse. The litany of pejoratives and viewpoints upheld by gender critical and trans exclusionary activists are numerous. Largely they centre on framing trans women as predatory men who pose a sexual risk to cis women in public toilets and other spaces; trans women as perverts or fetishists who receive sexual pleasure from dressing as women; trans people and trans advocacy as grooming children who are vulnerable to social contagion of being influenced by 'transgender ideology' or 'gender ideology'; an advocacy for the medical mutilation of child; the appropriation and potential replacement and erasure of women (see Ashley, 2020; Billard, 2023; Hines, 2020; Jones & Slater, 2020; Serano, 2020). This chapter does not have the scope to go into the full breadth of gender critical beliefs, in large part due to, as noted by Zanghellini (2020), proponents primarily publishing in non-traditional academic outlets such as blog posts, opinion pieces, and online essays, which have replaced scholarly production. Readers may wish to consult *inter alia* Hotine (2021), Williams (2020), and Zanghellieni (2020) for medical, philosophical, and ontological critiques of this discourse. However, we offer summarising arguments to contextualise gender critical and trans exclusion advocacy.

Gender critical activists largely argue that trans women are a risk to cis women's safety and frame their activism on the protection of single sex spaces by excluding trans and non-binary people, whom they argue are a risk of predation to cis women. As observed by Shaw (2022, p. 769) 'TERFs objectify trans people as the embodiment of gender and therefore sexism itself. Instead of focusing on the systemic architecture of sexism within society, as radical and trans feminists do, TERFs primarily focus upon the eradication of that which they believe has come to embody all that is oppressive about patriarchal culture: trans people'.

Gusmeroli (2023) argues that this gender critical discourse helps to politically feed the neo-conservative anti-gender rhetoric largely held by conservative and Christian circles, which are mirrored in a coalition of goals between the American Evangelical movements, who push anti-LGBTQ and anti-abortion positions, and gender critical or trans exclusionary activists. Indeed, Libby (2022) analyses materials (pamphlets, educational resources, advocacy leaflets etc.) produced by conservative evangelical Christian leaders and organisations, such as Focus on the Family, Family Policy Alliance, and Evangelical Alliance amongst others, and notes it is virtually impossible to find an evangelical opinion piece or text discussing transgender issues that does not draw upon or focus explicitly on gender critical and trans exclusionary radical feminist talking points. The language and advocacy used by these two unlikely bedfellows are almost exact in their phraseology. Both groups call for a rejection of 'gender ideology' and make 'use of panic-inducing terms such as *contagion*, *rape*, *invasion*, and *deception* to describe transgender subjects' (Libby, 2022, p. 437, original emphasis). Both groups pursue a 'politics of injury' (Libby, 2022, p. 436) to frame themselves as persecuted victims and to frame trans people as a destabilising force that threatens 'common-sense' understandings of pre-ordained sex dimorphism, the role of the family, and the perceived threat to women posed by trans existence.

Trans people, and debates on the social construction of sex and gender have been utilised as a tool to stoke a 'global battle of ideas' which, gender critical activists advocate that 'if not stopped in time—will eventually erase all differences between the sexes, depriving women, in particular, of their right to fulfil their biological destiny and pursue happiness' (Bassi & Lafleur, 2022, p. 312). They conceive that these movements heralded under gender critical feminism draw on essentialist notions of womanhood, have strong links to the evangelical right, and 'should be understood as a distinctively post-fascist feminism' (Bassi & Lafleur, 2022, p. 313) which draw on essentialist notions of womanhood. Further, analyses of the broadsheet and news media have found an overwhelmingly trans hostile approach (Shaw, 2022) with moral panics being stoked and created about trans people (Pepin-Neff & Cohen, 2021; Slothouber, 2020; Walker, 2023), and gender critical figureheads like Kathleen Stock retaining 'a disproportionate influence in the media and on government policy' to spread misinformation about trans issues (Shaw, 2022, p. 769).

Bassi and Lafleur (2022) trace these debates in the US and UK noting they are part of a larger political discourse, expedited by right-wing movements to bolster well established culture wars. Indeed, Lee Anderson, who, before defecting to the right-wing populist party Reform UK, served as Deputy Chairman to the Conservative Party (February 2023 until January 2024) publicly advocated that the next election should be fought on 'a mix of culture wars and trans debate' (Colbert, 2023). Additionally, then Conservative Prime Minister Rishi Sunak chided his opposition during a 2024 Prime Ministers Questions event for having difficulty 'defining a woman' whilst the mother of murdered trans teen Brianna Ghey was on the parliamentary estate having been invited by the opposition. Sunak refused to apologise for these comments (Courea, 2023). Further, then Conservative Equalities Minister Kemi Badenoch described trans women—whom she refers to as transsexuals (sic)—as men in a leaked tape (Bancroft, 2021) and has been accused of stoking culture wars in attempting to make unnecessary changes[3] to the Equality Act (2010) to enable organisations to legally exclude trans people from 'same-sex spaces' (Schofield, 2024).

The mainstreaming of anti-trans activism and advocacy by high-profile figures, the legacy media, and populist political discourse, has arguably created a heightened moral panic about trans people, shaping the decline in positive public attitudes cited at that start of this chapter. Whilst, of course, many gender critical or trans exclusionary activists have not engaged in violence and are not direct perpetrators of anti-trans hate crimes, we argue that it is against this social context in which trans perpetration, trans hostility, and trans hate crimes can and do flourish.

Thurlow (2022) traces the genealogy of how trans exclusionary radical feminists have reframed their identity as gender critical feminists to influence the overall 'culture war' discourse. Drawing on Serano's 2016, 2018, and 2021 work, Thurlow (2022) suggests three categories of trans hostile positions: the trans unaware (the uninformed), the trans antagonistic (the actively hostile who promote anti-trans agendas), and the trans suspicious (those who acknowledge trans people should in theory be protected, but ignore trans perspectives and largely distinguish between 'genuine trans people' and trans activists). Thurlow argues that gender critical advocates have filled the trans suspicious category in a move to gain access to mainstream discourse by framing their perspectives as having reasonable concerns, legitimate questions, and common-sense approaches to biology. This is mirrored in semantic changes from traditional TERF rhetoric, where 'reasonableness' is now the locus of advocacy; anti-trans is now pro-woman and trans erasure is now 'biology is real'. In the absence of empirical criminological study on anti-trans hate perpetrator profiles, these categories are useful when theorising anti-trans hate perpetrators and serve as a socio-cultural backdrop to the increases in anti-trans hostility.

Violence Against Transgender People

Whilst there is a growing body of victimological literature on transphobic hate crime (Blair-Woods & Herman, 2014; Bradley, 2020; Colliver, 2021; Jamel, 2018), there is a dearth of research on perpetrators. There is also very little data on the demographic profiles of transphobic perpetrators. Based on a small sample of 24 transgender victims of hate crime, Chakraborti et al. (2014) report that men overwhelmingly represent perpetrators, as individuals or as groups. Beyond this, much of our knowledge base is victim-centric. Studies which examine violence against LGBT people show that trans people are particularly susceptible to both direct (personal experiences) and indirect (knowing someone personally who has experienced) hate crimes. Walters et al., (2020, p. 4602) investigation of 593 LGBT people found that trans people are:

> …significantly more likely than non-trans LGB people to be direct victims of hate crime that involve physical assaults, physical assaults with weapons, verbal abuse, and online abuse… trans respondents were more than twice as likely to have experienced a hate-motivated physical assault over the past 3 years than LGB respondents. Trans respondents were also more than twice as likely to have experienced more than three incidents of hate-motivated verbal abuse over the past 3 years [preceding the study], and 9 times as likely to have experienced three or more hate-motivated physical assaults over the past 3 years [preceding the study], compared with non-trans respondents.

Anti-trans hostility is therefore a major social concern due to the disproportionate nature of the violence perpetrated towards gender-diverse people. Research examining violence against trans people largely relies on official reporting data and self-report rates, both of which depend on trans people acknowledging and reporting their experiences. This is problematic as research suggests that hate crime perpetration tends to be normalised by those who are targeted (Browne et al., 2011), which skew the true figure of hate crimes that is currently recorded. The full scope and extent of violence committed towards and against trans people is therefore difficult to ascertain. In England and Wales, hate crimes against transgender people have seen an annual increase since 2012 when official police monitoring began (Home Office, 2020), with a total of 4,732 offences recorded by police in the year ending March 2023. At the year of writing, hate crimes against transgender people stand as an outlier in contrast to other strands. Hate crimes against transgender people is the only category that saw an increase in reports to police; all other strands decreased (as shown in Fig. 1). The Home Office's (2020) own report makes direct reference to the mainstreaming of trans issues into the public realm as a potential factor in this increase, suggesting that 'transgender issues have been heavily discussed by politicians, the media and on social media over the last year, which may have led to an increase in these offences, or more awareness in the police in the identification and recording of these crimes'. Importantly, reports of anti-trans hate crimes to the police largely comprise of public order offences (36%) and offences of stalking and harassment (36%), making up 72% of all reports to the police (Home Office, 2020).

Hate crimes against transgender people in Scotland have fluctuated more than in England and Wales, with data showing slight increases and decreases depending on the year. The year ending 2021/22 showed the

Numbers and percentages						England and Wales, excluding Devon and Cornwall
Hate crime strand	**2018/19**	**2019/20**	**2020/21**	**2021/22**	**2022/23**	**% change 2021/22 to 2022/23**
Race	77,850	[x]	90,909	108,476	101,906	-6
Religion	8,460	[x]	6,288	8,602	8,241	-4
Sexual orientation	14,161	[x]	18,239	25,639	24,102	-6
Disability	8,052	[x]	9,690	13,905	13,777	-1
Transgender	2,253	[x]	2,728	4,262	4,732	11
Total number of motivating factors	110,776	[x]	127,854	160,884	152,758	-5

Fig. 1 Police recorded hate crime (*Source* Home Office Hate Crime Report 2023–24)

most dramatic increase in hate crime charges ($n = 88$) with the year 22/23 ending with 55 charges. In contrast, The Crime Survey for England and Wales shows a total of 7000 self-reports of victimisation from 2017–2020, indicating a higher rate of transphobic hate crime than currently being recorded by the police (Home Office, 2020). This is unsurprising as existing research indicates hate crimes, generally, are likely underreported, with trans people specifically facing certain reporting barriers. For example, previous research has suggested that trans people exhibit a distrust of the police (Jamel, 2018) and have expressed not wanting to disclose their trans identity (Jauk, 2013) to police officials. Indeed, the 2022 US trans survey, out of an unprecedent large sample of 92,329 respondents, found high levels of distrust towards the police, with 62% of respondents reporting that they were 'very uncomfortable' or 'somewhat uncomfortable' in asking the police for help because of their gender identity and expression (James et al., 2024).

Self-report studies often show a higher rate of transphobic violence than those found in official recording date. For instance, findings from GALOP indicate that 80% of survey participants had experienced a transphobic hate crime in the 12 months preceding participation (Bradley, 2020). Further, 60% of participants indicated that they had experienced transphobia online. There is no official data on transphobic perpetrators or their demographic profiles. However, self-report studies like GALOP have shown that 50% of respondents highlighted that they had been targeted by a 'transphobic activist', suggesting a causal link between the increase in anti-trans activism and discourse and hate crime perpetration. Given the high prevalence of online abuse, it is unsurprising that 50% of participants said they had also been targeted by a stranger. Although this chapter is mainly concerned with UK criminology, violence against transgender people is a global issue (Winter et al., 2016). Data taken from a European study, conducted by the European Agency for Fundamental Rights (FRA), found that 48% of trans respondents had experienced harassment and 17% had experienced physical or sexual violence (FRA, 2020). Additionally, the latest US Trans Survey found that 30% of respondents were verbally harassed within a 12-month period with 39% reporting being abused online (James, et al., 2024).

Globally, in the year 2023, the Human Rights Campaign report the deaths of at least 32 transgender and gender-diverse people, predominantly transgender people from the global majority. This is potentially a conservative estimate when data taken from 'Trans Murder Monitoring Project' reports significantly higher rates of murder, with 321 transgender and gender-diverse victims in the year ending October 2023. This project reveals that transgender women and transfeminine people are significantly over-represented as murder victims, with 94% of victims being transgender women or transfeminine. The murders of transgender people appear to be geographically clustered primarily in the South Americas. Discussing violence more broadly, Patel (2017) focuses on public bathrooms as a key site of verbal, physical, and spatial violence against transgender people in Cape Town, through the enforcement of rigid gendered expectations. Conclusively, there is strong evidence to suggest that trans people experience disproportionate violence to (a) the general public and (b) other LGB cisgender people. Further many jurisdictions around the world enact State violence against trans people. At the more extreme end, 14 countries actively criminalise the gender identity and expression of trans people using cross-dressing, 'impersonation' or 'disguise' laws. 12 countries impose the death penalty for same-sex activity, 6 of which implement capital punishment: Iran, Northern Nigeria, Saudi Arabia, Somalia and Yemen, with the death penalty having a legal possibility in Afghanistan, Brunei, Mauritania, Pakistan, Qatar, UAE, and Uganda (Human Dignity Trust, 2024).

There is an array of research that explores public attitudes towards transgender people, which evidence suggests influences rates of transphobic hate perpetration. Some studies have shown that women express more negative attitudes towards transgender people (King et al., 2009) whilst others have found that men are more likely to hold prejudicial views against transgender people (Norton & Herek, 2013). Regarding cisgender men, Conlin et al. (2020) found that conformity to the masculine expectation of heterosexual self-presentation was the biggest predictor for holding prejudicial views against transgender people. Alternatively, for cisgender women, conformity to feminine norms of sexual fidelity was a high indicator of transphobic views. Adams et al.'s (2016) research showed that discomfort of violating traditional gender norms was positively correlated with transphobia. Prejudicial attitudes towards transgender people have also been associated with lower levels of education about transgender people (Puckett et al., 2024), less support for general egalitarian ideals (King et al., 2009), and greater levels of religious fundamentalism (Tee & Hegarty, 2006).

These views have been found to be held on a global scale, particularly within Western society. Konopka et al. (2020) research exploring attitudes towards gender diversity in Poland affirms previous research that indicates cisgender men are more likely than cisgender women to be prejudiced against gender diversity. Elischberger et al. (2018) found religious-based disapproval contributed to generally negative attitudes towards transgender individuals in India. Research in Turkey highlights that negative attitudes towards homosexuality are also a significant predictor of prejudicial attitudes towards transgender people, with men indicating significantly higher levels of prejudice than women (Uluboy & Husnu, 2022). However, it is important to note that holding prejudicial views does not mean that an individual will enact violence towards transgender people, and there is a significant gap in criminological literature that explores the population of those who (a) incite violence against trans people an (b) who go on to enact transphobic violence directly. With this in mind, we turn to discuss UK legislation aimed at preventing and prosecuting transphobic hate perpetrators.

Legislating Against Transphobia

Despite the term 'hate crime' being socially recognisable, and widely used in academia, it does not appear in any legislation in England and Wales. Rather, there is an array of legislation in place that is used to police and prosecute crimes motivated by hostility or prejudice. The history of legislation dealing with hate crime in general is more extensive than the relatively brief history of legislation concerning transphobic hate crime and can be dated back to the introduction of the Race Relations Act (1965) concerned with racial discrimination. Over 30 years later, the Crime and Disorder Act was introduced in 1998, which created specific aggravated offences based on prejudice and hostility towards race and religion, creating new maximum penalties. No such legislation currently exists that creates specific aggravated offences for hostility or prejudice towards transgender identity.

The Criminal Justice Act introduced in 2003 required judges to consider prejudice or hostility towards sexual orientation or disability as an aggravating factor at sentencing, and if proved, impose a sentence uplift for perpetrators. However, it is important to note, that this legislation did not create new maximum penalties; rather, it required judges to impose the already existing maximum penalty. Transgender identity became a factor to be considered in 2012, when the Legal Aid, Sentencing and Punishment of Offenders Act amended the Criminal Justice Act of 2003 to include hostility or prejudice towards transgender identity as an aggravating factor at sentencing. This legislation also increased the minimum sentence for murder aggravated by hostility based on transgender identity from 15 years imprisonment to 30 years imprisonment. In 2020 the Sentencing Act superseded the Criminal Justice Act and is the most current piece of legislation used for considering prejudice and hostility towards transgender identity as an aggravating factor at sentencing. Whilst the legislation was updated, the disparity between the new maximum penalties introduced by the Crime and Disorder Act, and the sentence uplift outlined in the Sentencing Act still persist. This means that some forms of prejudice and discrimination are legislated against more punitively than others. This may symbolically contribute to the creation of a hierarchy of victims (Colliver, 2021).

The disparity in sentencing provisions was acknowledged in the 2021 Law Commission review of hate crime legislation (Law Commission, 2021). After a lengthy consultation, it has been recommended that both enhanced sentencing and aggravated offences continue to offer a dual approach, but that aggravated offences should be extended across all five protected characteristics, to offer equity across sentencing. The review acknowledged that England and Wales were a relative anomaly in the disparity of legal protection offered across characteristics, whilst acknowledging that other comparable jurisdictions treat characteristics that are recognised in the same way. The Law Commission (2021) also recognised that the language associated with the protected characteristic of 'gender reassignment' and its association with transgender identity should be expanded to include 'gender diversity' as a more explicit acknowledgement of non-binary people.

Whilst not directly related to the policing and sentencing of hate crime, there is a longer history of legislation that concerns transgender people and their experiences with the criminal justice system. The Police Reform Act of 2002 ushered in fresh guidelines addressing complaints regarding police discrimination linked to gender reassignment. In 2004, the implementation of the Gender Recognition Act (GRA) marked a pivotal moment, significantly enhancing the safeguarding of transgender individuals (Jamel, 2018). Nevertheless, whilst the GRA aimed at strengthening protections, it simultaneously reinforced the gender binary, failing to accommodate diverse gender expressions. However, the act explicitly prohibits the disclosure of a person's transgender identity without their consent. This required an extra level of sensitivity and vigilance from criminal justice agencies when working with transgender people.

In Scotland, more recent changes have been made to legislation with the introduction of the Hate Crime and Public Order (Scotland) Act which came into force in 2024. This legislation introduced new offences for threatening or abusive behaviour which is intended to stir up hatred based on prejudice against numerous characteristics including transgender identity. The legislation has been criticised publicly by several public figures, including J.K. Rowling and Elon Musk, who have expressed concern over the implications for free speech (Cook, 2024). The burden of evidence under this legislation is also lower as the prosecution only need prove that stirring up hatred was likely, rather than intentional. However, the legislation does include the opportunity for defence that an individual's actions were reasonable. Concerns around the use of harsher punishments for crimes motivated by prejudice and bias have been expressed by Hurd (2001). Hurd argues that criminalising bias moves from an act-centred, to character-centred approach to punishment. However, proponents of more punitive approaches to hate crime have argued that increased sentencing reflects the greater level of harm experienced by victims (Iganski & Lagou, 2015) and acts as a form of denunciation for perpetrators of transphobic hate crime.

Summary and Future Directions

This chapter has explored the multifaceted nature of transphobic hate discourse, situating it within its broader historical and political contexts. By examining the rise in anti-trans rhetoric, particularly within the framework of 'gender critical feminism', we have documented how such discourse has transitioned from academic claims to mainstream media and public policy, influencing societal attitudes and behaviours. This shift underscores the critical connection between political rhetoric and the perpetration of hate crimes, as highlighted by existing hate scholarship. By addressing the spectrum of transphobic hostility, from extreme violence to insidious prejudice, we emphasised the pervasive and harmful impact of transphobia on the lives of trans people globally. Furthermore, our discussion of legislative responses revealed significant disparities in the punishment of hate crime perpetrators, illustrating a structural system that often fails to adequately protect and value trans lives. These legal inconsistencies not only perpetuate a hostile environment but also highlight the urgent need for more equitable and effective policy interventions.

In England and Wales, there have recently been several high-profile homicide cases involving the murder and attempted murder of transgender young people, with anti-trans elements being recorded as part of a spectrum of motivating factors. Brianna Ghey (a murdered trans teenage girl) and Summer Betts-Ramsey (currently charged with attempted murder of a different teenage trans girl, alongside 3 other teenager perpetrators, whose details have not been revealed due to their ages). Cases of extreme hate-based violence involving murder is relatively rare in the UK context, and discussions of perpetrators cannot necessarily be taken to generalise all perpetrators of anti-trans violence, especially given the exceptionally rare instance of child-on-child murder involved in the cases of Briana Ghey. However, further work could be taken to examine the profiles of these perpetrators and explore how the spectrum of anti-trans hate-based violence and the rise in anti-trans rhetoric influences the likelihood of anti-trans violence.

Notes

1. Trans is an umbrella term that refers to a range of gender identities that differ from those originally assigned to people at birth. Cis or Cisgender is a term referring to individuals whose gender identity coheres with the identity assigned at birth.
2. Queer is an umbrella term used by a variety of people who identify with sexual and gender identities that are different to those considered straight and cisgender. Queer can, but not always, refer to a political dimension to these identities.
3. It is important to note that the Equality Act (2010) already provides legal exceptions for service providers to limit or modify access to services to single sex spaces if there is a proportionate and legitimate aim (for example, if there is a safeguarding risk).

Reference Lists

Adams, K. A., Nagoshi, C. T., Filip-Crawford, G., Terrell, H. K., & Nagoshi, J. L. (2016). Components of gender-nonconformity prejudice, *International Journal of Transgenderism*, 1–14.

Ashley, F. (2020). A critical commentary on 'rapid-onset gender dysphoria.' *The Sociological Review, 68*(4), 779–799. https://doi.org/10.1177/0038026120934693

Bancroft, H. (2021). Tory equalities minister Kemi Badenoch criticised for calling trans women 'men' in leaked tape, *Independent* (online), https://www.independent.co.uk/news/uk/politics/kemi-badenoch-transgender-transphobia-equalities-b1922103.html (Accessed 22/05/2024).

Bassi, S. & LaFleur, G. (2022). Introduction: TERFs, Gender-Critical Movements, and Postfascist Feminisms. *Transgender Studies Quarterly, 9*(3), 311–333.

Bem, S. (1993). *The lenses of gender*. Yale University Press.

Billard, T. J. (2023). Gender-Critical discourse as disinformation: Unpacking TERF strategies of political communication. *Women's Studies in Communication, 46*(2), 235–243. https://doi.org/10.1080/07491409.2023.2193545

Blair-Woods, J., & Herman, J. L. (2014). Anti-Transgender hate crime. In *The Routledge international handbook on hate crime* (pp. 278–288). Routledge.

Bracco, S. E., Sczesny, S. & Gustafsson Sendén, M. (2024). Media Portrayals of Trans and Gender Diverse People: A Comparative Analysis of News Headlines Across Europe. *Sex Roles, 90*, 491–507.

Bradley, C. (2020). *Transphobic Hate Crime Report*. GALOP.

Browne, K. (2004). Genderism and the bathroom problem: (Re)materialising sexed sites, (re)creating sexed bodies. *Gender, Place and Culture, 11*(3), 331–346.

Browne, K., Bakshi, L., & Lim, J. (2011). 'It's something you just have to ignore': Understanding and addressing contemporary lesbian, gay, bisexual and trans safety beyond hate crime paradigms. *Journal of Social Policy, 40*(4), 739–756. https://doi.org/10.1017/S0047279411000250

Butler, J. (1990). *Gender trouble: Feminism and the subversion of identity*. Routledge.

Chakraborti, N., Garland, J., & Hardy, S.-J. (2014). *Briefing paper 2: Gendered hostility*. University of Leicester.

Clery, E. (2023). *A liberalisation in attitudes?* Online: National Centre for Social Research.

Colbert, L. (2023). Lee Anderson's Culture Wars: How the Conservative Party is Flirting with Far-Right Hate to Appeal to its Base. Byline Times (online) available at: https://bylinetimes.com/2023/02/15/lee-andersons-culturewars-how-the-conservative-party-is-flirting-with-far-right-hate-to-appeal-to-its-base/

Colliver, B. (2021). *Reimagining hate crime: Transphobia*. Palgrave Macmillan.

Conlin, S., Douglass, R., & Mascardini, E. (2020). Predicting transphobia among cisgender women and men: The role of feminist identification and gender conformity. *Journal of Gay and Lesbian Mental Health, 25*(1), 5–19.

Conlin, S. E., Douglass, R., & Moscardini, E. H. (2021). Predicting transphobia among cisgender women and men: The roles of feminist identification and gender conformity. *Journal of gay & lesbian mental health, 25*(1), 5–19.

Cook, J. (2024). Scotland's new hate crime law comes into force, *BBC News,* 1st April. https://www.bbc.co.uk/news/uk-scotland-68703684. (Accessed 15th/May/2024).
Courea, E. (2023). Sunak refuses to apologise to Brianna Ghey's father over PMQs trans jibe. The Guardian (online) available at: https://www.theguardian.com/politics/2024/feb/08/rishi-sunak-refuses-apologise-brianna-gheyfather-pmqs-trans-jibe
Davidson, M. (2007). Seeking refuge under the umbrella: Inclusion, exclusion, and organizing within the category transgender. *Sexuality Research & Social Policy, 4*(4), 60–80. https://doi.org/10.1525/srsp.2007.4.4.60
Doan, P. L. (2010). The tyranny of gendered spaces: Reflections from beyond the gender dichotomy. *Gender, Place & Culture, 17*(5), 635–654.
DuBois, L. Z., & Shattuck-Heidorn, H. (2021). Challenging the binary: Gender/sex and the bio-logics of normalcy. *American Journal of Human Biology, 33*(5), Article e23623. https://doi.org/10.1002/ajhb.23623
Elischberger, H., Glazier, J., Hill, E., & Verduzco-Baker, L. (2018). Attitudes toward and beliefs about transgender youth: A cross-cultural comparison between the United States and India. *Sex Roles, 78*(1–2), 142–160.
Elliards, X. (2023). Who is Posie Parker? The anti-trans founder of standing for women, *The National* (online). https://www.thenational.scot/news/23299549.posie-parker-anti-trans-founder-standing-women/. (Accessed 20/05/2024).
European Union Agency for Fundamental Rights (FRA). (2020). *A Long Way to go For LGBTI Equality*. Publications Office of the European Union.
Fahs, B. (2024). The urgent need for radical feminism today, signs. *Journal of Women in Culture and Society, 49*(2), 479–497.
Gusmeroli, P. (2023). Is gender-critical feminism feeding the neo-conservative anti-gender rhetoric? Snapshots from the Italian public debate. *Journal of Lesbian Studies, 28*(3), 382–399.
Hines, S. (2010). Introduction. In S. Hines & T. Sanger (Eds.), *Transgender identities: Towards a social analysis of gender diversity* (pp. 1–22). Routledge.
Hines, S. (2013). Gender Diversity, Recognition and Citizenship: Towards a Politics of Difference. Palgrave Macmillan.
Hines, S. (2020). Sex wars and (trans) gender panics: Identity and body politics in contemporary UK feminism. *The Sociological Review, 68*(4), 699–717.

Home Office. (2020). *Hate crime, England and Wales, 2019 to 2020: appendix tables*. Online (Accessed 12th/March/2024). https://www.report-it.org.uk/files/hate-crime-1920-hosb2920.pdf

Hotine, E. (2021). Biology society and sex: Deconstructing anti-trans rhetoric and trans-exclusionary radical feminism. *JNDS, 2*(3), 1–5.

Human Dignity Trust. (2024). Map of jurisdictions that criminalise LGBT people. https://www.humandignitytrust.org/lgbt-the-law/map-of-criminalisation/. (Accessed 09/09/2024).

Human Rights Campaign. (2023). Fatal violence against the transgender and gender-expansive community in 2023. https://www.hrc.org/resources/fatal-violence-against-the-transgender-and-gender-expansive-community-in-2023

Hurd, H. M. (2001). Why liberals should hate 'hate crime legislation'. *Law and philosophy, 20*(2), 215–232.

Iganski, P., & Lagou, S. (2015). Hate crimes hurt some more than others: Implications for the just sentencing of offenders. *Journal of Interpersonal Violence, 30*(10), 1696–1718.

Jamel, J. (2018). *Transphobic hate crime*. Palgrave.

James, S. E., Herman, J. L., Durso, L. E., & Heng-Lehtinen, R. (2024). Early Insights: A Report of the 2022 U.S. Transgender Survey. National Center for Transgender Equality, Washington, DC.

Jauk, D. (2013). Gender violence revisited: Lessons from violent victimization of transgender identified individuals. *Sexualities, 16*(7), 807–825.

Jeffreys, S. (1997). Transgender activism: A lesbian feminist perspective. *Journal of Lesbian Studies, 1*(3–4), 55–74.

Jones, C., & Slater, J. (2020). The toilet debate: Stalling trans possibilities and defending 'women's protected spaces.' *The Sociological Review, 68*(4), 834–851. https://doi.org/10.1177/0038026120934697

Kessler, S. J., & McKenna, W. (1978). *Gender: An ethnomethodological approach*. University of Chicago Press.

King, M. E., Winter, S., & Webster, B. (2009). Contact reduces transprejudice: A study on attitudes towards transgenderism and transgender civil rights in Hong Kong. *International Journal of Sexual Health, 21*(1), 17–34. https://doi.org/10.1080/19317610802434609

Konopka, K., Prusik, M., & Szulawski, M. (2020). Two sexes, two genders only: Measuring attitudes toward transgender individuals in Poland. *Sex Roles, 82*(9–10), 600–621.

Law Commission. (2021) *Hate crime laws: Final report*. Law Commission.

Libby, C. (2022). Sympathy, fear, hate: Trans-exclusionary radical feminism and evangelical Christianity. *Transgender Studies Quarterly, 9*(3), 425–442. https://doi.org/10.1215/23289252-9836078

Macdonald, E. (1998). Critical Identities: Rethinking Feminism Through Transgender Politics. *Critical Studies in Gender, Culture and Social Justice, 23*(1) 3–12.

Mediatique,. (2020). *Examining trends in editorial standards in coverage of transgender issues*. Independent Press Standards Organisation.

Murphy, A. (2021). Political rhetoric and hate speech in the case of Shamima Begum. *Religions, 12*(10), 834–851.

National Centre for Social Research. (2021). Britain's attitudes towards moral issues have become much more liberal (online press release). https://natcen.ac.uk/news/britains-attitudes-towards-moral-issues-have-become-much-more-liberal. Accessed (22/05/2024).

Norton, A. T., & Herek, G. M. (2013). Heterosexuals' attitudes toward transgender people: Findings from a national probability sample of US adults. *Sex Roles, 68*(11–12), 738–753. https://doi.org/10.1007/s11199-011-0110-6

Patel, N. (2017). Violent cistems: Trans experiences of bathroom space. *Agenda (Durban). [Online], 31*(1), 51–63.

Pearce, R., Erikainen, S., & Vincent, B. (2020). TERF wars: An introduction. *The Sociological Review, 68*(4), 677–698. https://doi.org/10.1177/0038026120934713

Pearce, R., Steinberg, D. L., & Moon, I. (2018). Introduction: The emergence of 'trans.' *Sexualities*. https://doi.org/10.1177/1363460717740261

Pepin-Neff, C., & Cohen, A. (2021). President Trump's transgender moral panic. *Policy Studies, 42*(5–6), 646–661. https://doi.org/10.1080/01442872.2021.1952971

Puckett, J., Hanson, C., Dunn, T., Kuehn, K., & DuBois, Z. (2024). An examination of predictors of prejudice against transgender individuals. *Journal of Homosexuality, 71*(3), 645–665.

Raymond, J. G. (1979). *The transsexual empire: The making of the she-male*. Beacon Press.

Rogers, B. A. (2024). TERFs aren't feminists: Lesbians stand against trans exclusion. *Journal of Lesbian Studies, 28*(1), 24–43. https://doi.org/10.1080/10894160.2023.2252286

Schofield, K. (2024). 'Don't call it culture wars': Kemi Badenoch clashes with journalist over single-sex spaces. *The Huffington Post* (online). https://www.huffingtonpost.co.uk/entry/dont-call-it-culture-wars-kemi-badenoch-clashes-with-journalist-over-single-sex-spaces_uk_6631ef97e4b0849b2edd86fb. (Accessed 22/05/2024).
Serano, J. (2020). Autogynephilia: A scientific review, feminist analysis, and alternative 'embodiment fantasies' model. *The Sociological Review, 68*(4), 763–778. https://doi.org/10.1177/0038026120934690
Shaw, D. (2022). A tale of two feminisms: Gender critical feminism, trans inclusive feminism and the case of Kathleen Stock. *Women's History Review, 32*(5), 768–780. https://doi.org/10.1080/09612025.2022.2147915
Slothouber, V. (2020). (De)trans visibility: Moral panic in mainstream media reports on de/retransition. *European Journal of English Studies, 24*(1), 89–99. https://doi.org/10.1080/13825577.2020.1730052
Tate, C. C., & Pearson, M. D. (2016). Toward an inclusive model of lesbian identity development: Outlining a common and nuanced model for cis and trans women. *Journal of Lesbian Studies, 20*(1), 97–115. https://doi.org/10.1080/10894160.2015.1076237
Tee, N., & Hegarty, P. (2006). Predicting opposition to the civil rights of trans persons in the United Kingdom. *Journal of Community and Applied Social Psychology, 16*(1), 70–80. https://doi.org/10.1002/casp.851
Trans Murder monitoring project - https://transrespect.org/en/trans-murder-monitoring-2023/
Thurlow, C. (2022). From TERF to gender critical: A telling genealogy? *Sexualities, 0*(0), Online First. https://doi.org/10.1177/13634607221107827
Uluboy, Z., & Husnu, S. (2022). Turkish speaking young adults attitudes toward transgender individuals: Transphobia, homophobia and gender ideology. *Journal of Homosexuality, 69*(1), 101–119.
Walker, A. (2023). Transphobic discourse and moral panic convergence: A content analysis of my hate mail. *Criminology, 61*, 994–1021. https://doi.org/10.1111/1745-9125.12355
Walters, M. A., Paterson, J., Brown, R., & McDonnell, L. (2020). Hate crimes against trans people: Assessing emotions, behaviors, and attitudes toward criminal justice agencies. *Journal of Interpersonal Violence, 35*(21–22), 4583–4613. https://doi.org/10.1177/0886260517715026
Worthen, M. G. F. (2022). This is my TERF! lesbian feminists and the stigmatization of trans women. *Sexuality & Culture, 26*, 1782–1803. https://doi.org/10.1007/s12119-022-09970

Winter, S., Settle, E., Wylie, K., Reisner, S., Cabral, M., Knudson, G., & Baral, S. (2016). Synergies in health and human rights: A call to action to improve transgender health. *The Lancet, 388*, 318–321.
Williams, C. (2020). The ontological woman: A history of deauthentication, dehumanization, and violence. *The Sociological Review, 68*(4), 718–734. https://doi.org/10.1177/0038026120938292
Zanghellini, A. (2020). Philosophical problems with the gender-critical feminist argument against trans inclusion. *Sage Open, 10*(2). https://doi.org/10.1177/2158244020927029

Offender Motivation

Populism and Hate Feelings

Cristhian A. Martínez

Introduction

The populist worldview portrays society as an antagonism between the 'pure people' and 'corrupt elites' which exploit them and rule them against their general will (Mudde, 2007). A new wave of left and right-wing populism has been on the rise in Europe, Latin America, and North America since the 90s. Over the last two decades for example, support for both left and right-wing populist parties and leaders has tripled in Europe (Verbalyte et al., 2024). On the left, parties such as *Podemos* in Spain, *Die Linke* in Germany, or the *Socialistische Partij* (SP) in the Netherlands advocate for 'the people' appealing to different variations of anti-elitism and direct democracy. On the right, parties such as the *Front National* (FN) in France, or *Alternative für Deutschland* (AfD) in Germany, and

C. A. Martínez (✉)
Department of Social Psychology, University of Groningen, Groningen, Netherlands
e-mail: c.a.martinez@rug.nl

J. Garland et al. (eds.), *Hate Crime Perpetrators: New Perspectives from Theory, Research and Practice, Volume I*, Palgrave Hate Studies,
https://doi.org/10.1007/978-3-031-92666-2_7

populist leaders such as Victor Orban in Hungary, Mateo Salvini in Italy, or Geert Wilders in the Netherlands, advocate for protecting 'the people' from external threats, appealing to different variations of nationalist and anti-globalist rhetoric.

In Latin America the political landscape is not very different, in the last decade left-wing populists such as Nicolás Maduro in Venezuela, or Evo Morales in Bolivia, and right-wing populists like Jair Bolsonaro in Brazil or Javier Milei in Argentina have been elected as advocates of the 'true people' according to their own interpretations, leading to a wave of unprecedented polarization in the region (McCoy, 2022). In North America, populism arguably found its prototype in Donald Trump's election as U.S. president in 2016, when he promised to make America great again for the 'true Americans' through an anti-expertise, anti-elitism, and nationalist discourse (Oliver & Rahn, 2016).

Along with the new wave of populism, scholarly interest in the phenomenon has surged (e.g., Mudde, 2007; Rhodes-Purdy et al., 2021; Rico et al., 2017; Yilmaz & Morieson, 2021). Populism is broadly addressed in the scientific literature from two perspectives: the *supply side*, which studies the strategies that populist parties employ to attract followers, and the *demand side*, which focuses on the individual variables that facilitate the reception of the populist worldview and the development of populist attitudes. The supply side of populism has been extensively explored. Researchers have investigated various aspects, including the role of communication (Jagers & Walgrave, 2007), the use of nationalist rhetoric (Custodi, 2021), the framing of past, present, and future (Mols & Jetten, 2014), the impact of misinformation (Hameleers, 2022), and the appeal to emotional content (Alonso-Muñoz & Casero-Ripollés, 2023; Kinnvall, 2018) on the rise of populist leaders and movements. The demand side of populism, however, has only recently gained traction. Some studies have begun to examine the role of psychological variables on individuals' susceptibility to developing populist attitudes. These variables include personality (Bakker et al., 2021), gullibility, credibility, conspiracy thinking, need for cognition, and moral disengagement (Erisen et al., 2021; van Prooijen et al., 2022). Other factors explored include political trust (Akkerman et al., 2017) and a variety of demographic characteristics (Kriesi et al., 2008).

Both from the demand and supply perspectives, a crucial aspect of understanding populism is how it mobilizes emotions among people. Support for populist views is typically driven by 'gut feelings' and emotion-driven attitudes rather than deliberate and reasoned decision-making (Demertzis, 2006). Populist rhetoric is heavily laden with intense emotional content-invoking images of a bright past, the motherland, the struggles of the working class, the true patriots, or the corrupt elites—to spread its message and gain support (Alonso-Muñoz & Casero-Ripollés, 2023; Martella & Bracciale, 2022). Anger and fear are perhaps the most studied emotions in relation to populism (e.g., Rico et al., 2017). However, other emotions such as nostalgia, disgust, sadness, contempt, and even positive emotions like joy, enthusiasm, hope, and pride, have recently been included in the palette of emotions that populism instills within and between groups (Verbalyte et al., 2024). Despite the extensive literature on the relationship between populism and these emotions, more complex and strong negative feelings such as hate, which are critical for understanding political polarization and ideologically based conflicts (Halperin et al., 2009, 2012; Staub, 2011), have surprisingly not yet been thoroughly studied in relation to populist attitudes.

Hate is one of the most destructive and at the same time understudied human feelings (Ben-Ze'ev, 2000). So far, we know that populist attitudes are positively associated with hate, that their association is stable over time, and that populist attitudes seem to pave the way for developing interpersonal and intergroup hate and not the other way around (Martínez et al., 2023). We also know that hate comprises other primary negative emotions previously associated with populism, specifically anger, contempt, and disgust (Fischer et al., 2018; Sternberg, 2003; Sternberg & Sternberg, 2008), but these emotions have been so far addressed on their own and not as a composite second-order emotional experience, which can lead to qualitatively different outcomes (Matsumoto et al., 2017). In this chapter, I argue that hate matches particularly well the core ingredients of the populist worldview better than other discrete negative emotions alone.

Through the lens of hate's unique composite second-order nature, appraisals, antecedents, and goals, and based on the established associations between the populist worldview and hate's component emotions,

I propose a three-phase model in which the populist worldview progressively adds the necessary and sufficient ingredients for the emergence of hate feelings over time. The model establishes links between the three main features of populism (i.e., people-centrism, anti-elitism, and Manicheism) and characteristic negative emotions which blend together to constitute the recipe for hate. Accordingly, in the present chapter, I briefly review the main features of the populist worldview and the role of emotions in populism. I then provide an overview of the distinctive features of hate and outline the three-phase model of the emergence of hate in the context of populism. Finally, I discuss the implications of populism instilling hate compared to other discrete negative emotions for intergroup conflict.

The Populist Worldview

Populism is an ideology predicated on the idea that society is divided into two homogeneous and antagonistic groups: the 'pure people' and the 'corrupt elites' who aim to exploit and take advantage of them (Akkerman et al., 2014; Mudde, 2007). It is also conceptualized as a thin-centered ideology that needs to attach to stronger host ideologies, such as conservatism or socialism, thus emerging at both ends of the political spectrum (Akkerman et al., 2017). Three main features characterize the populist worldview. First, populism is *people-centered*, portraying 'the people'—also referred to as 'the silent majority' or 'the ordinary decent people'—as sovereign, pure, wise, and moral beyond politicians or elites, and viewing politics as the expression of their *volonté générale*, or people's will (Oliver & Rahn, 2016). Second, populism is *anti-elitist,* and characterizes 'the elites' as corrupt and intended to exploit 'the people'. Elites are often political, economic, intellectual, or cultural (Jagers & Walgrave, 2007), but sometimes also rather abstract such as 'a deep state', or simply 'outside forces' (Erisen et al., 2021). Finally, populism is *Manicheist,* meaning that it characterizes the antagonism between 'the people' and 'the elites' as a moral clash between good and evil (Erisen et al., 2021).

With this general template, the role of populist rhetoric is to define the placeholders of who is 'the people' and 'the elites', grant political power to the people, and promote a charismatic leader embodying their will (Abts & Rummens, 2007). Depending on the political leaning of the host ideology, these placeholders can take different forms. For instance, right-wing populist parties often use exclusionary populism based on nativist, nationalist, and xenophobic ideas, leading to anti-immigration sentiments. On the other hand, left-wing populist parties employ anti-elitist populism, focusing on fighting powerful elites and advocating for equality (Bernhard & Kriesi, 2019; Jagers & Walgrave, 2007). The antagonism between 'the people' and 'the elites' is characterized on both a vertical axis, with 'the elites' on top and 'the people' at the bottom, and a horizontal homogeneity/exclusion axis, with the homogeneous 'good decent people' on one side and other groups within society—referred to as 'the not real people', 'the enemies of the state' or 'the anti-patriots'—on the other (Custodi, 2021; Jagers & Walgrave, 2007).

Populism and Emotions

Not surprisingly, once settled, the populist worldview mobilizes a variety of positive in-group and negative out-group emotions. Overall, populist parties tend to use more emotional appeals compared to non-populist parties (Caiani & Di Cocco, 2023). Typically, emotions such as fear and outrage are strategically employed by populist leaders to engage online users and potential voters with their agendas (Martella & Bracciale, 2022). For instance, fear, uncertainty, and resentment have been revealed as the most frequent feelings spread in populist communication online in Europe (Alonso-Muñoz & Casero-Ripollés, 2023). Regarding in-group positive emotions, populist radical right-wing parties often appeal to the nostalgia of a romanticized past, 'the heartland', or the 'good old days', to establish a contrast with the current decay of societies and the grim future ahead (Mols & Jetten, 2014), an idea that resonates particularly well with people's societal pessimism (Steenvoorden & Harteveld, 2018). Moreover, both right- and left-wing populist parties often appeal to pride (e.g., of national, class, or minority memberships), as a mechanism to transform anger and humiliation into strong in-group cohesion within 'the people' (Salmela & von Scheve, 2017); they also instill feelings of joy, enthusiasm, or hope within their party lines to reinforce existing attitudes and party identification (Verbalyte et al., 2024). Nevertheless, negative out-group emotions prevail in the populist discourse. For the sake of the argument, I will mainly focus here on anger, contempt, and disgust, which are hate's component emotions.

Anger is crucial in the process of forming populist attitudes, and it goes hand in hand with fear and anxiety (Rico et al., 2017). The populist discourse often spreads fear and anxiety towards alleged external threats such as immigrants, powerful elites, 'enemies of the state', or 'anti-patriots', portrayed as posing realistic and symbolic threats to 'the people'. These initial feelings of fear and anxiety capitalize later in anger and resentment towards these targets and their sympathizers (Nguyen et al., 2022). For instance, recent evidence reveals that anxiety about personal well-being and economic instability predicts anger towards the government and the elites, which in turn predicts populist attitudes across fifteen European countries (Abadi et al., 2024). Anger has also been associated with the raise of populist attitudes across diverse contexts, for example as a response to economic turmoil in Spain (Rico et al., 2017); right-wing anti-elitist attitudes in the U.S. (Oliver & Rahn, 2016); higher populist vote intentions in France after the 2015 terrorist attacks (Vasilopoulos et al., 2019). The extent to which people in the U.S. believe that their anger towards politicians is representative of the anger of most Americans predicts populist attitudes via feelings of deprivation and lack of representation (Gaffney et al., 2018). Thus, anger towards politicians, elites, and their followers is essential in the formation of populist attitudes. Anger seems to stem from feelings of fear and anxiety towards out-groups perceived as threatening to 'the people', independently of how this placeholder has been filled by social identity processes crafted by right or left-wing populist movements.

The research on the role of contempt in the development of populist attitudes is less extensive, but it yields important findings. Contempt consists of 'looking down' at others viewed as inferior, and its goal is to derogate and exclude them (Schriber et al., 2017). The alleged moral superiority of the 'true people', also associated with national collective narcissism (Marchlewska et al., 2018), sets the stage for experiencing contempt towards the elites and other threatening out-groups perceived as inferior. For example, Elad-Strenger and Kessler (2024) reveal that when German participants feel their national identity threatened, they experience contempt towards the elites, rejection of national minorities, and support for right-wing populism. Moreover, U.S. participants experience higher contempt towards political opponents when their populist attitudes target a mix of economical and cultural elites (Barker & DeTamble, 2022). From the supply side, populist parties tend to publicly express and instill contempt towards their opponents, based on perceptions of moral superiority (Vahter & Jakobson, 2023), or populist-nationalist rhetoric (Yi et al., 2019). Overall, contempt serves as a powerful tool in populist strategies, reinforcing in-group moral superiority, identity, and intensifying antagonism towards out-groups and elites perceived as inferior.

Similarly, the role of disgust in the development of populist attitudes has not been extensively explored, but the existing literature reveals relevant insights (Herpen, 2021). Moral disgust is evoked when people appraise others as immoral or undesirable, and its goal is to avoid them and the moral contamination they harbor (Tybur et al., 2009). In the context of populism, the function of disgust becomes evident when considering the alleged symbolic threats posed to people's pure morality by the elites, their supporters, and other minority out-groups. A notable example are the anti-immigration sentiments fostered by right-wing populism. It has been shown that disgust can shape anti-immigration attitudes via the activation of the behavioral immune system, leading to the avoidance of intergroup contact and opposition to immigration, particularly among people with high disgust sensitivity (Aaroe et al., 2017; Karinen et al., 2019). Right-wing populism often appeals to disgust by using (moral) disease metaphors when referring to immigrants or other minorities in order to achieve this goal (Brown et al., 2019). Compared to non-populist parties, populist parties in Europe exhibit the highest levels of disgust appeals on Twitter, surpassing other negative emotions including anger, fear and sadness (Widmann, 2021). In the U.S., Donald Trump's frequent and visceral signs of disgust towards Mexicans, Muslims, Chinese, Democrats, and other minorities in his political communication has been identified as one of the primary affective drivers of his success, particularly given the conservative inclination to be moved by disgust (Richardson, 2017). In sum, the strategic use of disgust in populist rhetoric intensifies peoples' in-group cohesion and heightens aversion towards out-groups based on moral grounds, further solidifying populist support.

Anger, contempt, and disgust are emotions strategically triggered by the populist worldview to achieve its goals. However, two important aspects are often overlooked in the literature on populism. First, these emotions have qualitatively different appraisals, goals, functions, and outcomes. For instance, anger targets individuals' behavior and aims to change it in the short term, while contempt and disgust target individuals' stable dispositions, aiming to derogate and avoid the targets, respectively (Fischer & Giner-Sorolla, 2016; Tybur et al., 2009). In the context of populism, these differences are highly relevant for the societal outcomes they facilitate, especially when these emotions are present simultaneously. This leads to the second aspect: the individual characteristics of these emotions change qualitatively when they are blended and evoked simultaneously (Heavey et al., 2017). Anger, contempt, and disgust, also known as the CAD triad (Rozin et al., 1999), are moral emotions that, when combined, account for the emergence of the distinctive second-order feeling of hate (Sternberg & Sternberg, 2008). The following section provides a brief conceptualization of hate and its unique characteristics compared to its composite emotions alone.

Hate

Hate is a distinctive, intense negative feeling involving an extreme negative view of its targets, aiming to eliminate them physically, socially, or symbolically (Fischer et al., 2018). It can develop towards individuals as close as family members or romantic partners (Aumer et al., 2016) as well as towards entire out-groups, even without direct contact (Halperin, 2008; Halperin et al., 2009). Compared to other emotions, hate is more intense and long-lasting, sometimes transcending time and space across generations, remaining dormant until a new trigger emerges (Sternberg & Sternberg, 2008). Hate is at the heart of many social, political, ethnic, and religious conflicts globally (Sternberg & Sternberg, 2008), breeding aggression, prejudice, polarization, conflict, violence, and genocide (Baumeister & Butz, 2005; Staub, 2005; Sternberg, 2003). Hate is so profound that shares with love its intensity and commitment to its targets (Ben-Ze'ev, 2018). Unfortunately, feeling hatred is more prevalent than one might think (Martínez et al., 2022a). Whether aimed at a manager, coworker, ex-partner, or an entire ethnic group, hate is a detrimental force that undermines the well-being of individuals and societies and can, in the worst cases, lead to the loss of human lives.

Despite ongoing debate around its affective nature (Fischer et al., 2018), I conceptualize hate as a second-order composite feeling comprising anger, contempt, and disgust. According to Sternberg's theory (Sternberg & Sternberg, 2008), hate shows a triangular structure encompassing passion, commitment, and distance towards the targets. These three motives, are driven respectively by anger, contempt, and disgust, and the co-occurrence of these three emotions lead to the second-order feeling of hate. This specific blend of emotions makes hate a distinctive and unique emotional experience (Fischer et al., 2018; Sell et al., 2022), with qualitatively different features, antecedents, functions, and outcomes compared to its composite emotions in isolation. For instance, compared to anger, contempt, and disgust alone, hate is more emotionally arousing, targets are perceived as more personally threatening, it leads to a higher degree of attack-oriented behaviors (Martínez et al., 2022a), predicts more hostile cognitions (Matsumoto et al., 2017), and takes longer to dissipate (Verduyn & Lavrijsen, 2015), sometimes not dissipating completely and becoming a latent disposition (Sternberg & Sternberg, 2008). These unique features make hate a more intense, enduring, and taxing emotional experience compared to other negative emotions, including its composite emotions.

Hate has unique appraisals, antecedents, and motivational goals compared to other emotions. Hate targets are perceived as undesirable, unfair, morally inappropriate, inferior, and threatening to individual or in-group identity, personality, values, and worldviews (Martínez et al., 2022b; Staub, 2005; Sternberg, 2003). They are seen as intrinsically evil, unchangeable, and their offenses as unfair and intentional, leading to the perception that coping with them in the future is impossible, thus the goal becomes their elimination (Baumeister & Butz, 2005; Fischer et al., 2018; Roseman & Steele, 2018). Compared to other emotions, hate is particularly triggered by perceived moral violations and injustice (Pretus et al., 2022; Van Doorn, 2018). It also plays a role in political behavior, serving functions such as group affiliation, unification, and maintaining shared goals to preserve the status quo (Halperin et al., 2012). Additionally, hate may serve a prospective control function, keeping the emotional drive active to face perceived latent threats or injustices (Roseman & Steele, 2018). Interestingly, hate might also fulfill abstract human needs, as new evidence suggests that hate towards out-groups, institutions, or social issues may bolster a sense of meaning and purpose in life (Elnakouri et al., 2022).

Although the elimination of the target is often seen as the primary goal of hate, it is associated with a wide range of outcomes varying in severity. These include non-verbal indicators of contempt, mild discrimination, moral exclusion, hate speech, mild physical aggression, torture, irreversible injuries, mutilation, and murder (Opotow & McClelland, 2007). Recent theories propose that hate's broader goal is to cause harm, suffering, and loss to the targets (Rempel & Sutherland, 2016). This extends beyond physical elimination to include social (e.g., excluding, ostracizing, ignoring), psychological (e.g., humiliating, taking revenge), and symbolic (e.g., burning a flag, refusing to recognize a country) forms of elimination (Fischer et al., 2018). Ultimately, expanding hate's goal to the broader aim of keeping the targets out of one's life (Aumer et al., 2016; Roseman & Steele, 2018).

In summary, hate appears to protect the self from perceived enduring threats to core psychological constructs such as identity, personality, autonomy, affiliation needs, values, and worldviews. It thrives when people perceive their circumstances as fundamentally unfair and hostile, view their targets as essentially evil, and feel powerless and humiliated. Due to its unique characteristics, hate is more complex and might pose more severe outcomes compared to its component emotions separately.

How Populism Leads to Hate Feelings

I argue that the populist worldview sets the stage for the emergence of hate feelings in three phases. First, it establishes the tension and anxiety-related emotions necessary for intergroup conflict by asserting that power is in the wrong hands, that there is an urgent need to reclaim it for the sake of democracy, and that an upcoming unique opportunity (e.g., elections) exists to restore it to the people. This logic is based on the premise that democratic systems are based on leaving the locus of power empty, and populism aims to place 'the people' in this position with the aid of a charismatic leader embodying their will (Abts & Rummens, 2007). In this first phase, *people-centrism* is the predominant feature of populism, evoking emotions of generalized *fear, powerlessness, uncertainty, and anxiety*—components of a broader feeling of ressentiment (Capelos & Demertzis, 2018)—which ultimately lead to anger and hate (Salmela & von Scheve, 2017).

Against this backdrop, in the second phase populism divides society into adversarial groups vying for power by filling the placeholders of the oppressed 'people', the oppressive 'elites', their supporters, and the threatening minorities or out-groups. Social identity processes are crucial in this division, particularly in defining 'the people' (Elad-Strenger & Kessler, 2024), toward whom populist rhetoric is directed. The political leaning of the populist movement determines these definitions: left-wing populism focuses on class and socio-economic identities (e.g., blue-collar workers, the working class), targeting economic elites, while right-wing populism emphasizes national or native identities (e.g., patriots, local settlers), targeting cultural and allegedly corrupt elites (e.g., mainstream media, the deep state, the experts) (Mudde & Rovira Kaltwasser, 2013). These antagonisms are structured vertically, with 'the elites' on top and 'the people' at the bottom, and horizontally, with 'the people' on one side and elite sympathizers and threatening out-groups on the other. In this second phase, *anti-elitism* is the most salient feature. The identity of 'the people' is bolstered by in-group emotions such as *pride, hope, or nostalgia,* while intergroup conflict is fueled by out-group emotions such as *indignation, resentment, and anger*.

Finally, in the third phase populism moralizes the political confrontation, framing it as a battle between good and evil, thus steering the out-group emotions towards the moral kind (Hutcherson & Gross, 2011). The elites, their supporters, and the out-groups are depicted not only as realistic threats to 'the people' but also as symbolic threats to their values and identity. The elites and their sympathizers are portrayed as dispositionally evil, and the threatening out-groups as dangerous to the people's values (Ruzza, 2020). These threats to peoples' moral convictions, now embodied in a charismatic populist leader seen as a people's messiah, even reach religious connotations quite often (Wagenvoorde, 2019) and trigger moral outrage and strong related moral emotions (Skitka et al., 2005). In this phase, *Manicheism* becomes the most prominent feature of populism, with moral emotions such as *contempt* and *disgust* being added to the mix. In this way, the simultaneous activation of anger, contempt, and disgust, along with other negative emotions like ressentiment, paves the way for the emergence of hate feelings. The theoretical model is summarized in Fig. 1.

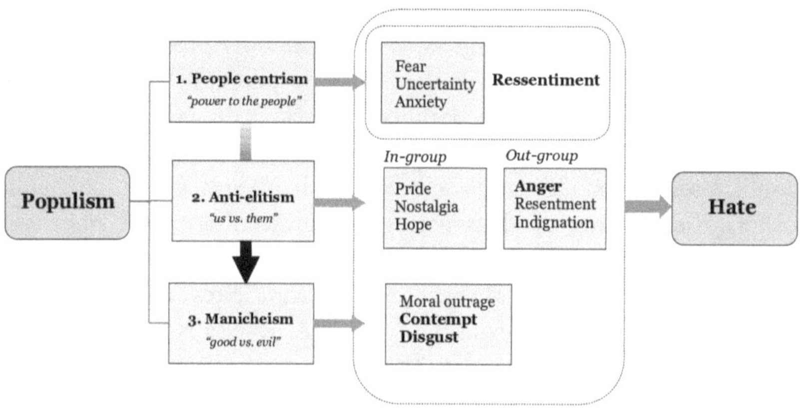

Fig. 1 A three-phase model of how populism leads to hate feelings (*Note* Emotions within squares are close (yet unique) in valence, appraisals, goals, and behavioural outcomes. Emotions grouped together within dotted squares indicate second order feelings. Emotions in bold have been associated with hate and proposed as hate's composite emotions. The gradient arrow indicates the progression of the three phases over time)

The model in Fig. 1 depicts the most common emotions associated with populism in the literature. However, this list is not exhaustive, as other emotions might also play a role in the formation of populist attitudes (see Verbalyte et al., 2024). Horizontally, the model flows from left to right, based on evidence suggesting that populist attitudes pave the way for hate feelings over time, rather than individuals prone to experiencing hate adopting populist attitudes (Martínez et al., 2023). However, it is likely that once hate emerges, it further strengthens populist attitudes and the discrete emotions involved in a vicious cycle. The model links the three characteristic features of populism with specific emotions, indicating associations between each feature of populism and the most salient emotions in each phase, but these links are not exclusive. For example, people-centrism might also inspire in-group and out-group emotions to some degree in the second phase, or the Manichean outlook might instill emotions leading to ressentiment in the first phase. Nevertheless, the match between each populist feature and the corresponding emotions follows the logic of linking a generalized feeling of societal unrest with corresponding anxiety-related emotions, a more direct intergroup conflict with confrontational and attack-oriented emotions, and the moralization of the conflict with moral emotions. Although all these emotions have been broadly associated with populism, this model aims to provide a more nuanced picture, accounting for their connections with specific features of populism, as well as the second-order emergent feelings derived from their joint configuration.

The three phases in the model follow a progressive sequence (see the vertical arrow in Fig. 1). This sequence follows an escalation logic, moving from the broadest to the most concrete features of populism, and correspondingly, from the most generalized to the most target-focused emotions. For instance, a populist campaign might begin by highlighting the generalized decay of institutions in society and the lack of representation of the people's will. It then moves on to fuel intergroup confrontation by filling the placeholders of 'the people' and their enemies through social identification strategies. Finally, it moralizes these vertical and horizontal confrontations by appealing to the perceived evil character of the targets. Following this logic, the corresponding emotions also spiral down from generalized fear to behavior-focused emotions like anger, and then to dispositional-focused emotions such as disgust. In the third phase, when all the ingredients are present, the model reaches a state of simultaneous activation of co-occurring emotions, which together lead to the emergence of second-order feelings of hate.

It is still possible that all three features of populism, along with the corresponding emotions, appear simultaneously in varying degrees from the very beginning of a populist agenda. We know that people typically experience blends of emotions rather than isolated, discrete emotions (Lange et al., 2020). Also, the patterns of emotional activation (e.g., sequential, prevalent, simultaneous) depend heavily on fluctuations in emotional ambivalence and tension (Oceja & Carrera, 2009). However, the discrete emotions in the model also seem to naturally follow an escalation sequence. For example, the initial fear and anxiety instilled by populism usually leads later to anger (Nguyen et al., 2022; Rico et al., 2017). Moreover, anger, contempt, and disgust progress from the least to the most severe (Hutcherson & Gross, 2011), and from the least to the most closely related to hate across multiple dimensions (Martínez et al., 2022a), supporting the progressive and cumulative pattern of the three phases in the model.

Implications

The model above summarizes how the populist worldview might lead to hate feelings. It is based not only on the aggregation of hate's component emotions through the three phases I propose, but more generally, on the fit between hate's unique appraisals and the goals of populism. Overall, hate is an intense and enduring distinct feeling, rooted in perceived symbolic threats to individuals' moral values and identity. It motivates the physical, social, and symbolic elimination of its targets based on stable dispositional attributions of evilness and immorality. Hate finds fertile ground in political worldviews that capitalize on these features, such as populism, which portrays the elites and their sympathizers as inferior, morally corrupt, evil, and as symbolic threats to 'the people's' identity and pure values. Populist parties also benefit from instilling a feeling such as hate among people. Inducing a feeling that fuels strong in-group identification, a heightened perception of identity threats, and a conflict of moral values proves efficient for achieving their goals. However, when gaining voters in the polls before elections escalates to the elimination of political opponents and alleged threatening out-groups, the scope of hate might go beyond these goals and become damaging to interpersonal and intergroup relations.

Compared to other negative emotions, the behavioral tendencies and outcomes associated with hate are far more severe. Anger is temporary and dissipates faster once the target's behavior changes. The social unrest, powerlessness, and uncertainty raised in the first phase, and the anger resulting from the second phase, may actually motivate social change. Anger can indeed foster political participation and collective action (Erisen, 2020; Valentino et al., 2011) within the limits of healthy political exercise and can even be constructive for conflict resolution as long as it is not accompanied by hate (Halperin et al., 2011). However, when positive in-group emotions and other negative out-group emotions such as resentment, contempt, or disgust are added, the emotional tone becomes more hostile and destructive. The behavioral change goals of anger transform into a deeper, dispositional-based, and moralized feeling such as hate, with more extreme goals like aggression and elimination.

Similarly, fear, contempt, and disgust are avoidant-oriented emotions, and their goals do not necessarily involve direct harm or elimination of the targets. While both contempt and hate involve appraising targets as inferior, bad, incompetent, and loathsome (Fischer & Giner-Sorolla, 2016), contempt alone results in looking down on, ignoring, excluding, and derogating targets without necessarily aiming to hurt or eliminate them, as hate does (Schriber et al., 2017). For example, immigrants might be perceived as less competent, warm, or distant but not necessarily dangerous (Sevillano & Fiske, 2013). Similarly, disgust might trigger visceral reactions towards moral violations (Fischer & Giner-Sorolla, 2016) and be associated with anti-immigrant attitudes (Aaroe et al., 2017). However, it primarily aims to avoid contact with targets considered infectious without necessarily translating into actions to harm or eliminate them.

A different picture emerges when all these emotions are simultaneously evoked by a single individual or group. When targets are portrayed as incompetent, distant, entitled, endorsing entirely different values and worldviews, immoral, dispositionally evil, unchangeable, and as posing realistic and symbolic threats to the in-group (i.e., the pure common people), they inspire feelings beyond fear, anger, contempt, or disgust alone. The most fitting emotion encompassing elements from all these discrete emotions is hate (Fischer et al., 2018; Sternberg & Sternberg, 2008). Beyond derogating or avoiding the targets or seeking to change their behaviors, the emergent second-order feeling of hate aims to actively harm, devalue, and ultimately eliminate them through behaviors ranging from hate speech and public humiliation to extreme violence and physical elimination (Opotow & McClelland, 2007). This unleashes a series of destructive outcomes detrimental to interpersonal and intergroup relations, societal stability, and peace.

The negative effects of hate can endure over time, establishing lasting divisions and polarization between groups. Hate dissipates much more slowly compared to other emotions (Verduyn & Lavrijsen, 2015), often transcending generations and becoming a stable disposition (Sternberg & Sternberg, 2008). Since targets are perceived as unchangeable, latent hate feelings persist until the threat is eliminated (Roseman & Steele, 2018). Once entrenched, hate is difficult to overcome and transform; it is easy to turn love into hate but almost impossible to turn hate into love, resulting in a constant negative and taxing experience that distorts attitudes and behaviors, often worsening over time (Ben-Ze'ev, 2018). This lingering feeling, rooted in moral and identity threats, can turn conflicts spurred by the populist worldview into intractable ones. Unlike tractable conflicts, protracted intractable conflicts are deeply meaningful and central to the parties involved, characterized by intense and escalatory social processes, polarized collective identities, and a prolonged duration marked by historical rivalries and intergenerational perpetuation paired with intense emotionality (Coleman, 2003). Thus, beyond fear, anger, and other discrete emotions associated with populism, hate can turn vertical and horizontal antagonisms into intractable intergroup conflicts.

Concluding Remarks

Hate is likely to transcend the political goals of parties during elections, breeding moral divides, intractable conflicts, and affective polarization among people, posing long-term negative effects on individual and group relations. The populist worldview aligns well with the appraisals, goals, and unique features of hate, potentially instilling more than resentment, anger, or contempt among groups. Understanding the nuances and second-order configuration of the affective drives of populism might help in realizing and assessing its negative impact. Beyond the immediate goals of populist parties in their political campaigns, these strategies might sow the seeds for prolonged divisions deeply rooted in identity and moral conflicts, fueled by intense, long-lasting, and destructive feelings such as hate. Recognizing how the necessary ingredients of hate are progressively added to the mix is crucial for preventing its emergence and difficult de-escalation.

References

Aaroe, L., Petersen, M. B., & Arceneaux, K. (2017). The behavioral immune system shapes political intuitions: Why and how individual differences in disgust sensitivity underlie opposition to immigration. *American Political Science Review, 111*(2), 277–294. https://doi.org/10.1017/S0003055416000770

Abadi, D., Bertlich, T., Duyvendak, J. W., & Fischer, A. (2024). Populism versus nativism: Socio-economic, socio-cultural, and emotional predictors. *American Behavioral Scientist*. https://doi.org/10.1177/00027642241240336/ASSET/IMAGES/LARGE/10.1177_00027642241240336-FIG4.JPEG

Abts, K., & Rummens, S. (2007). Populism versus democracy. *Political Studies, 55*(2), 405–424. https://doi.org/10.1111/J.1467-9248.2007.00657.X

Akkerman, A., Mudde, C., & Zaslove, A. (2014). How populist are the people? Measuring populist attitudes in voters. *Comparative Political Studies, 47*(9), 1324–1353. https://doi.org/10.1177/0010414013512600

Akkerman, A., Zaslove, A., & Spruyt, B. (2017). 'We the people' or 'we the peoples'? A comparison of support for the populist radical right and populist radical left in the Netherlands. *Swiss Political Science Review, 23*(4), 377–403. https://doi.org/10.1111/SPSR.12275
Alonso-Muñoz, L., & Casero-Ripollés, A. (2023). The appeal to emotions in the discourse of populist political actors from Spain, Italy, France and the United Kingdom on Twitter. *Frontiers in Communication, 8*, 1159847. https://doi.org/10.3389/FCOMM.2023.1159847/BIBTEX
Aumer, K., Bahn, A. C. K., Janicki, C., Guzman, N., Pierson, N., Strand, S. E., & Totlund, H. (2016). Can't let it go: Hate in interpersonal relationships. *Journal of Relationships Research, 7*, Article e2. https://doi.org/10.1017/jrr.2016.2
Bakker, B. N., Schumacher, G., & Rooduijn, M. (2021). The populist appeal: Personality and antiestablishment communication. *Journal of Politics, 83*(2), 589–601. https://doi.org/10.1086/710014
Barker, D. C., & DeTamble, R. (2022). American populism: Dimensions, distinctions, and correlates. *Global Public Policy and Governance, 2*(1), 22–46. https://doi.org/10.1007/S43508-022-00033-2/TABLES/8
Baumeister, R., & Butz, D. (2005). Roots of hate, violence, and evil. In R. Sternberg (Ed.), *The psychology of hate* (pp. 87–102). American Psychological Association.
Ben-Ze'ev, A. (2018). Is hate worst when it is fresh? The development of hate over time. *Emotion Review, 10*(4), 322–324. https://doi.org/10.1177/1754073918787233
Ben-Ze'ev, A. (2000). *The subtlety of emotions*. MIT Press.
Bernhard, L., & Kriesi, H. (2019). Populism in election times: A comparative analysis of 11 countries in Western Europe. *West European Politics, 42*(6), 1188–1208. https://doi.org/10.1080/01402382.2019.1596694
Brown, M., Keefer, L. A., Sacco, D. F., & Bermond, A. (2019). Is the cure a wall? Behavioral immune system responses to a disease metaphor for immigration. *Evolutionary Psychological Science, 5*(3), 343–356. https://doi.org/10.1007/S40806-019-00191-3/FIGURES/3
Caiani, M., & Di Cocco, J. (2023). Populism and emotions: A comparative study using machine learning. *Italian Political Science Review/rivista Italiana di Scienza Politica, 53*(3), 351–366. https://doi.org/10.1017/IPO.2023.8
Capelos, T., & Demertzis, N. (2018). Political action and resentful affectivity in critical times. *Humanity and Society, 42*(4), 410–433. https://doi.org/10.1177/0160597618802517

Coleman, P. T. (2003). Characteristics of protracted, intractable conflict: Toward the development of a metaframework-I. *Peace and Conflict: Journal of Peace Psychology, 9*(1), 1–37. https://doi.org/10.1207/S15327949PAC0901_01

Custodi, J. (2021). Nationalism and populism on the left: The case of Podemos. *Nations and Nationalism, 27*(3), 705–720. https://doi.org/10.1111/NANA.12663

Demertzis, N. (2006). Emotions and populism. *Emotion, Politics and Society*, 103–122. https://doi.org/10.1057/9780230627895_7

Elad-Strenger, J., & Kessler, T. (2024). *The role of misrecognition in driving support for right-wing populism.* https://doi.org/10.1177/00027642241240338

Elnakouri, A., Hubley, C., & McGregor, I. (2022). Hate and meaning in life: How collective, but not personal, hate quells threat and spurs meaning in life. *Journal of Experimental Social Psychology, 98*, Article 104227. https://doi.org/10.1016/J.JESP.2021.104227

Erisen, C. (2020). Anger in political decision making. *Oxford Research Encyclopedia of Politics.* https://doi.org/10.1093/ACREFORE/9780190228637.013.997

Erisen, C., Guidi, M., Martini, S., Toprakkiran, S., Isernia, P., & Littvay, L. (2021). Psychological correlates of populist attitudes. *Political Psychology*. https://doi.org/10.1111/POPS.12768

Fischer, A., Halperin, E., Canetti, D., & Jasini, A. (2018). Why we hate. *Emotion Review, 10*(4), 1–12. https://doi.org/10.1177/1754073917751229

Fischer, A., & Giner-Sorolla, R. (2016). Contempt: Derogating others while keeping calm. *Emotion Review, 8*(4), 346–357. https://doi.org/10.1177/1754073915610439

Gaffney, A. M., Hackett, J. D., Rast, D. E., Hohman, Z. P., & Jaurique, A. (2018). The state of American protest: Shared anger and populism. *Analyses of Social Issues and Public Policy, 18*(1), 11–33. https://doi.org/10.1111/ASAP.12145

Halperin, E. (2008). Group-based Hatred in intractable conflict in Israel. *Journal of Conflict Resolution, 52*(5), 713–736. https://doi.org/10.1177/0022002708314665

Halperin, E., Canetti-Nisim, D., & Hirsch-Hoefler, S. (2009). The central role of group-based hatred as an emotional antecedent of political intolerance: Evidence from Israel. *Political Psychology, 30*(1), 93–123. https://doi.org/10.1111/j.1467-9221.2008.00682.x

Halperin, E., Russell, A. G., Dweck, C. S., & Gross, J. J. (2011). Anger, Hatred, and the quest for peace: Anger can be constructive in the absence of Hatred. *Journal of Conflict Resolution, 55*(2), 274–291. https://doi.org/10.1177/0022002710383670

Halperin, E., Cannetti, D., & Kimhi, S. (2012). In love with Hatred: Rethinking the role Hatred plays in shaping political behavior. *Journal of Applied Social Psychology, 42*(9), 2231–2256. https://doi.org/10.1111/j.1559-1816.2012.00938.x

Hameleers, M. (2022). *Populist disinformation in fragmented information settings: Understanding the nature and persuasiveness of populist and post-factual communication.* Routledge.

Heavey, C. L., Lefforge, N. L., Lapping-Carr, L., & Hurlburt, R. T. (2017). Mixed emotions: Toward a phenomenology of blended and multiple feelings *9*(2), 105–110. https://doi.org/10.1177/1754073916639661

Hutcherson, C. A., & Gross, J. J. (2011). The moral emotions: A social–functionalist account of anger, disgust, and contempt. *Journal of Personality and Social Psychology, 100*(4), 719–737. https://doi.org/10.1037/a0022408

Jagers, J., & Walgrave, S. (2007). Populism as political communication style: An empirical study of political parties' discourse in Belgium. *European Journal of Political Research, 46*(3), 319–345. https://doi.org/10.1111/J.1475-6765.2006.00690.X

Karinen, A. K., Molho, C., Kupfer, T. R., & Tybur, J. M. (2019). Disgust sensitivity and opposition to immigration: Does contact avoidance or resistance to foreign norms explain the relationship? *Journal of Experimental Social Psychology, 84*, Article 103817. https://doi.org/10.1016/J.JESP.2019.103817

Kinnvall, C. (2018). Ontological insecurities and postcolonial imaginaries. *Humanity & Society, 42*(4), 523–543. https://doi.org/10.1177/0160597618802646

Kriesi, H., Grande, E., Lachat, R., Dolezal, M., Bornschier, S., & Frey, T. (2008). West European politics in the age of globalization. In *West European politics in the age of globalization.* Cambridge University Press. https://doi.org/10.1017/CBO9780511790720

Lange, J., Dalege, J., Borsboom, D., van Kleef, G. A., & Fischer, A. H. (2020). Toward an integrative psychometric model of emotions. *Perspectives on Psychological Science*, 174569161989505. https://doi.org/10.1177/1745691619895057

Marchlewska, M., Cichocka, A., Panayiotou, O., Castellanos, K., & Batayneh, J. (2018). Populism as identity politics: Perceived in-group disadvantage,

collective narcissism, and support for populism. *Social Psychological and Personality Science, 9*(2), 151–162. https://doi.org/10.1177/194855061773 2393
Martella, A., & Bracciale, R. (2022). Populism and emotions: Italian political leaders' communicative strategies to engage Facebook users. *Innovation: The European Journal of Social Science Research, 35*(1), 65–85. https://doi.org/ 10.1080/13511610.2021.1951681
Martínez, C. A., van Prooijen, J. W., & Lange, P. A. M. V. (2022a). Hate: Toward understanding its distinctive features across interpersonal and intergroup targets. *Emotion, 22*(1), 46–63. https://doi.org/10.1037/EMO000 1056
Martínez, C. A., van Prooijen, J.-W., & Van Lange, P. A. M. (2022b). A threat-based hate model: How symbolic and realistic threats underlie hate and aggression. *Journal of Experimental Social Psychology, 103*, Article 104393. https://doi.org/10.1016/J.JESP.2022.104393
Martínez, C. A., van Prooijen, J. W., & Van Lange, P. A. M. (2023). The hateful people: Populist attitudes predict interpersonal and intergroup hate. *Social Psychological and Personality Science, 14*(6), 698–707. https://doi.org/ 10.1177/19485506221127491/ASSET/IMAGES/LARGE/10.1177_1948 5506221127491-FIG1.JPEG
Matsumoto, D., Hwang, H. C., & Frank, M. G. (2017). Emotion and aggressive intergroup cognitions: The ANCODI hypothesis. *Aggressive Behavior, 43*(1), 93–107. https://doi.org/10.1002/ab.21666
McCoy, J. (2022). Reflections on populism and polarization in Latin America, and consequences for democracy. *Desafíos, 34*(2). https://doi.org/10.12804/ REVISTAS.UROSARIO.EDU.CO/DESAFIOS/A.11307
Mols, F., & Jetten, J. (2014). No guts, no glory: How framing the collective past paves the way for anti-immigrant sentiments. *International Journal of Intercultural Relations, 43*(PA), 74–86. https://doi.org/10.1016/ J.IJINTREL.2014.08.014
Mudde, C., & Rovira Kaltwasser, C. (2013). Exclusionary vs. Inclusionary populism: Comparing contemporary Europe and Latin America. *Government and Opposition, 48*(2), 147–174. https://doi.org/10.1017/GOV.201 2.11
Mudde, C. (2007). Populist radical right parties in Europe. In *Populist radical right parties in Europe*. Cambridge University Press. https://doi.org/10.1017/ CBO9780511492037
Nguyen, C. G., Salmela, M., & von Scheve, C. (2022). From specific worries to generalized anger: The emotional dynamics of right-wing political populism.

The Palgrave handbook of populism (pp. 145–160). https://doi.org/10.1007/978-3-030-80803-7_8
Oceja, L., & Carrera, P. (2009). Beyond a single pattern of mixed emotional experience. *Psychological Assessment, 1*, 58–67. https://doi.org/10.1027/1015-5759.25.1.58
Oliver, J. E., & Rahn, W. M. (2016). Rise of the Trumpenvolk: Populism in the 2016 election. *Annals of the American Academy of Political and Social Science, 667*(1), 189–206. https://doi.org/10.1177/0002716216662639
Opotow, S., & McClelland, S. I. (2007). The intensification of hating: A theory. *Social Justice Research, 20*(1), 68–97. https://doi.org/10.1007/s11211-007-0033-0
Pretus, C., Ray, J. L., Granot, Y., Cunningham, W. A., & Van Bavel, J. J. (2022). The psychology of hate: Moral concerns differentiate hate from dislike. *European Journal of Social Psychology*. https://doi.org/10.1002/EJSP.2906
Rempel, J. K., & Sutherland, S. (2016). Hate: theory and implications for intimate relationships. In K. Aumer (Ed.), *The psychology of love and hate in intimate relationships* (pp. 105–129). Springer International Publishing. https://doi.org/10.1007/978-3-319-39277-6_7
Rhodes-Purdy, M., Navarre, R., & Utych, S. M. (2021). Populist psychology: Economics, culture, and emotions. https://doi.org/10.1086/715168
Richardson, M. (2017). The disgust of Donald Trump. *Continuum, 31*(6), 747–756. https://doi.org/10.1080/10304312.2017.1370077
Rico, G., Guinjoan, M., & Anduiza, E. (2017). The emotional underpinnings of populism: How anger and fear affect populist attitudes. *Swiss Political Science Review, 23*(4), 444–461. https://doi.org/10.1111/SPSR.12261
Roseman, I. J., & Steele, A. K. (2018). Concluding commentary: Schadenfreude, Gluckschmerz, jealousy, and hate—What (and when, and why) are the emotions? *Emotion Review, 10*(4), 327–340. https://doi.org/10.1177/1754073918798089
Rozin, P., Lowery, L., Imada, S., & Haidt, J. (1999). The CAD triad hypothesis: A mapping between three moral emotions (contempt, anger, disgust) and three moral codes (community, autonomy, divinity). *Journal of Personality and Social Psychology, 76*(4), 574–586.
Ruzza, C. (2020). Civil society between populism and anti-populism. *IMISCOE Research Series*, 221–235. https://doi.org/10.1007/978-3-030-41694-2_14

Salmela, M., & von Scheve, C. (2017). Emotional roots of right-wing political populism. *Social Science Information, 56*(4), 567–595. https://doi.org/10.1177/0539018417734419
Schriber, R. A., Chung, J. M., Sorensen, K. S., & Robins, R. W. (2017). Dispositional contempt: A first look at the contemptuous person. *Journal of Personality and Social Psychology, 113*(2), 280–309. https://doi.org/10.1037/pspp0000101
Sell, A., Scrivner, C., Landers, M., & Lopez, A. (2022). *The neutralization theory of Hatred*. https://doi.org/10.31234/OSF.IO/KXDVU
Sevillano, V., & Fiske, S. T. (2013). Ambivalence toward immigrants: Invaders or allies? In *U.S. immigration and education: Cultural and policy issues across the lifespan.* (pp. 97–118). Springer Publishing Company.
Skitka, L. J., Bauman, C. W., & Sargis, E. G. (2005). Moral conviction: Another contributor to attitude strength or something more? *Journal of Personality and Social Psychology, 88*(6), 895–917. https://doi.org/10.1037/0022-3514.88.6.895
Staub, E. (2005). The origins and evolution of hate, with notes on prevention. In R. Sternberg (Ed.), *The psychology of hate.* (pp. 51–66). American Psychological Association. https://doi.org/10.1037/10930-003
Staub, E. (2011). *Overcoming evil: Genocide, violent conflict, and terrorism.* Oxford University Press.
Steenvoorden, E., & Harteveld, E. (2018). The appeal of nostalgia: The influence of societal pessimism on support for populist radical right parties. *West European Politics, 41*(1), 28–52. https://doi.org/10.1080/01402382.2017.1334138
Sternberg, R. J., & Sternberg, K. (2008). https://doi.org/10.1017/CBO9780511818707
Sternberg. (2003). A duplex theory of hate: Development and application to terrorism, massacres, and genocide. In *Review of General Psychology, 7*(3), 299–328. https://doi.org/10.1037/1089-2680.7.3.299
Tybur, J. M., Lieberman, D., & Griskevicius, V. (2009). Microbes, mating, and morality: Individual differences in three functional domains of disgust. *Journal of Personality and Social Psychology, 97*(1), 103–122. https://doi.org/10.1037/a0015474
Vahter, M., & Jakobson, M. L. (2023). The moral rhetoric of populist radical right: The case of the Sweden Democrats. *Journal of Political Ideologies.* https://doi.org/10.1080/13569317.2023.2242795
Valentino, N. A., Brader, T., Groenendyk, E. W., Gregorowicz, K., & Hutchings, V. L. (2011). Election night's alright for fighting: The role of emotions

in political participation. *The Journal of Politics, 1*, 156–170. https://doi.org/10.1017/S0022381610000939
Van Doorn, J. (2018). Anger, feelings of revenge, and hate. *Emotion Review, 10*(4), 321–322. https://doi.org/10.1177/1754073918783260
van Herpen, M. H. (2021). *The end of populism: Twenty proposals to defend liberal democracy*. Manchester University Press.
van Prooijen, J. W., Cohen Rodrigues, T., Bunzel, C., Georgescu, O., Komáromy, D., & Krouwel, A. P. M. (2022). Populist gullibility: conspiracy theories, news credibility, bullshit receptivity, and paranormal belief. *Political Psychology, 43*(6), 1061–1079. https://doi.org/10.1111/POPS.12802
Vasilopoulos, P., Marcus, G. E., Valentino, N. A., & Foucault, M. (2019). Fear, anger, and voting for the far right: Evidence from the November 13, 2015 Paris Terror Attacks. *Political Psychology, 40*(4), 679–704. https://doi.org/10.1111/POPS.12513
Verbalyte, M., Bonansinga, D., & Capelos, T. (2024). Introduction to the triple special issue "The emotional side of populist support: Key affective mechanisms at test." *American Behavioral Scientist*. https://doi.org/10.1177/00027642241240360
Verduyn, P., & Lavrijsen, S. (2015). Which emotions last longest and why: The role of event importance and rumination. *Motivation and Emotion, 39*(1), 119–127. https://doi.org/10.1007/s11031-014-9445-y
Wagenvoorde, R. (2019). The religious dimensions of contemporary European populism. *Religion and European Society: A Primer*, 111–123. https://doi.org/10.1002/9781119162766.CH7
Widmann, T. (2021). How emotional are populists really? Factors explaining emotional appeals in the communication of political parties. *Political Psychology, 42*(1), 163–181. https://doi.org/10.1111/POPS.12693
Yi, J., Phillips, J., & Lee, W. (2019). Manufacturing contempt: State-linked populism in South Korea. *Society, 56*(5), 494–501. https://doi.org/10.1007/S12115-019-00404-2/METRICS
Yilmaz, I., & Morieson, N. (2021). A systematic literature review of populism, religion and emotions. *Religions, 12*(4), 272. https://doi.org/10.3390/REL12040272

Genocide: An Alternative Lens to Explore Hate Crime Offending

William Bergstroem

Introduction

The 'crime of crimes' is a phrase often used to describe genocide, distinguishing it from other forms of criminal offending (Rafter, 2016; Schabas, 2000). This argument can be seen to stem from several key premises, in particular, an assessment that the nature, impact and scale of genocide is above that often associated with other crimes. An influential aspect contributing to this exceptionality is the *mens rea* of genocide, i.e. the intent and motivation, which plays an important part in the distinction between genocide and other mass-scale atrocities (O'Brien, 2020; Williams & Pfeiffer, 2017).

However, this very distinction in intent is what arguably connects genocide to hate crime, with both resulting from a level of prejudice towards a specific group. According to the 1948 Convention on the

W. Bergstroem (✉)
Department of Sociology, University of Surrey, Guildford, UK
e-mail: W.bergstroem@surrey.ac.uk

J. Garland et al. (eds.), *Hate Crime Perpetrators: New Perspectives from Theory, Research and Practice, Volume I*, Palgrave Hate Studies,
https://doi.org/10.1007/978-3-031-92666-2_8

Prevention and Punishment of the Crime of Genocide, listed acts will constitute genocide if they are committed against one of the groups specified in the Convention, and importantly, if they are intended to destroy that group in whole or in part. Despite the exceptionality this is deemed to bring to genocide, this specificity leads to key similarities with hate crime. Since other chapters in this book explore the definitional discussions around the concept of hate crime, these will not be repeated here. Instead, hate crime will be taken to mean 'a criminal act which is motivated by bias or prejudice towards a specific group of people' (OSCE ODIHR, 2020).

The similarities between the two definitions arguably provide a unique opportunity to explore the two concepts in a more interdisciplinary way, offering new insights into the reasons and nature of offending. In addition to a number of more practical definitional parallels, arguably the most significant overlap is the *mens rea* in both offences. For genocide, the intent must be to destroy a group of people, inherently suggesting a level of prejudice or bias towards that group. For hate crime, this is generally specifically mentioned as the key motivating factor for committing targeted crimes. As such, this need for a level of prejudice or bias in the *mens rea*, without which neither crime is made out, makes genocide and hate crime unique within legal jurisprudence and inherently related to each other. In fact, while it may be too simplistic to suggest that the only real difference between the crimes is the mass-scale and systematic nature of genocide, thus essentially making genocide a collection of hate crimes, the similarities between the two phenomena nevertheless raise interesting and important considerations and applications (Martson Danner, 2002; Schweppe & Perry, 2022).

Despite the similarities between the two definitions, a significant gap can be identified in the research around these two concepts and, in particular, discussions of the relationship between the two. This leads to both subjects often being considered in isolation due to their perceived exceptionality, differing historical background and international legal framework. As such, this chapter aims to provide a new and unique lens through which to explore genocide and hate crime offending through a combined exploration of relevant theories. While there are many theories and models available to investigate the relationship between the two crimes, many of which are explored in other parts of this book, this chapter will utilise a selection of these as examples to demonstrate the value of applying an interdisciplinary approach to the two topics, thus providing new insights into explanations of hate crime and genocide offending.

Explanations of Hate Offending

Models of Hate Offending

Many theories on the development of hate provide invaluable insights into the process through which hateful attitudes can spread and physical expressions of such views encouraged. However, despite their insights, they are often simplistic and over-reliant on a single factor, thus not accounting for the complexity and interactive elements which influence the given circumstances (Hall, 2013). Instead, Hakwe et al. (2022) summarise key literature in this area to develop a new model of 5 archetypes or sources of normalisation and polarisation as related to hate acts, which contributes to a more nuanced understanding of the topic. These archetypes are: (1) attitudes (such as shifts in stereotypes and vilification); (2) affiliation (such as group identity and group narratives); (3) interaction (for example a lack of positive inter-group interactions); (4) interests (including group power and group interests); (5) norms (group reinforcement of norms and normalisation). Importantly, these factors overlap and interact with each other, thus providing a useful model to explain more deeply how an environment can develop which can be conducive to and promote escalation in perceptions and thus actions towards hated groups (Hakwe et al., 2022). In this context, such an environment can directly be linked to what Perry and others describe as a 'climate of hate' (Perry & Scrivens, 2018; Syed & Ali, 2021).

Another key criticism of many theories is that they are often prescriptive, suggesting that this process is automatic, which seems oversimplified and reductionist in that the importance of individual agency and rational choice is often overlooked or excluded (Schweppe & Perry, 2022). This creates an important limitation in being able to fully explain such behaviours and the reasons why some people become involved in different forms of hate crime. However, several models have been developed to categorise possible hate offenders, arguably to some degree avoiding this issue of overly prescriptive explanations of individuals' roles and involvement in the commission of hateful acts (Barna, 2021; Davis, 2020; Stefaniak & Winiewski, 2022). Although still inherently simplistic and generalised, these provide a useful platform to explore the complexities around who is involved in hate crime (and genocide as shown later), as well as some of the reasons why.

One such model, often referred to by scholars, was developed by Levin and McDevitt (1993) and later expanded on by McDevitt et al. (2002) (Barna, 2021; Davis, 2020). This model describes 4 types of offenders: thrill seekers; defensive offenders; retaliators; and mission offenders (added later) (McDevitt et al., 2002). Thrill seekers can be described as those motivated by the excitement involved in the act and sometimes the power felt by subjugating the victim, while defensive offenders act due to a perceived threat from the target group. Retaliators often respond to specific events, whereas mission offenders are the ones most closely associated with an extreme ideology of hatred in which the aim is to completely remove the target group from their community. Of interest is that researchers have argued that only around 1% of hate crime offenders fall within the category of mission offenders, a point which has formed the foundation for some criticism of the concept of hate crime (Davis, 2020). While introducing an alternative examination of reasons for offending, and even if adapting the model to allow for intersectionality between the offenders, these categories can still be considered somewhat reductive and limited, as well as raising some questions around the validity of the methodology behind the model.

In contrast to this model, the one by Jacobs and Potter (1998) (see Fig. 1) is based on a matrix of levels of hostility and causation to the offence, rather than a typological categorisation of offenders. As such, it could be argued that this model is slightly more nuanced and representative of a wider demographic of hate crime offenders, which in part contributes to its use to argue against a concept of hate crime (Iganski, 1999; Perry, 2002). Based on this model, hate crimes can be broken down into four situations: (1) a high level of hatred towards the victim group which is the key motivator for the offence (such as a Neo-Nazi attacking a Jewish person to instigate a race war); (2) a high level of hatred but a low level of causality to the offence (for example the same neo-Nazi damaging a Jewish person's car without initially knowing that the owner is Jewish); (3) a low level of hatred but high causality (in this case, for example a member of a neo-Nazi group who damages a Jewish shop due to peer pressure without being anti-Semitic themself); (4) a low level of hatred and low causality (e.g. a shoplifter, who is not overly anti-Semitic, using a slur while stealing from a Jewish shop for financial reasons).

Despite its development over 20 years ago and its criticism of the concept of hate crime, this model nevertheless provides a useful tool to explore a range of aspects within the topic of hate crime, ranging from the nature of the concept itself, legal discussions around the purpose and efficacy of legislation, to practical applications within cases of hate crime and associated acts. In addition, since the model is based on levels of hate and causality, it could potentially be expanded to include levels between the four types originally outlined, for example offenders whose level of hatred is between 'low' and 'high'. Finally, the model provides an

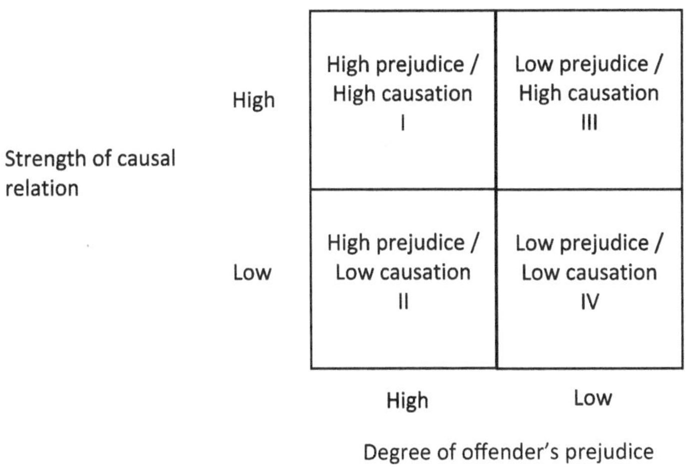

Fig. 1 Jacobs and Potter's model of hate crime offender typologies (Jacobs & Potter, 1998)

interesting opportunity to explore the intersection between types of hate acts, such as hate crime and genocide, as demonstrated later. While it is argued here that no model or theory in and of itself can fully explain all aspects and reasons for the commission of hate crime, when combined and considered in addition to other theories outlined in this book, a picture starts to emerge of how individual and social factors can come together to create a situation which may lead to such acts taking place.

Social Factors in Hate Formation and Development

The dual-attitude model suggests that recent developments in society have led to two separate types of prejudice: 'old-fashioned prejudice' which is argued to result in more blatant and clear forms of discriminatory acts; and 'modern prejudice' which is proposed as more subtle and implicit due to the changing nature of societal scrutiny of prejudice (Pérez Ramírez et al., 2022). This suggests that societal attitudes not only play a role in fostering an environment more conducive to hate offending, but also in moderating such behaviours. For example, research has demonstrated that individuals and groups may exhibit varying levels of tolerance of prejudicial behaviour, which can in some circumstances predict their willingness to express prejudicial views and even their justification to condone or commit prejudicial acts (Hoover et al., 2021; Hunt et al., 2021). Furthermore, such levels of tolerance are not only individually held, but shaped and informed by group values and influences (Hoover et al., 2021). Hence, group identities can play a role in both promoting or preventing prejudicial actions. In addition, these studies suggest that tolerance of prejudicial views and acts exist on a scale, from low tolerance to various levels of justification or condoning of such acts and active willingness to engage in prejudicial behaviour.

This exploration of how prejudicial views may turn into action is crucial to better understand the intersection between hate crime and genocide offending. It is important to consider this both in the sense of what is often considered every-day acts of hate crime and wider societal forms, including genocide. A key element of this process which repeatedly presents in the literature is the question of normalisation, both on an individual psychological level as well as group-based social and even societal levels, thus providing a bridge between the various levels (Barna, 2021; Stefaniak & Winiewski, 2022; Vendrell Ferran, 2021). In this sense, normalisation can generally be described as the process in which previously unusual or exceptional perceptions or acts become acceptable and considered more mainstream, in essence, a lowering of the threshold of what is considered unacceptable (Bieńkowski et al., 2022; Hunt et al., 2021). In terms of hate crime specifically, this can mean negative views about identifiable groups, which were previously deemed unacceptable, becoming increasingly normal and thus reducing the barrier to such views being expressed and potentially acted upon.

This normalising process is often continuous, which means that views and acts can increasingly be pushed towards more extremes (Bieńkowski et al., 2022; Stefaniak & Winiewski, 2022). For example, if hateful stereotypes become normalised, expressions of such stereotypes become less unacceptable. Once such expressions are experienced more widely within society, it can be a small step towards expressions turning into actions, which can over time create an environment where the targeting becomes increasingly extreme, potentially leading to mass-scale atrocities against a group. As such, it becomes clear how normalisation can play a crucial part in the commission of hate acts on both an individual, group-based and societal level. In addition, it is worth noting that these three paradigms coexist and interact with each other. For example, normalisation on an individual level is inherently connected to what that individual experiences and the reactions of their in-group, as well as society more broadly (Barna, 2021; Vendrell Ferran, 2021).

This process of escalation is also essential in starting to explore the relationship and link between hate crime and genocide, and will therefore form a basis of later discussions, in combination with other theories. For example, more recent research draws on new technologies to create simulations incorporating graph theory in order to explore how prejudices held by individuals can quickly spread within and subsequently between groups, thus spreading to a wider audience (Bieńkowski et al., 2022; Stefaniak & Winiewski, 2022). This is especially the case in modern times where social media can significantly expand the spread of such messages. In addition, these models also demonstrate how this 'drip-drip' effect and normalisation of views can push people towards increasingly extreme opinions, which has been associated with an increased likelihood of acting on such views (Bieńkowski et al., 2022; Hoover et al., 2021; Stefaniak & Winiewski, 2022). Furthermore, a noteworthy finding is that this process not only affects like-minded individuals but also those who had no connection to the originator of the views and did not initially hold such beliefs or opinions (Bieńkowski et al., 2022). Equally, through this spread, general views can become more targeted towards a specific group, increasing the likelihood of targeted action (Bieńkowski et al., 2022; Hoover et al., 2021; Vendrell Ferran, 2021).

Societal Frameworks of Hate

Role of the State

As has already been established, individual and group-based explanations of hatred and hate acts are directly interconnected with the societal context in which they exist. For example, the normalisation of such views and behaviours can easily spread between various groups, thus expanding to wider society (Bieńkowski et al., 2022; Bilewicz & Soral, 2020). Similarly, society can play a crucial role in enabling or creating barriers within this process. Tolerance to racism both on an individual and wider level can for example contribute to determining the likelihood of such attitudes spreading, as well as the willingness to act on such views (Bilewicz & Soral, 2020; Hoover et al., 2021; Hunt et al., 2021). Equally, drawing on models of how hatred spreads among groups, as well as findings by Allport, it is suggested that the deliberate avoidance of the target group can play a key role in the spread of hatred and acts as one of the early steps in this process (Allport, 1979; Bieńkowski et al., 2022). Hence, conversely, a lack of avoidance, or in other words, an increased exposure to out-groups, can mitigate this process (Allport, 1979; Denti et al., 2023; Levine & Brenman, 2019). This importantly suggests that societal set-ups and systems can play a key role in the ease with which hatred can spread, introducing the idea that governments can thus equally play an important role.

This role of societal control is also highlighted by the impact of potential responses by governments to hate crime and related acts, which can both play a preventative role, as well as send a message to victims, perpetrators and communities more broadly. Many theories, such as Routine Activities Theory, have been applied to hate crime and suggest that crimes require three factors in order to occur: the presence of a likely offender, a suitable target and the absence of a capable guardian (Cohen & Felson, 1979; Davis, 2020; Felson & Cohen, 1980). The first two arguably relate more to the explanations of offending explored elsewhere, however, the third factor is an interesting one in considering the potential relationship between hate crime and genocide, especially considering genocide as a systematic form of hate crime and given the involvement of a government or other state actor in genocide perpetration (Karstedt et al., 2021). Hence, it could be suggested that a state's approach in the role of capable guardians (for example through legal and criminal justice responses to hate) can be an indicator of the state's views of such behaviours, with a lack of responses potentially indicating a lack of interest or even condoning of the acts. Hence, a question may be raised as to whether this can be used as an indicator of the likelihood of escalation, potentially to the level of genocide.

However, the lack of barriers is not the only way in which states can play an enabling role in hate crime and genocide (Sinnar, 2022). As suggested by research, governing bodies not only play a role in the encouragement or commission of genocide (as is to an extent inherent in the international definition of genocide), but also in the commission of hate crimes (Akca et al., 2020; Dugan & Chenoweth, 2020; Koski & Bantley, 2020). A multitude of societal factors have been linked to the commission of hate crime and genocide, in addition to those mentioned previously, including aspects such as community disorganisation, urban demographics, racial balance, economic and residential stability, as well as messaging through media and other outlets (Barna, 2021). Again, these factors should be taken in context and as a combination of interacting elements, rather than in isolation. However, regardless of the interplay of factors, it can be seen that these elements together can easily lead to a form of scapegoating or transference of frustrations or negative feelings towards a group of people, which in turn develops into hostility through various processes mentioned above (Allport, 1979).

Hate Crime and Genocide on a Continuum of Hate

As has been alluded to, the systematic nature of genocide sets it apart from the majority of hate crimes; however, this appears slightly oversimplified when examined more closely (Schweppe & Perry, 2022). While it cannot be contested that not all hate crimes form part of a wide-scale strategy, nevertheless, more nuanced examinations suggest that the majority of hate crimes are in some ways linked to a systematic context, even in the case of individual acts of hate crime, because they happen within the context of a societal system (James & McBride, 2022; Perry, 2002). This will be explored further in this chapter, however, as Stefaniak and Winiewski (2022) argue, all hate crimes are to varying levels the result of and part of inter-group interactions. Furthermore, as outlined, hate crimes often result from a climate of hate, which can be seen as a form of systematic hostility (James & McBride, 2022; Perry, 2002; Walters, 2022). This is perhaps most clearly evidenced through the role and potential impact of hate speech. While not always necessarily a part of hate crime in the strictest sense, there is undeniably a close relationship between the two, and in some cases a causal relationship (Akca et al., 2020; Schweppe & Perry, 2022).

Exploring models related to the development and stages of genocide, it becomes apparent that the initial stages and acts demonstrate clear similarities with what would generally be considered hate crime. In fact, as Allport states, it can be suggested that genocidal violence is always preceded by milder manifestations of prejudice (Allport, 1979; Barna, 2021). As Perry and Scrivens (2018) outline, this can be described as the development of a climate of hate, which equally includes the potential for hate crime as well as genocide, depending on the circumstances. Hence, this argument leads Perry and others to the assertion that hate crimes exist on a so-called continuum of hatred, which includes a range of acts related to hatred or prejudice (Schweppe & Perry, 2022). This suggestion of a continuum of hate has started to emerge as a relatively new angle through which to explore hate crime and other hate-related acts (Baider, 2020; Perry, 2020; Schweppe & Perry, 2022).

As demonstrated in the models and stages describing the development and lifecycle of genocide featured in Figs. 2 and 3, as well as scholarly theories and case study evidence, it is clear that genocides do not exist in a vacuum and do not occur abruptly without any preceding signs (Dunlap, 2021; Marston Danner, 2002; Meiches, 2019). Hate crime, arguably, plays a key role in this, as well as within the commission of the genocide itself. This is because, although genocide is often described in academia as one incident, in reality, genocides by their very nature are a collection of acts which together, as part of a systematic approach, are aimed at destroying a group of people (Martson Danner, 2002). Hence, it does not seem unreasonable to suggest that the individual acts that make up a genocide are also in themselves forms of hate crimes. In fact, the inclusion of the need to address hate crime within genocide prevention programs and laws, by both international and national bodies, is a good example of the recognition of the role hate crime plays within genocide (OSCE, n.d.; Schweppe & Perry, 2022).

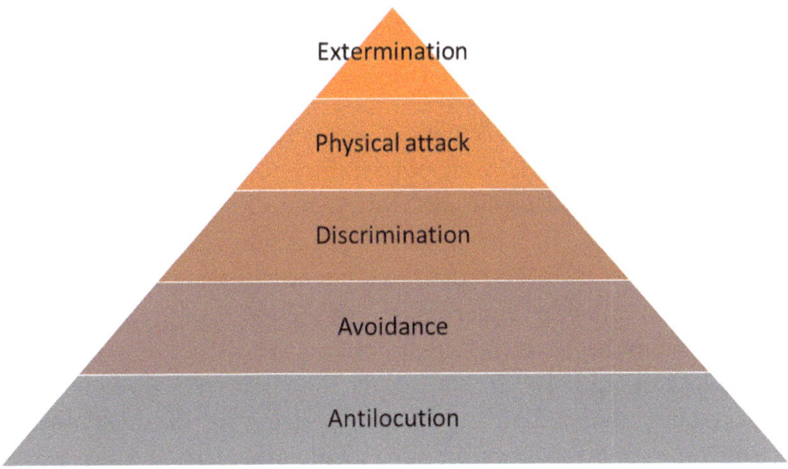

Fig. 2 Allport's model of the stages of genocide (Allport, 1979)

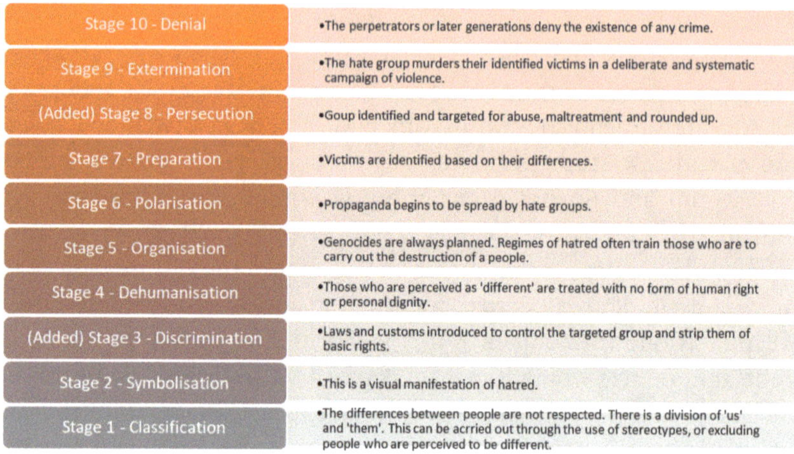

Fig. 3 Stanton's model of the stages of genocide (Burleson & Giordano, 2016; Stanton, 2004)

Offender Roles Within Hate Crime and Genocide Commission

Application of Hate Crime Offender Typologies Within Genocide

Given the clear interconnectedness and overlap between hate crime and genocide, this provides an opportunity to explore hate offending through a more interdisciplinary lens. As mentioned previously, Jacobs and Potter's typology of hate crime offenders provides a valuable framework through which to examine these nuances. As outlined, the model describes four types of offenders, based on their level of prejudice and the level of causality between this prejudice and the commission of the hate act (Jacobs & Potter, 1998) (see Fig. 1). The first type of offender with high levels of hatred and high causality is perhaps the one most obviously related to the traditional notion of genocide offenders. In this case, this would likely describe those offenders who are more commonly referred to as the instigators of the genocide, or as labelled by Levin & McDevitt (1993), the 'mission' offenders (Weisband, 2018). While it could be argued that a high level of hatred is not necessarily always an essential motivator of those behind the planning of a genocide, as explored later, it is nevertheless clear how such offenders form a key demographic among those who commit genocide (Hollows & Fritzon, 2012; Sternberg, 2003). Equally, within the context of individual acts of hate crime, such offenders often cite larger-scale aims as a reason for their offending, whether this be due to their involvement in hate groups (whose narratives often evoke or directly relate to genocide), or for example the motivation of instigating a race war (which has been a prevalent motivator in recent cases) (Buckingham & Alali, 2020; Lowe, 2022; Taylor, 2019). While it is not the purpose to claim that all 'mission' hate crimes are committed in order to instigate a genocide, there is an evidenced overlap and it is clear that such offenders have a role in genocide (Hollows & Fritzon, 2012; Lowe, 2022; Sternberg, 2003).

The second type of offenders, those whose acts demonstrate a low level of hatred but high causality to the offence, is a particularly interesting one within the context of genocide, as it relates to the idea of 'ordinary' people committing 'extraordinary' crimes (Hollows & Fritzon, 2012; Waller, 2007). In Jacobs and Potter's model, this type is often described as someone who for example commits hate crime due to peer pressure from others with a hatred towards the group (Jacobs & Potter, 1998; Phillips, 2009). It is easy to see this being the case in some circumstances within the context of genocide as well, where historical records suggest ordinary people have often felt forced to take part in genocides such as the Holocaust (Mann, 2000; Scull et al., 2016; Straus, 2006; Waller, 2007). This can either be the result of direct pressure, or a perception of indirect pressure from others or society on a larger scale. For example, research shows that some offenders act not so much due to their own hatred, but rather due to a perceived benefit of such actions, often socially, from being associated with the wider in-group (Davis, 2020). As such, an individual may feel that the benefits of for example social or even personal security may outweigh the moral implications and risks of the action. This is especially the case with genocide where the societal and governmental acceptance often involved mean that the benefits are wider and the risks of punishment are likely to be relatively low. While it has been suggested that such offenders who do not demonstrate extreme levels of hatred are more likely to take part in indirect or symbolic forms of hate acts, discussions above have demonstrated how this can easily escalate due to normalisation over time (Scull et al., 2016; Stefaniak & Winiewski, 2022). Hence, it is equally important to note that these typologies are flexible, in that individuals can move between types, and someone with low hatred can develop higher levels of hate over time or through activity.

The last two types in the model are perhaps less clearly directly related to genocide, however, given their inclusion in a model explaining involvement in hate crime, this suggests a role for these types within the context of genocide as well. The third type of high hatred but low causality is perhaps the more difficult one to apply. This generally describes individuals who possess a strong hostility towards the target group, but this hostility is not inherently related to their actions. Nevertheless, two examples can be used to demonstrate the relevance of this offender within genocide. Firstly, this introduces a thought-provoking analysis and consideration of the purpose of genocide. For example, a question can be raised as to whether the planners of genocide, often state actors, commit genocide purely to exterminate a hated group, or if genocide can sometimes perform a different purpose. It could for example be proposed that genocide has often played, at least to some extent, a political purpose for instigators, often related to the acquisition or maintenance of power, for example by redirecting societal frustrations towards a specific group (Powell, 2011; Straus, 2006). Hence, it is possible to argue that some planners of genocide may use hatred as a tool to achieve more personal goals, demonstrating the idea that hatred is not necessarily always the primary cause of the action. Equally, another example can be drawn from the more ground-level offenders. Given the systematic nature of genocide, these acts often become part of the day-to-day activities and experiences of those involved, both as victims and offenders (as also suggested by the escalation and stages of genocide) (Bieńkowski et al., 2022; Stefaniak & Winiewski, 2022). Therefore, while after a time, the normalisation of hatred often means these views are widely held within the society in question, many may act as part of their every-day roles. For example, soldiers or camp guards may feel hostility towards the target group, but see their activities as part of their job, without having a sense of or seeing their part in the wider process (Mann, 2000; Scull et al., 2016; Waller, 2007).

Importantly, this differentiation again demonstrates the potential movement between types of offenders mentioned earlier, for example from initially being unaware or perhaps purposefully ignorant of the larger picture, but increasingly finding meaning in their actions. This evolution is perhaps equally relevant to the final category, those who demonstrate relatively low levels of hostility and who are not directly involved in the offence. Again, this group presents a number of interesting considerations, in that many will argue that it is this group that ultimately allows genocides to take place, namely the 'passive bystanders' (Baum, 2008; Waller, 2007; Wilson, 2023). Despite perhaps being somewhat of a departure from the original model, the passive bystander nevertheless arguably fits quite well into this type of offender due to their role within the situation. The traditional view of genocide as the 'crime of crimes' may suggest that the systematic nature of genocide means the involvement of the entire society, however, historical records clearly contradict this, in that a large proportion of the population often act as silent observers (Baum, 2008; Moerland, 2022). While not removing culpability from these individuals, the distinction is important in order to recognise the nuances and complexity within offender roles. Added to this complexity is the question of whether this category can truly be deemed 'offenders', slightly in line with the original use of the model to question the conceptualisation of hate crime, given their relative low association to the criminal acts themselves. It is argued here that although perhaps not offenders in the traditional sense, this typology nevertheless plays a key role within a genocide, and therefore importantly, contributes to the understanding of the phenomenon (Moerland, 2022; Wilson, 2023). In addition, as has been demonstrated, the normalisation and large-scale prejudice spread as part of the process of genocide means that individuals in this group may over time become involved in other ways.

Relationship Between Hate Sentiment and Perpetration

The reasons for why offenders may belong to these various types is to some extent explored in other parts of this book. However, drawing on the model above, two key features can be highlighted: the level of hatred held and expressed by the individual; and the level to which this hatred is directly linked to their actions. Interestingly, research has found that involvement in hateful acts is less dependent on the level of hatred, but rather the willingness to take action against others (Davis, 2020; Hunt et al., 2021). This leads Davis (2020) to conclude that programs to address hate are perhaps over-reliant on the sentiment, rather than wider factors. Equally, this could be extended to genocide, to argue that the level of prejudice in a society is perhaps not enough to indicate the likelihood of a genocide, but that the willingness to act on such prejudice, as demonstrated by the commission of certain forms of hate crime, can be a key factor in predicting genocide. Another important aspect to consider is the distinction between systematic and symbolic violence, or direct and indirect hate acts (James & McBride, 2022; Pérez Ramírez et al., 2022; Stefaniak & Winiewski, 2022). While research has often focused on the systematic and direct acts within genocide, the arguably more symbolic and indirect elements are equally important and inherent within the wider process of genocide. These can be an indication of the early stages of the process, as well as send a message to victims and potential offenders, while also demonstrating the lack of barriers to prevent escalation.

Escalation is often deemed the primary factor in determining and defining genocide in the sense of the ultimate aim being the intent to destroy, in whole or in part, the target group, as outlined by the Genocide Convention. An alternative parallel can be drawn from the remit of extremism to further explore this argument and how it relates to the relationship between hate crime and genocide. Wintrobe (2006) suggests three types of extremists: (1) those who are extreme by method but not by goal; (2) those who are extreme by goal but not by method; (3) and those who are extreme by both goal and method (Schweppe & Perry, 2022). A surprising similarity is visible in this explanation and the model by Jacobs and Potter (1998) used above in the approach of using two variables and their strength to identify types of offenders. For example, parallels can be drawn between extremists with extreme goals and those hate offenders with high levels of hatred, while the extreme method is more akin to the acts in the framework of hate crime. Furthermore, the definition of extremism is often the combination of an extreme ideology and willingness to utilise extreme methods to achieve this aim, rather than purely being ideology-based (Cassam, 2022; Richards, 2015). This arguably resonates strongly with the typologies discussed above and how they fit within the longer process of genocide. Hence, this provides an insight not only into the nature of offending, but also the concepts and processes of hate crime and genocide.

Conclusion

This chapter has utilised a selection of key theories and models on hate crime offending to explore how these can be applied to an intersectional assessment of hate crime and genocide. The chapter has outlined offender typologies, as well as discussed the role of social and societal processes and systems which may lead to the normalisation and escalation of hate. In addition, the chapter has identified key similarities between hate crime and genocide through the idea of a 'continuum of hate', using this relationship to apply models of hate crime offending to the concept of genocide. By doing so, the chapter has demonstrated how hate crime offending can link to and in some cases lead to genocide, as well as investigated the role of hate crime offending within genocide. As such, the chapter has introduced three key arguments: (1) there is a clear relationship between the concepts of hate crime and genocide, which warrants an interdisciplinary approach to the topics; (2) hate crime can play a key role in the development and stages of genocide; (3) models of hate crime offending can be applied to demonstrate the role of and overlap between hate crime and genocide commission. While more in-depth explorations of the relationship between hate crime and genocide are required, which is the subject of this author's PhD research, this chapter has nevertheless demonstrated the benefit and importance of such approaches in discovering new perspectives and knowledge around hate crime and genocide. As such, the chapter argues that an interdisciplinary exploration of hate crime and genocide can fill an important knowledge gap, providing new insights to the subject areas with significant potential applications for genocide prediction and prevention.

References

Akca, D., Karakus, F., Bastug, M. F., & Perry, B. (2020). Planting hate speech to harvest hatred: How does political hate speech fuel hate crimes in Turkey? *International Journal for Crime, Justice and Social Democracy, 9*(4), 195–211.

Allport, G. W. (1979). *The nature of prejudice* (3rd ed.). Perseus Books.

Baider, F. (2020). Pragmatics lost? Overview, synthesis and proposition in defining online hate speech. *Pragmatics and Society, 11*(2), 196–218.

Barna, I. (2021). The genealogy of social hatred. *Hungarian Journal of Legal Studies, 61*(3), 296–312.

Baum, S. K. (2008). *The psychology of genocide: Perpetrators, bystanders, and rescuers*. Cambridge University Press.

Bieńkowski, M., Soral, W., & Bilewicz, M. (2022, April 27). *Why does online hate speech spread so fast? The social psychological perspective* [Video lecture]. https://mediapeaceproject.smpa.gwu.edu/2209-2/3472-2/.

Bilewicz, M., & Soral, W. (2020). Hate speech epidemic. The dynamic effects of Derogatory language on intergroup relations and political radicalization. *Political Psychology, 41*(S1), 3–33.

Buckingham, L., & Alali, N. (2020). Extreme parallels: A corpus-driven analysis of ISIS and far-right discourse. *New Zealand Journal of Social Sciences, 15*(2), 310–331.

Burleson, S. J., & Giordano, A. (2016). Spatiality of the stages of genocide: The armenian case. *Genocide Studies and Prevention: An International Journal, 10*(3), 39–58.

Cassam, Q. (2022). *Extremism: A philosophical analysis*. Routledge.

Cohen, L. E., & Felson, M. (1979). Social change and crime rate trends: A routine activity approach. *American Sociological Review, 44*(4), 588–608.

Davis, E. (2020). Race hate crime and the criminal justice response. *British Journal of Community Justice, 16*(2), 92–102.

Denti, D., Crociata, A., & Faggian, A. (2023). Knocking on Hell's door: Dismantling hate with cultural consumption. *Journal of Cultural Economics, 47*, 303–349.

Dugan, L., & Chenoweth, E. (2020). Threat, Emboldenment or both? The effects of political power on violent hate crimes. *Criminology, 58*(4), 714–746.

Dunlap, A. (2021). The politics of ecocide, genocide and megaprojects: Interrogating natural resource extraction, identity and the normalization of erasure. *Journal of Genocide Research, 23*(2), 212–235.

Felson, M., & Cohen, L. E. (1980). Human ecology and crime: A routine activity approach. *Human Ecology, 8*, 389–406.

Hakwe, J., El Mawla, M., Gichuhi, C., & Puig Laurrari, H. (2022, March 30). *Responses to polarization archetypes on social media* [Video lecture]. https://mediapeaceproject.smpa.gwu.edu/2209-2/3472-2/.

Hall, N. (2013). *Hate crime* (2nd ed.). Routledge.

Hollows, K., & Fritzon, K. (2012). "Ordinary Men" or "Evil Monsters"? An action systems model of genocidal actions and characteristics of perpetrators. *Law and Human Behavior, 36*(5), 458–467.

Hoover, J., Atari, M., Mostafazadeh Davani, A., Kennedy, B., Portillo-Wightman, G., Yeh, L., & Deghani, M. (2021). Investigating the role of group-based morality in extreme behavioral expressions of prejudice. *Nature Communications, 12*, n.p.

Hunt, J. S., Folberg, A. M., & Ryan, C. S. (2021). Tolerance of racism: A new construct that predicts failure to recognize and confront racism. *European Journal of Social Psychology, 51*(3), 551–571.

Iganski, P. (1999). Why make 'Hate' a crime? *Critical Social Policy, 19*(3), 386–395.

Jacobs, J. B., & Potter, K. (1998). *Hate crimes: Criminal law & identity politics*. Oxford University Press.

James, Z., & McBride, K. (2022). Critical hate studies: A new perspective. *International Review of Victimology, 28*(1), 92–108.

Karstedt, S., Nyseth Brehm, H., & Frizzell, L. C. (2021). Genocide, mass atrocity, and theories of crime: Unlocking criminology's potential. *Annual Review of Criminology, 4*, 75–97.

Koski, S. V., & Bantley, K. (2020). Dog whistle politics: The Trump administration's influence on hate crimes. *Seton Hall Legislative Journal, 44*(1), 39–60.

Levine, D., & Brenman, M. (2019). *When hate groups march down main street: Engaging a community response*. Rowman & Littlefield.

Lowe, D. (2022). Far-right extremism: Is it legitimate freedom of expression, hate crime, or terrorism? *Terrorism and Political Violence, 34*(7), 1433–1453.
Mann, M. (2000). Were the perpetrators of genocide "Ordinary Men" or "Real Nazis"? Results from fifteen hundred biographics. *Holocaust and Genocide Studies, 14*(3), 331–366.
Marston Danner, A. (2002). Bias crimes and crimes against humanity: Culpability in context. *Buffalo Criminal Law Review, 6*(1), 389–450.
McDevitt, J., Levin, J., & Bennett, S. (2002). Hate crime offenders: An expanded typology. *Journal of Social Issues, 58*(2), 303–317.
Meiches, B. (2019). *The politics of annihilation: A genealogy of genocide.* University of Minnesota Press.
Moerland, R. (2022). Individuals as bystanders to atrocity crimes. In B. Holá, H. Nyseth Nzitatira, & M. Weerdesteijn (Eds.), *The Oxford handbook on atrocity crimes* (pp. 303–328). Oxford University Press.
O'Brien, M. (2020). Defining genocide. *Journal of International Peacekeeping, 22*(1–4), 149–169.
OSCE. (n.d.). *ODIHR hate crime reporting.* Retrieved from: hate-crime.osce.org/what-do-we-know.
OSCE ODIHR. (2020). *Hate crime victims in the criminal justice system: A practical guide.* OSCE ODIHR.
Pérez Ramírez, M., Chiclana, S., Méndez, R. C., & Suárez, A. (2022). Sociodemographic and psycho-social differences between hate crime offenders and other non-bias-motivated criminals: Implications for prison rehabilitation programs. *International Journal of Offender Therapy and Comparative Criminology,* n.p.
Perry, B. (2002). Hate crime and identity politics. *Theoretical Criminology, 6*(4), 485–491.
Perry, B. (2020). Hate in the peaceable kingdom. *Directions: Research and studies on race relations in Canada, 8*, 65–74.
Perry, B., & Scrivens, R. (2018). A climate of hate? An exploration of the right-wing extremist landscape in Canada. *Critical Criminology, 26*, 169–187.
Phillips, N. D. (2009). The prosecution of hate crimes: The limitations of the hate crime typology. *Journal of Interpersonal Violence, 24*(5), 883–905.
Powell, C. (2011). *Barbaric civilization: A critical sociology of genocide.* McGill-Queen's University Press.
Rafter, N. (2016). *The crime of all crimes: Toward a criminology of genocide.* New York University Press.

Richards, A. (2015). From terrorism to 'Radicalization' to 'Extremism': Counterterrorism imperative or loss of focus? *International Affairs, 91*(2), 371–380.
Schabas, W. A. (2000). *Genocide in international law: The crime of crimes*. Cambridge University Press.
Schweppe, J., & Perry, B. (2022). A continuum of hate: Delimiting the field of hate studies. *Crime, Law and Social Change, 77*, 503–528.
Scull, N. C., Mbonyingabo, C. D., & Kotb, M. (2016). Transforming ordinary people into killers: A psychological examination of Hutu participation in the Tutsi Genocide. *Peace and Conflict: Journal of Peace Psychology, 22*(4), 334–344.
Sinnar, S. (2022). The conundrums of hate crime prevention. *Journal of Criminal Law and Criminology, 112*(4), 801–846.
Stanton, G. H. (2004). Could the Rwandan genocide have been prevented? *Journal of Genocide Research, 6*(2), 211–228.
Stefaniak, A., & Winiewski, M. (2022). Differentiating between direct and indirect hate crime: Results from Poland. *Journal of Social and Political Psychology, 10*(1), 86–105.
Sternberg, R. J. (2003). A Duplex theory of hate: Development and application to terrorism, massacres, and genocide. *Review of General Psychology, 7*(3), 299–328.
Straus, S. (2006). *The order of genocide: Race, power, and war in Rwanda*. Cornell University Press.
Syed, J., & Ali, F. (2021). A Pyramid of hate perspective on religious bias, discrimination and violence. *Journal of Business Ethics, 172*, 43–58.
Taylor, H. (2019). Domestic terrorism and hate crimes: Legal definitions and media framing of mass shootings in the United States. *Journal of Policing, Intelligence and Counter Terrorism, 14*(3), 227–244.
Vendrell Ferran, Í. (2021). Hate: Toward a four-types model. *Review of Philosophy and Psychology*, n.p.
Waller, J. (2007). *Becoming evil: How ordinary people commit genocide and mass killing* (2nd ed.). Oxford University Press.
Walters, M. (2022, November 1). *Criminalizing hate: Law as social justice liberalism* [Lecture].
Weisband, E. (2018). *The Macabresque: Human violation and hate in genocide, mass atrocity, and enemy-making*. Oxford University Press.

Williams, T., & Pfeiffer, D. (2017). Unpacking the mind of evil: A sociological perspective on the role of intent and motivations in genocide. *Genocide Studies and Prevention, 11*(2), 72–87.
Wilson, P. E. (2023). *The degradation of ethics through the holocaust*. Palgrave Macmillan.

Female Hate Crime Offenders: The Theoretical and Policy Implications of an Under-Researched Phenomenon

Brendan Lantz and Lexi Faulkner

Introduction

While theories of bias crime have been well-established in recent years—especially at the macro-level—very few of these theories explicitly incorporate gender variation. Those studies that do incorporate gender in some way, generally do so by including a static control measure in their analytic models (see Bufkin, 1999; Lantz, 2022). The fundamental presumption behind such an approach is in part the implicit—and sometimes explicit—assumption that hate-motivated violence is similar to many other forms of violence, such that it is predominantly committed by men and is thus the product of gender role socialization which

B. Lantz (✉) · L. Faulkner
College of Criminology and Criminal Justice, Florida State University, Tallahassee, FL, USA
e-mail: blantz@fsu.edu

L. Faulkner
e-mail: arf18c@fsu.edu

J. Garland et al. (eds.), *Hate Crime Perpetrators: New Perspectives from Theory, Research and Practice, Volume I*, Palgrave Hate Studies,
https://doi.org/10.1007/978-3-031-92666-2_9

contributes to increased aggression among men and willingness to engage in interpersonal violence, relative to women (see Comstock, 1991; Hamm, 1993; Lantz, 2022; Levin & McDevitt, 1993).

Gender, however, is not a static or fixed measure, but is instead a process that is itself the product of human interaction (Connell, 1985, 1987, 1989; West & Zimmerman, 1987). Gender, along with other social characteristics, like race, is the product of social construction (West & Zimmerman, 1987); it is the primary thesis of this chapter that these construction processes have important theoretical significance for understanding hate crime offending. This significance has been acknowledged regularly in the literature regarding the role of racial boundaries and bias-motivated violence (see, Perry, 2002) but has been acknowledged only sporadically regarding gender (Bufkin, 1999; Lantz, 2022). Broader studies on hate crime often fail to consider the influence of gender socialization in any significant theoretical detail, however. Of the few studies that do address gender differences, there is a tendency to focus exclusively on women's involvement in bigoted behaviors without comparing it to men's, implicitly assuming the significance of gender (e.g., Borgeson, 2003). Consequently, the lack of gender-focused analysis and appropriate comparative frameworks has significantly impeded our grasp of gender in hate crime offending and victimization.

Existing Research on Female Hate Crime Offending

Recent research challenges these existing gendered assumptions by highlighting that women do indeed engage in hate crimes, albeit in different ways and contexts compared to men. For instance, Lantz (2022) found that between 2010 and 2016, more than 21% of reported hate crimes in the National Incident-Based Reporting System (NIBRS) data, which is the primary source of incident-level crime data in the United States, involved female perpetrators, acting alone, in female-only groups, or in conjunction with male offenders. Lantz also found significant differences in the incident characteristics associated with hate crimes according to the gender of the offense perpetrators. Research on hate groups—most notably by Blee (2003, 2007, 2012)—has also noted female participation in organized racist groups, specifically arguing that women "participate in acts of racially-directed violence whose nature, targets, and social organization vary considerably" (Blee, 2007, p. 422).

While Lantz's (2022) research is the most direct, and recent, examination of the gendered dynamics of hate crime, earlier researchers noted the omission of attention to gender as well. Cunningham (2007, p. 15) noted this most directly by pointing to the omission of gender information in the United States-based Federal Bureau of Investigation (FBI) hate crime statistics, arguing that the implication was to otherwise conclude that all offenders must be male. Blee (2012, p. 256) also lamented the lack of focus on women in racial extremist groups, referring to a problematic "template of the rightist as male." Yet existing research tends to either focus exclusively on male offending, or to combine all hate crime offenders together, a practice that Jolliffe and Farrington (2020, p. 5) argued has the potential to bias results because of gender differences that may instead be perceived as differences in hate crime offender motivation (see also, Lantz, 2022). Taken together, these findings suggest that a more nuanced understanding of gender in hate crimes is necessary and potentially beneficial from a theoretical standpoint.

An Intersectional Theoretical Framework for Understanding Female Hate Crime Offending

The prevailing issue in existing hate crime research is the tendency to oversimplify or homogenize gender as a social category. We cannot, however, invoke or analyze gender in isolation if we wish to fully understand gendered patterns. In this chapter, we emphasize the critical need to adopt a framework of intersectionality in order to better understand not just gendered patterns in hate crime offending, but patterns in hate crime offending more generally. Put simply, intersectionality frameworks posit that social divisions operate jointly in the production of social relations and outcomes. Gender, for example, does not operate independently, but is also impacted by other social categories, including race and class, as well as any other characteristics promoting social division (e.g., sexuality, religion, disability). Together these social characteristics are understood to be mutually constitutive (Anthias, 2012; Brah & Phoenix, 2004). Women, therefore, are not homogenous, but are also subject to differential processes of racialization, along with other forms of differentiation.

Intersectionality is important not just to the understanding of gender dynamics, but is also fundamental to the understanding of violence. In her seminal work, Collins (1998) argued that addressing violence as a social problem requires sufficiently sophisticated approaches which account for the role of intersecting power relations in the production of violence (see also, Collins, 2017). Specifically, Collins outlined the ways in which hierarchical power relations in the United States were related to systemic and interpersonal violence. In doing so, she noted that power relations themselves structure the ability to legitimate or delegitimate violence. One need only think of former U.S. President Trump's reference to "very fine people" in the wake of the infamous Unite the Right Rally[1]—which featured a deadly hate crime—to understand the ability of those in power to undermine or promote the legitimacy of acts of violence. Second, and perhaps more importantly, Collins noted how routinized institutionalized violence normalized interpersonal violence targeting some specific groups. Interpersonal acts of violence, in turn, act to sustain and maintain these traditional power structures. Collins further argued that violence represents a saturated site of intersectionality wherein the intersection of power relations is especially visible (see also, Collins, 1998). This is even more so the case for hate-motivated violence, which can be conceptualized as a more intensely saturated site of intersectionality, given its basis in identity.

In our view, intersectionality is not just a value-added framework which can enhance our understanding of hate crime, or a "formula" to be mentioned (see Knapp, 2005), but a fundamental component for understanding the complexities of power dynamics underlying hate crimes as a social phenomenon. Intersectionality approaches focus on interactions between actors operating within unequal social structures that are context specific and complex (Winker & Degele, 2011). Critical to understanding the importance of intersectionality in the process of hate crime offending is understanding the notion that group positioning itself is not static and does not exist as a matter of fact. As noted in the classic work of West and Zimmerman (1995), individual actions and interactions are structured such that individuals are constantly categorizing those they interact with by gender (or by race), while at the same time acting in ways that facilitate their own categorization. In doing so, our actions are both informed by and inform social structures, by outlining the "rules" or normative expectations for interactions; gender and race thus act as structured actions (Groves & Lynch, 1990; Messerschmidt, 1993, 1997).

In other words, group positioning is the outcome of group-making processes and related patterns of interaction; intergroup conflict, including hate crime offending, can be a particularly effective means for group making. In this context, many theoretical formulations of hate crime have argued that hate crimes function as a means of inferiorisation of the other. In committing a hate crime, the offender constructs their social positioning as superior within the existing social order, while simultaneously casting the victim as inferior or subordinate. In some cases, the backdrop of the prevailing social order might serve to reinforce these actions. This might be the case, for example, in instances of White supremacist motivated violence directed toward a racial minority, in that existing systems of systemic racism and White privilege leave little room for doubt for understanding social positioning as differentiated by race. In other cases, the social positioning of the victim and offender may be less clear; in such situations, hate crimes might even be understood as a mechanism for "jockeying" for position within a system that is subject to change. These instances are those wherein we should most expect women to engage in hate crimes, and for these hate crimes to potentially be structured by other intersectional qualities (e.g., race).

Yet, the prevailing characterization of power hierarchies within the extant hate crime literature has been too simplistic, focusing predominantly on one single axis of power, and most often on race. But hierarchies and power relations in America are more complex than that, encompassing power differentials across class, ethnicity, nationality, sexuality, age, gender, ability, religion, and a litany of other characteristics. Put simply, each of these social categories is associated with boundary and hierarchy-making processes in unique ways (Anthias, 2012). More importantly, the impact of each of these categories will differ over time and across situations (Pieterse, 1997). Take, for example, the case of a White woman active in a local White supremacist group. In the home, this woman is likely to subscribe to traditional gendered normative expectations and is likely to position herself as subordinate to her husband or male partner, as is often the case among women in such movements. In this context, her gender is the predominant social characteristic defining her positioning within relational hierarchies, not her Whiteness. Outside the home, or in other contexts, she may position herself the opposite, even when in social interactions with non-White men; in this context, the gendered context of the interaction is no longer the predominant hierarchy-making feature. Instead, race is the primary differentiator. These dynamics are fundamental to social interactions of all types, but rarely acknowledged in the literature on hate crimes and intergroup conflict as a possible precursor to female offending.

Structured Action Theory, Hegemonic Masculinity, and Gendered Differences in Offending

The few existing studies of gendered patterns of hate crime offending largely draw from structured action theory as a theoretical lens (see Bufkin, 1999). Less often acknowledged is the importance of intersectionality to these theories. In his work, Messerschmidt (1993, 1997) draws attention to the concept of hegemonic masculinity, which is a structurally based form of masculinity that contributes to the maintenance of existing power structures, by upholding not just the subordination of women, but also Whiteness, and heterosexism, among other processes (see also, Connell, 1987).

Enter the importance of considering intersectionality within this framework. Past research has largely operated under the assumption that, because crime is associated with power, and women are structurally excluded from power structures relative to men, then women should also be unlikely to commit crimes, and especially unlikely to commit violent bias crimes (Bufkin, 1999; Messerschmidt, 1993). And that indeed should be the case for bias crimes that are most traditionally conceptualized as situated within masculine power structures, like bias crimes toward women and sexual and gender minorities, who are frequently victimized for violating heteronormative gender expectations. Men have more motivation and opportunity to commit these acts, and there is little reason to expect women to engage in this behavior. For these crimes, bias-motivated violence may also serve the dual purpose of exercising power and "doing gender," allowing men to demonstrate their masculinity through their willingness and ability to engage in violence (Messerschmidt, 1993).

We agree with the notion that women should be less likely to be involved in such crimes. Indeed, some past research has suggested that female involvement in bias crimes is "minute" (Bufkin, 1999). Bufkin, albeit without quantitative data on the subject, argued that when women are involved in hate crimes, they rarely act as instigators and are frequently in the company of men, especially those they are dating or otherwise in a relationship with. Bufkin's (1999) research made a critical first step in theorizing these processes; we push this theoretical conceptualization one step further, however, arguing that understanding hate crimes as a mechanism of difference can explain not just the victimization of women, but also the perpetration of hate crimes *by* women. As Bufkin (1999, p. 157) noted, the typical hate crime victim is "antithetical to the hegemonic ideal," in that they tend to be oppressed groups (e.g., women, people with disabilities, LGBTQ+ people) that "stand in opposition to hegemonic masculinity by virtue of their existence." Where we diverge from this past research, however, is in our expectation that women should be unlikely to engage in hate crimes in all forms; we believe this assumption is too narrowly constructed around gender, without sufficient attention to other axes of difference.

Recent research using large United States-based national-level data has suggested that women commit hate crimes with a frequency that exceeds expectations, and that they often do so by themselves or with other women, and without the company of men (Lantz, 2022). In the current study, we present an explanation for these patterns. We start with two foundational assumptions, both of which align with this previous research. First, bias-motivated violence—including the threat of violence—is an instrument of power, useful as a tool for defining difference. Second, women are excluded from accessing traditional gendered power structures relative to men. These two assumptions have led previous scholars to suggest or imply that women should thus be unlikely to engage in bias-motivated violence (Bufkin, 1999; McDevitt et al., 2002). In some circumstances—those most clearly embedded within traditional patriarchal and heteronormative power structures—we agree that this is most likely to be the case. But we also think the opposite is possible: given that violence is an instrument of power, and women lack such power (at least relative to men), they may sometimes engage in bias-motivated violence to demonstrate powerful statuses within other social dynamics, or even in a response to their perceived lack of power. As a behavior, this would be consistent with prior theoretical conceptions of female violence as an attempt to gain power within the bounds of existing male-dominated social structures (e.g., Adler, 1975; Bottcher, 1995; Simon, 1975; Thorne, 1993). Bufkin (1999) even acknowledged as much, but still suggested that "for male and female bias offenders, the suggested end is gender accomplishment." We think this framing is too narrow.

To be sure, in the absence of an intersectional framework, the perpetration of bias-motivated violence by women might seem random or senseless. If hate crimes are fundamentally rooted in the maintenance of traditional power structures, why would women—as a traditionally subordinated group—engage in acts of violence that uphold such systems? As Crenshaw (1989) noted, however, it is this very single-axis analysis that tends to distort our understanding. This single-axis framework acts to erase the differences between Black women and White women, for example, by conceptualizing these groups as equally subordinated. Yet, few would argue that the experiences of oppression among White women and Black women are equal. If we understand there to be inherent and obvious differences between these groups, we must also accept the potential that they may also be differentially inclined toward hegemonically embedded violence. To do otherwise is to risk oversimplifying a complex phenomenon.

Hegemonic power structures are not simply about the valorization of masculinity; racism, ableism, and homophobia are all hegemonic in the ways that they contribute to the maintenance of traditional power structures. Crenshaw's poignant basement metaphor is useful here. In this metaphor, Crenshaw (1989, pp. 151–152) asks the reader to:

> Imagine a basement which contains all people who are disadvantaged on the basis of race, sex, class, sexual preference, age, and/or physical ability. These people are stacked – feet standing on shoulders – with those on the bottom being disadvantaged by the full array of factors, up to the very top, where the heads of all those disadvantaged by a singular factor brush up against the ceiling. Their ceiling is actually the floor above which only those who are not disadvantaged in any way reside.

In this metaphor, those above the floor are the portrait of privilege in America: White, cisgender, heterosexual, abled men. Just below the floor—or the ceiling, depending on perspective—are the singularly disadvantaged White heterosexual women. Crenshaw (1989) further asks the reader to envision a hatch, permitting travel through the ceiling to above the floor, but which is only accessible to those who can position themselves to crawl and squeeze through. Unfortunately, the only way to establish this position is by climbing on the backs of the multiply disadvantaged people below. Unfortunately, applying this metaphor to the power dynamics of hate crimes, one way to establish this position is to elevate oneself above those below through force, using targeted violence as a means for establishing difference. Metaphorically speaking, one method for getting closer to and accessing the hatch is to employ group-based violence in a way that emphasizes axes of difference which are hegemonically valued (e.g., Whiteness), while de-emphasizing those that are not. In this way, White women and other singularly disadvantaged folks are left with an outlet for escape, while the multiply marginalized are left jockeying for position below the floor; hate crimes may also be employed in this process.

A Descriptive Account of Female Offending in America, 2000–2019

To better interrogate our theoretical framework and demonstrate the plausibility of this conceptualization, we compiled twenty years of data (2000–2019) on interpersonal hate crimes from the United States-based National Incident-Based Reporting System (NIBRS). The NIBRS data are the only national-level incident-based data in America, and are now the primary source of American crime statistics, given a recent transition to the NIBRS-based system from the Uniform Crime Reporting Summary Reporting System (Lantz, 2020). We focus only on those incidents for which the gender of the offender is known. For this analysis, we also exclude incidents involving mixed-sex offending in order to focus exclusively on male- and female-perpetrated crimes, resulting in 21,133 hate crimes. We then analyze these incidents in two ways, first focusing on the differences between male- and female-perpetrated crimes by type of motivation (i.e., bias motivation). Then, in the second stage of the analysis, we examine differences between White female and Black female-perpetrated hate crimes, in order to evidence our key points regarding the need for an intersectional lens.

First, Table 1 presents differences in male and female-perpetrated hate crimes by bias motivation type, with a focus on the frequency of motivation type and the percentage of female- or male-perpetrated hate crimes that involved that motivation. We note that we focus only on those motivation types which occurred with enough frequency to permit statistical tests for differences in means; those which occurred so infrequently (e.g., anti-Mormon, $N = 3$, including one committed by a female and two committed by men) that we could not draw reliable conclusions are omitted from the table. Turning to the table, we first note that nearly 17% of hate crimes are perpetrated *exclusively* by women who are otherwise not operating within a partnership with male offenders. This finding alone points to the relative importance of considering female offending: not doing so risks excluding nearly one-fifth of hate crimes from our empirical and theoretical consideration.

Next, we draw attention to three critical patterns, each of which points to the importance of focusing on various axes of difference. First, we

Table 1 Differences in male and female-perpetrated hate crimes, by bias motivation (selected motivation types)

Hate crime type (Bias motivation)	Female-perpetrated		Male-perpetrated		Sig
Race/ Ethnicity-Motivated	N	%	N	%	
Anti-White	922	25.73	2,629	14.98	***
Anti-Black	1,141	31.84	6,280	35.78	***
Anti-Hispanic	201	5.61	1,407	8.02	n.s
Anti-AIAN	85	2.37	329	1.87	n.s
Anti-Asian	67	1.87	360	2.05	n.s
Anti-Multi-Racial	60	1.67	283	1.61	n.s
Religion-Motivated					
Anti-Jewish	49	1.37	350	1.99	*
Anti-Catholic	14	0.39	71	0.40	n.s
Anti-Islamic	80	2.23	474	2.70	n.s
Anti-Other Religion	31	0.87	140	0.80	n.s
Anti-Multi-Religion	20	0.56	78	0.44	n.s
Anti-Sexual Orientation/Gender					
Anti-Gay	126	3.52	1,829	10.42	***
Anti-Lesbian	147	4.10	319	1.82	***
Anti-LGBT Mixed	129	3.60	1,120	6.38	***
Anti-Bisexual	27	0.75	81	0.46	*
Anti-Heterosexual	23	0.64	63	0.36	*
Anti-Male	13	0.36	40	0.23	n.s
Anti-Female	9	0.25	74	0.42	–
Anti-Transgender	14	0.39	99	0.56	n.s
Anti-Disability					
Anti-Physical Disability	42	1.17	129	0.74	**
Anti-Mental Disability	85	2.37	312	1.78	*
Total	3,583		17,550		

Note '*'= $p < 0.05$; '**'= $p < 0.01$; '***'= $p < 0.001$; n.s.= not significant

note that female-perpetrated hate crimes are more likely to be race-based (roughly 57.6% of all offenses) than male-perpetrated hate crimes (50.8% of all offenses). Put simply, men are more likely to "spread" their motivation around, a pattern that is consistent with their more powerful positioning within traditional hegemonic power structures, at least when focusing on gender alone. Interestingly, we also observe differences within racial motivation, such that women are significantly more likely to perpetrate anti-White hate crimes ($p < 0.001$), and significantly less likely to perpetrate anti-Black hate crimes ($p < 0.001$) relative to men; we further interrogate these findings below by disaggregating these patterns by the race of female perpetrators.

Second, also in Table 1, we see important differences in the frequency of anti-sexual orientation and gender-based hate crimes. Each of these differences is consistent with the expectations we outline regarding the notion that women would engage in these crimes less than men, given that these crimes represent those hate crimes most embedded within traditional hegemonic power structures. Specifically, we find that women are substantially and significantly less likely to engage in anti-gay hate crimes compared to men, such that anti-gay hate crime offending represents only about 3.5% of female offending, but more than 10% of male-perpetrated hate crimes ($p < 0.001$). Women are also less likely to engage in anti-LGBT mixed hate crimes ($p < 0.001$) and anti-bisexual hate crimes ($p < 0.05$), relative to men. Anti-lesbian hate crime, however, represents an exception to these patterns, in that women are significantly more likely than men to commit such hate crimes (4.1% of female hate crimes, compared to 1.8% of male hate crimes; $p < 0.001$). This pattern is in direct alignment with our theoretical conceptualization of female-perpetrated hate crime as a mechanism for emphasizing relational differences beyond male/female gender structures, given that anti-lesbian hate crime committed by women can be interpreted as a form of violence meant to emphasize the heterosexual/homosexual axis of difference between heterosexual and lesbian women. That this pattern does not extend to the victimization of gay men—who occupy both subordinated and traditionally superior roles at the same time—by heterosexual women is further evidence for the importance of considering the complex nature of power differentials across multiple domains simultaneously.

Finally, we observe patterns regarding disability which also align with our theoretical framework, such that women are significantly more likely than men to engage in both anti-physical disability ($p < 0.01$) and anti-mental disability-motivated hate crimes ($p < 0.05$). For bias-motivated female offenders, the abled/disabled axis of difference may once again represent a theoretical point of emphasis which positions the offender above the victim through the perpetration of violence, allowing women to exercise power through hate crime perpetration despite their subordinated gender status. Men, on the other hand, have more entry points for emphasizing power differentials within a hegemonic system—as evidenced by their increased perpetration of anti-gay hate crimes, for example—and are thus less likely to engage in disability-motivated hate crime, at least from a proportionality standpoint.

Next, in order to demonstrate the critical need to consider female offenses from an intersectional perspective, we examine differences in hate crimes committed by White women, relative to Black women, in Table 2. Because of the relative infrequency of hate crime offending in the NIBRS data among women of other races, such hate crimes are omitted. Again, we also omit hate crimes that occur too infrequently for reliable statistical comparisons to be conducted from this analysis, resulting in a sample of 3,346 hate crimes, 2,066 (or 61.7%) of which were perpetrated by White women, and 1,280 (or 38.3%) of which were perpetrated by Black women.

Again, we note five important findings. First, there are clear and pronounced patterns regarding racial differences, such that White women are considerably more likely to commit anti-Black racially motivated hate crimes (about 43% of offenses), and Black women are significantly more likely to engage in anti-White violence (about 50% of offenses). Within our theoretical framework, both of these patterns are likely related to power differentials, albeit in different ways. White women may employ anti-Black violence as a mechanism of racial subordination, simultaneously emphasizing race as a primary axis of difference, while de-emphasizing their own gendered subordination. Anti-White violence committed by Black women, on the other hand, is likely a mechanism through which to resist that subordination, or to gain power. Taken together, these patterns reflect the critical importance of employing an intersectional lens for understanding gendered patterns in bias-motivated violence.

Second, these patterns indicate that White women are significantly more likely than Black women to engage in anti-Hispanic bias-motivated

Table 2 Differences in white- and black-perpetrated female hate crimes, by bias motivation (selected offenses)

Hate crime type (Bias motivation)	White women		Black women		Sig
Race/Ethnicity-motivated	N	%	N	%	
Anti-White	233	11.28	646	50.47	***
Anti-Black	896	43.37	150	11.72	***
Anti-Hispanic	181	8.76	57	4.45	***
Anti-AIAN	49	2.37	35	2.73	n.s
Anti-Asian	43	2.08	19	1.48	n.s
Anti-Multi-Racial	29	1.40	25	1.95	n.s
Religion-Motivated					
Anti-Jewish	39	1.89	5	0.39	**
Anti-Islamic	57	2.76	18	1.41	*
Anti-Sexual Orientation/Gender					
Anti-Gay	64	3.1	47	3.67	n.s
Anti-Lesbian	101	4.89	41	3.20	*
Anti-LGBT Mixed	64	3.10	55	4.30	n.s
Anti-Disability					
Anti-Physical Disability	23	1.11	13	1.02	n.s
Anti-Mental Disability	57	2.76	27	2.11	n.s
Total	2,066		1,280		

Note '*'= $p < 0.05$; '**'= $p < 0.01$; '***'= $p < 0.001$; n.s.= not significant

violence ($p < 0.001$), such that anti-Hispanic hate crimes represent nearly 9% of White female offenses, but only 4% of Black female offenses. Again, these patterns are likely the product of White females employing bias-motivated violence as a mechanism for emphasizing Hispanic/non-Hispanic as an axis of difference. This axis of difference is likely more effective as a point of emphasis for White women than Black women. Within traditional racial/ethnic hierarchies which uphold White supremacy over non-White racial/ethnic identities, Hispanic ethnicity is clearly subordinate to Whiteness, but less clearly positioned relative to Black racialization. We observe no significant differences in anti-American Indian/Alaskan Native or anti-Asian bias-motivated violence, although small sample sizes preclude drawing strong conclusions from these patterns.

Third, White women exercise more religiously motivated subordination than Black women, engaging in significantly more anti-Jewish hate crime ($p < 0.01$) and anti-Islamic hate crime ($p < 0.05$); again, however, these crimes are relatively infrequent for women in general. Fourth, White women engage in significantly more anti-lesbian hate crime, compared to Black women ($p < 0.05$). Again, this pattern is likely the product of intertwined hierarchies of difference, such that lesbian women are clearly subordinate to White, heterosexual, female offenders within traditional hegemonic structures, thus facilitating the use of anti-lesbian hate crime as a mechanism for emphasizing heterosexual/homosexual points of difference; the positionality of Black heterosexual women relative to White lesbian women, however, is considerably more complex, given that each of these women would possess qualities that are traditionally subordinated, but in different domains. Taken together, these patterns likely explain the increased tendency for White women to employ anti-lesbian violence, relative to Black women.

Finally, we observe no significant differences in the frequency of anti-gay and anti-disability-motivated hate crimes between White women and Black women, suggesting that hate crimes emphasizing these axes of difference (e.g., abled/disabled) are employed by both groups with similar frequency. Again, this supports the notion that women may sometimes engage in non-gender motivated hate crimes which emphasize their more powerful positionalities (e.g., abled, rather than disabled; heterosexual, rather than homosexual), while de-emphasizing their subordinate positionalities.

Implications and Future Directions

Existing research on hate crime offending has largely ignored the study of gender differences in hate crime offending, either by focusing exclusively on men, or by ignoring the potential etiological and theoretical significance of women offenders. This omission has facilitated the presumption that most hate crime offenders are men (Cunningham, 2007), while also hampering theoretical development that insight into gender differences can provide (Lantz, 2022). In this work, we have attempted to address this issue by elucidating an intersectional theoretical framework for understanding hate crime offending as a mechanism for "doing difference" across multiple social domains. Put simply, while women occupy subordinate gender roles within traditional systems of hegemonic masculinity, they may also occupy other roles that facilitate their participation in subordination across other domains. We posit that understanding hate crime offending within this framework has fundamental implications for understanding hate crimes as a mechanism of social stratification and the production of societal inequality.

As evidenced by the data we compiled, women do commit hate crimes. And, while they do so less than men, they still do so at rates that exceed those that might be considered trivial or non-consequential. In other words, women commit hate crimes to such an extent and frequency that they must be accounted for within our theoretical explanations for hate crime. We suggest that a good theoretical account prioritizes an intersectional lens, noting that hate crimes may serve as a mechanism of doing difference not only among those with no marginalized characteristics (i.e., White, non-Hispanic, heterosexual, men), but also among those who possess both marginalized and non-marginalized characteristics (e.g., White women). In this context, the examination of hate-motivated violence perpetrated by women provides an entry point into broader research understanding the complex interaction of multiple systems of power in the generation of hate crime offending. Racism, heterosexism, and similar systems of power all play a role in the motivation of power-embedded violence. The maintenance of power is inherently built on systems of oppression, and oppression relies on violence (Collins, 2017). In this chapter, we have also touched on female-perpetrated hate crimes as a tool not just for maintaining power, but for gaining power. While we must be careful not to enter into discourse which places blame on individual victims, these patterns also suggest the potential for considering bias-motivated violence committed by women—and particularly minority women—as a kind of tool of resistance. We observe, for example, that many hate crimes committed by racial/ethnic minority women are anti-White in nature; these crimes should be the subject of future research, and viewing them through a lens of resistance to oppression may prove fruitful.

We also note several promising areas for future research. In our research, we note particular differences in hate crime perpetration between White women and Black women, for example. Unfortunately, due to the limitations of the data at hand, we are unable to explore other stratifying characteristics, like class or religion, as structuring positional differences that might underlie female-perpetrated hate crime. Class, in particular, is a central factor in the production of social divisions and should be the subject of future research on hate crime offending moving forward. Next, if these patterns are occurring within—and as a product of—hegemonic patriarchal power structures, then it should also be noted that such structures vary across space. Some communities, for example, exhibit greater gender inequality than others. Individual adherence and belief in traditional gender values also vary across locales. Following this, one particularly promising avenue for future research may be the focus on gendered variation in hate crime offending within spatial and temporal contexts. It is possible, for example, that female offending is more frequent in communities with traditional patriarchal structures (e.g., gender inequality in wages); future research should investigate this possibility. Finally, while the data we employ includes information only on the incident details of the hate crime itself (e.g., bias motivation), it does not include information regarding individual histories *prior to* hate crime perpetration. There is significant heterogeneity, however, in pathways into hate crime offending, and there may be important differences by gender. Future research should thus consider the potential for gender-related pathways into offending.

Conclusions

Previous research and scholarship on hate crime has consistently emphasized the role that traditional power hierarchies play in structuring hate crime offending (Perry, 2002). This power hierarchy framework—at least in terms of gender—has predominantly been interpreted in narrow terms, however, leading researchers to often frame female hate crime offending as unlikely or uncommon because of the subordinated nature of women, relative to men, within traditional hegemonic power hierarchies. In this chapter, we have argued for the need to go beyond a focus on unilateral hierarchies—as traditionally conceptualized in hate crime literature—to include a broader view of the complex, interactional, social landscapes of power and hierarchy. While women do commit less hate crime than men, they still engage in bias-motivated violence with non-trivial frequency, and our analyses suggest that such female-perpetrated hate crimes tend to convene along axes of difference that highlight hierarchical differences other than gender, including racial/ethnic differences (e.g., anti-Black and anti-Hispanic hate crimes by White women, anti-White hate crimes by Black women), differences in sexual orientation (e.g., anti-lesbian hate crimes), and disability.

Notes

1. As a matter of background, the "Unite the Right Rally" took place in Charlottesville, VA on August 12th, 2017, ostensibly as a matter of protest of the planned removal of the city's Robert E. Lee statue. During the rally, James Alex Fields Jr., a twenty-two-year-old from Ohio, deliberately drove his car into a group of counter protestors, resulting in the death of one woman and injuries to dozens more. At his plea hearing on March 27, 2019, Fields admitted under oath that he targeted the crowd based on their actual and perceived race, color, national origin, and religion (U.S. Department of Justice, 2022a). He confessed that his actions caused the death of Heather Heyer and that he intended to kill others he struck with his vehicle. Fields also acknowledged that, prior to the rally, he used social media to express and promote white supremacist views and advocate violence against racial, ethnic, and religious groups he deemed non-white (U.S. Department of Justice, 2022b). Fields pled guilty to twenty-nine counts of violating the federal Matthew Shepard and James Byrd Jr. Hate Crimes Prevention Act, 18 U.S.C § 249, including one count of a hate crime resulting in the death of Heather Heyer and twenty-eight counts of hate crimes causing bodily injury and involving an attempt to kill others in the crowd (U.S. Department of Justice, 2022b).

References

Adler, F. (1975). *Sisters in crime*. McGraw-Hill.

Anthias, F. (2012). Intersectional what? Social divisions, intersectionality and levels of analysis. *Ethnicities, 13*(1), 3–19.

Blee, K. M. (2003). *Inside organized racism: Women in the hate movement*. Univ of California Press.

Blee, K. M. (2007). Women and organized racial terrorism in the United States. *Female terrorism and militancy* (pp. 215–230). Routledge.

Blee, K. M. (2012). Does gender matter in the United States far-right? *Politics, Religion & Ideology, 13*(2), 253–265.

Borgeson, K. (2003). Culture and identity among skinhead women. *Michigan Sociological Review*, 99–118.

Bottcher, J. (1995). Gender as social control: A qualitative study of incarcerated youths and their siblings in Greater Sacramento. *Justice Quarterly, 12*, 33–57.

Brah, A., & Phoenix, A. (2004). Ain't I a woman? Revisiting intersectionality. *Journal of International Women's Studies, 5*(3), 75–86.

Bufkin, J. L. (1999). Bias crime as gendered behavior. *Social Justice, 26*(1), 155–176.

Collins, P. H. (1998). The tie that binds: Race, gender, and US violence. *Ethnic and Racial Studies, 21*(5), 917–938.

Collins, P. H. (2017). On violence, intersectionality and transversal politics. *Ethnic and Racial Studies, 40*(9), 1460–1473.

Comstock, G. D. (1991). *Violence against lesbians and gay men*. Columbia Press.

Connell, R. W. (1985). Theorizing gender. *Sociology (Oxford), 19*, 260–272.

Connell, R. W. (1987). *Gender and power*. Stanford University Press.

Connell, R. W. (1989). Cool guys, swots, and wimps: The interplay of masculinity and education. *Oxford Review of Education, 15*, 291–303.

Crenshaw, K. (1989). Demarginalizing the intersection of race and sex: A Black Feminist critique of antidiscrimination doctrine, feminist theory and antiracist politics. *University of Chicago Legal Forum*, 139–167.

Cunningham, K. J. (2007). Countering female terrorism. *Studies in Conflict & Terrorism, 30*(2), 113–129.

Groves, W. B., & Lynch, M. J. (1990). Reconciling structural and subjective approaches to the study of crime. *Journal of Research in Crime and Delinquency, 27*, 348–375.

Hamm, M. S. (1993). *American skinheads*. Praeger.

Jolliffe, D., & Farrington, D. P. (2020). The criminal careers of those imprisoned for hate crime in the UK. *European Journal of Criminology, 17*(6), 936–955.

Knapp, G. (2005). Race, class, gender, reclaiming baggage in fast travelling theories. *European Journal of Women's Studies, 12*(3), 249–265.

Lantz, B. (2020). Why more agencies and researchers should embrace the upcoming NIBRS transition: Contributions and promise of the NIBRS data. *American Journal of Criminal Justice, 47*(3), 462–484.

Lantz, B. (2022). Women who commit hate-motivated violence: Advancing a gendered understanding of hate crime. *Social Science Research, 104*, Article 102682.

Levin, J., & McDevitt, J. (1993). *Hate crimes: The rising tide of bigotry and bloodshed*. Springer.

McDevitt, J., Levin, J., & Bennett, S. (2002). Hate crime offenders: An expanded typology. *Journal of Social Issues, 58*(2), 303–317.

Messerschmidt, J.W. (1993). *Masculinities and crime*. Rowman and Littlefield.

Messerschmidt, J. W. (1997). *Crime as structured action*. Sage.

Perry, B. (2002). Defending the color line: Racially and ethnically motivated hate crime. *American Behavioral Scientist, 46*(1), 72–92.

Pieterse, J. N. (1997). Deconstructing/reconstructing ethnicity. *Nations and Nationalism, 3*, 365–395.

Simon, R. (1975). *Women and crime*. DC Heath.

Thorne, B. (1993). *Gender play: Girls and boys in school*. Rutgers University Press.

U.S. Department of Justice. (2022a). Ohio man pleads guilty to 29 federal hate crimes for August 2017 car attack at rally in Charlottesville. Office of Public Affairs, United States Department of Justice. https://www.justice.gov/opa/pr/ohio-man-pleads-guilty-29-federal-hate-crimes-august-2017-car-attack-rally-charlottesville

U.S. Department of Justice. (2022b). Ohio man sentenced to life in prison for federal hate crimes related to August 2017 car attack at rally in Charlottesville, Virginia. Office of Public Affairs, United States Department of Justice. https://www.justice.gov/opa/pr/ohio-man-sentenced-life-prison-federal-hate-crimes-related-august-2017-car-attack-rally

West, C., & Zimmerman, D. H. (1987). Doing gender. *Gender and Society, 1*, 125–151.

West, C., & Zimmerman, D. H. (1995). Doing difference. *Gender and Society, 9*, 8–37.

Winker, G., & Degele, N. (2011). Intersectionality as multi-level analysis: Dealing with social inequality. *European Journal of Women's Studies, 18*(1), 51–66.

Conclusion

Jon Garland, Irene Zempi, and Jo Smith

In October 2024, the Office for National Statistics released their annual hate crime statistics for the year ending March 2024 (ONS, 2024). The data collected by the ONS shows a rise in police-recorded hate crime from around 42,255 per year in 2012–2013 (the first year such data was collected) to peak at around 163,322 in 2021–2022 (ONS, 2024). Since then, we have seen a decline in the number of hate crimes recorded

J. Garland (✉)
Department of Sociology, University of Surrey, Guildford, UK
e-mail: j.garland@surrey.ac.uk

I. Zempi
Department of Criminology & Criminal Justice, Nottingham Trent University, Nottingham, UK
e-mail: irene.zempi@ntu.ac.uk

J. Smith
Brighton Law School, School of Business and Law, University of Brighton, Brighton, UK
e-mail: j.smith12@brighton.ac.uk

J. Garland et al. (eds.), *Hate Crime Perpetrators: New Perspectives from Theory, Research and Practice, Volume I*, Palgrave Hate Studies,
https://doi.org/10.1007/978-3-031-92666-2_10

by the police, to 140,561 in 2023–2024 (ONS, 2024). This, of course, does not present the whole picture: omitted are the many hate incidents that are a normalised everyday occurrence, the incidents and crimes that individuals do not feel confident to report to the police, and the reports made to the police which are not recorded as either crimes or as hate motivated.

As a society trying to understand—and trying to address—hate crime we need to understand perpetration. Without such an understanding, how can we design policies and practices to educate people about the effects of hate crime, aid those who want to leave hate groups or rehabilitate themselves, design our technologies to avoid them allowing or encouraging hate speech, or address that 'mundane' everyday hate that is often overlooked? Throughout this book, perpetration as an individual act as been examined: from the analysis of the everyday 'hate relationships', to consideration of differences in recidivism between hate and non-hate offenders, to looking at those who perpetrate hate in particular contexts and against particular groups.

However, if we examine hate crime only as a series of individual acts, we overlook how the societies in which we live can create a climate of intolerance that can play an important role in perpetration. Chapters of this book have highlighted this in a variety of contexts: policymakers overlooking Islamophobic offenders acting in cyberspace; the legal system failing to protect trans lives and instead perpetuating a hostile environment; the rise of populism since the 1990s; and the links between hate crime by individuals and genocide by the state, for example. This book has therefore sought to explore perpetration of hate crime as both an individual act, and as something that is sanctioned by societies. Throughout these chapters, the authors have offered the reader theoretical understandings of hate crime, scholarly analysis of responses to hate crime, and showcased some of the current research into hate crime, in the hopes that this will help us come closer to effectively tackling prejudice, hatred and intolerance. But to achieve this, we must look at both what shapes the individual hate crime offenders and also consider how the state, our political leaders, and wider society allow hate to flourish.

The idea for this book first began in 2016, around the time of the Brexit referendum. Whilst intolerance, prejudice and hate were nothing new in the UK before then, the campaigning around Brexit emphasised to us how intolerant society was becoming. This was not only at an individual level but seemed to be coming from the politicians leading or seeking to lead the country, whose political discourse was moving closer and closer to something that we recognised as prejudice and even hate. Again, this was nothing new to us—as hate crime scholars we are familiar with state-sanctioned and state-led hatred, but this felt like something more overt and yet mundane than we had seen in previous years. The 'vote leave' campaign increasingly centralised the important of restricting immigration (Vote Leave, no date) and the need to 'take back control of our borders', as we were at 'breaking point' (Stewart & Mason, 2016). We saw reports on the 42% rise in recorded hate crime in the week before and the week after the Brexit referendum (Dodd, 2016), which spoke to us of the impact that the campaigning was having on attitudes towards others. We have continued to see anti-migrant fear mongering (Green, 2022) and calls to 'send *them* back' (Page, 2024), attempts to remove asylum seekers and migrants to Rwanda (*R (on the application of AAA and others) v Secretary of State for the Home Department*, 2023; Gov.UK, 2024b; United Nations, 2024), the rolling back of trans rights (Gov.UK, 2024a; The White House, 2025; Trans Legislation Tracker, 2025), failures by political parties to condemn Islamophobia and antisemitism (EHRC, 2020; Merrick, 2021; Syal, 2021) and so it continues.

And yet despite this, there are things to celebrate: the insightful and informative work of those researching in hate studies; those organisations supporting the victims of hate crime, educating the public about hate crime, and working with perpetrators to encourage change; the politicians and political organisations trying to address the structural and societal factors that make hate seem acceptable; and the efforts of activists trying to raise awareness of hate crime and stand against those whose hateful rhetoric is otherwise unchallenged. We hope this book also provides inspiration to readers in their own work.

References

Dodd, V. (2016, July 11). Police blame worst rise in recorded hate crime on EU referendum. *The Guardian*. https://www.theguardian.com/society/2016/jul/11/police-blame-worst-rise-in-recorded-hate-on-eu-referendum (Accessed: 7 March 2025).

EHRC. (2020). *Investigation into antisemitism in the Labour Party finds unlawful acts of discrimination and harassment*. https://www.equalityhumanrights.com/media-centre/news/investigation-antisemitism-labour-party-finds-unlawful-acts-discrimination-and (Accessed: 7 March 2025).

Gov.UK. (2024a). *Ban on puberty blockers to be made indefinite on experts' advice, GOV.UK*. https://www.gov.uk/government/news/ban-on-puberty-blockers-to-be-made-indefinite-on-experts-advice (Accessed: 7 March 2025).

Gov.UK. (2024b). *Safety of Rwanda (Asylum and Immigration) Bill: factsheet, GOV.UK*. https://www.gov.uk/government/publications/the-safety-of-rwanda-asylum-and-immigration-bill-factsheets/safety-of-rwanda-asylum-and-immigration-bill-factsheet-accessible (Accessed: 7 March 2025).

Green, L. A. (2022). *We need to send them back, Migration Watch*. https://www.migrationwatchuk.org/news/2022/04/11/we-need-to-send-them-back (Accessed: 7 March 2025).

Merrick, R. (2021). *The key findings from the Tory Islamophobia report, The Independent*. https://www.independent.co.uk/news/uk/politics/conservative-party-racism-inquiry-islamophobia-b1853354.html (Accessed: 7 March 2025).

ONS. (2024). *Hate Crime, England and Wales, year ending March 2024, GOV.UK*. https://www.gov.uk/government/statistics/hate-crime-england-and-wales-year-ending-march-2024/hate-crime-england-and-wales-year-ending-march-2024 (Accessed: 7 March 2025).

Page, M. (2024) *Trump's crowd chants 'Send them back,' claims immigrants 'destroyed' London and Paris, The Independent*. https://www.independent.co.uk/news/world/americas/us-politics/trump-rally-crowd-immigrants-london-paris-b2617865.html (Accessed: 7 March 2025).

R (on the application of AAA and others) v Secretary of State for the Home Department. (2023). https://www.supremecourt.uk/cases/uksc-2023-0093#judgment-details (Accessed: 7 March 2025).

Stewart, H., & Mason, R. (2016, June 16). Nigel Farage's anti-migrant poster reported to police. *The Guardian*. https://www.theguardian.com/politics/2016/jun/16/nigel-farage-defends-ukip-breaking-point-poster-queue-of-migrants (Accessed: 7 March 2025).

Syal, R. (2021, May 25). Tory Islamophobia report a "whitewash", say Muslims in party. *The Guardian.* https://www.theguardian.com/news/2021/may/25/tory-islamophobia-report-criticises-boris-johnson-over-burqa-remarks (Accessed: 7 March 2025).

The White House. (2025). *Defending women from gender ideology extremism and restoring biological truth to the Federal Government, The White House.* https://www.whitehouse.gov/presidential-actions/2025/01/defending-women-from-gender-ideology-extremism-and-restoring-biological-truth-to-the-federal-government/ (Accessed: 7 March 2025).

Trans Legislation Tracker. (2025). *2025 anti-trans bills: Trans legislation tracker, trans legislation tracker.* https://translegislation.com (Accessed: 7 March 2025).

United Nations. (2024). *UK's newly passed 'Safety in Rwanda' bill is anything but safe: UN officials.* https://news.un.org/en/story/2024/04/1148901 (Accessed: 7 March 2025).

Vote Leave. (n.d.). *Briefing: The EU immigration system is immoral and unfair, Vote Leave.* http://www.voteleavetakecontrol.org/briefing_immigration (Accessed: 7 March 2025).

Index

J. Garland et al. (eds.), *Hate Crime Perpetrators: New Perspectives from Theory, Research and Practice, Volume I*, Palgrave Hate Studies,
https://doi.org/10.1007/978-3-031-92666-2

Kolibri 360 GmbH
Ferdinand-Jühlke-Straße 7
99095 Erfurt, Deutschland
produktsicherheit@kolibri360.de